Philanthropy and the Future of Science and Technology

An increasingly important and often overlooked issue in science and technology policy is recognizing the role that philanthropies play in setting the direction of research. In an era where public and private resources for science are strained, the practices that foundations adopt to advance basic and applied research needs to be better understood. This first-of-its-kind study provides a detailed assessment of the current state of science philanthropy. This examination is particularly timely, given that science philanthropies will have an increasingly important and outsized role to play in advancing responsible innovation and in shaping how research is conducted.

Philanthropy and the Future of Science and Technology surveys the landscape of contemporary philanthropic involvement in science and technology by combining theoretical insights drawn from the responsible research and innovation (RRI) framework with empirical analysis investigating an array of detailed examples and case studies. Insights from interviews conducted with foundation representatives, scholars, and practitioners from a variety of sectors add real-world perspective. A wide range of philanthropic interventions are explored, focusing on support for individuals, institutions, and networks, with attention paid to the role that science philanthropies play in helping to establish and coordinate multi-sectoral funding partnerships. Novel approaches to science philanthropy are also considered, including the emergence of crowdfunding and the development of new institutional mechanisms to advance scientific research. The discussion concludes with an imaginative look into the future, outlining a series of lessons learned that can guide how new and established science philanthropies operate and envisioning alternative scenarios for the future that can inform how science philanthropy progresses over the coming decades.

This book offers a major contribution to the advancement of philanthropic investment in science and technology. Thus, it will be of considerable interest to researchers and students in public policy, public administration, political science, science and technology studies, sociology of science, and related disciplines.

Evan S. Michelson is a Program Director at the Alfred P. Sloan Foundation, New York, USA.

The Earthscan Science in Society Series

Series Editor: Steve Rayner
Institute for Science, Innovation and Society, University of Oxford

Editorial Board: Jason Blackstock, Bjorn Ola Linner, Susan Owens, Timothy O'Riordan, Arthur Petersen, Nick Pidgeon, Dan Sarewitz, Andy Stirling, Chris Tyler, Andrew Webster, Steve Yearley

The Earthscan Science in Society Series aims to publish new high-quality research, teaching, practical and policy-related books on topics that address the complex and vitally important interface between science and society.

Assessing the Societal Implications of Emerging Technologies
Anticipatory Governance in Practice
Evan Michelson

Aid, Technology and Development
The Lessons from Nepal
Edited by Dipak Gyawali, Michael Thompson and Marco Verweij

Climate Adaptation Policy and Evidence
Understanding the Tensions between Politics and Expertise in Public Policy
Peter Tangney

Cities and the Knowledge Economy
Promise, Politics and Possibilities
Tim May and Beth Perry

Institutional Capacity for Climate Change Response
A New Approach to Climate Politics
Theresa Scavenius and Steve Rayner

Geoengineering Our Climate?
Ethics, Politics and Governance
Edited by Jason J. Blackstock and Sean Low

Philanthropy and the Future of Science and Technology
Evan S. Michelson

Philanthropy and the Future of Science and Technology

Evan S. Michelson

Routledge
Taylor & Francis Group

LONDON AND NEW YORK

earthscan
from Routledge

First published 2020
by Routledge
2 Park Square, Milton Park, Abingdon, Oxon OX14 4RN

and by Routledge
605 Third Avenue, New York, NY 10017

First issued in paperback 2022

Routledge is an imprint of the Taylor & Francis Group, an informa business

Publisher's Note
The publisher has gone to great lengths to ensure the quality of this reprint but points out that some imperfections in the original copies may be apparent.

British Library Cataloguing-in-Publication Data
A catalogue record for this book is available from the British Library

Library of Congress Cataloging-in-Publication Data
A catalog record has been requested for this book

ISBN 13: 978-0-367-49883-2 (pbk)
ISBN 13: 978-1-138-33492-2 (hbk)
ISBN 13: 978-0-429-44411-1 (ebk)

DOI: 10.4324/9780429444111

Typeset in Bembo
by Taylor & Francis Books

To Ilysa, Mira, and Seth:
I just love it when you YOU!

Contents

List of illustrations

Figure

Tables

Acknowledgments

Taking on a large-scale book writing project in addition to regular professional and personal responsibilities is a rather foolhardy task, one that is deeply satisfying in retrospect but hard to appreciate during the process. Although I vowed after my first book not to write another one, at least for a while, the opportunity presented by a number of supportive people throughout my life to dive into issues related to philanthropy, science and technology, and public policy—issues that I care passionately about and have interested me for years—was just too good to pass up.

I made it through due to the kindness, support, understanding, and generosity of spirit of many, many people. First and foremost, many thanks to the late Steve Rayner—among many other distinguished accomplishments, editor of The Earthscan Science in Society Series—who saw value in this project from the outset and provided inspiration to many scholars in the fields of science and technology policy and science and technology studies to undertake extended analyses of complex, pressing topics in need of attention. Although I never had the opportunity to meet Steve in person, he was so kind, generous, gracious, and constructive with his thinking and feedback. He will be deeply missed. Many thanks go to the excellent editorial team at Routledge for their interest and guidance throughout this project. Rebecca Brennan, Leila Walker, and Rosie Anderson have been supportive throughout every stage of writing this book, from encouraging the original development of this idea to providing invaluable assistance of every kind along the way. Much appreciation goes to Jane Woodhead for catching all the grammatical mistakes before this went to press.

Second, I extend my thanks to all the individuals—foundation representatives, scholars, and practitioners—who were willing to take time out of their busy schedules to speak with me about the issues at hand. Collectively, they are the ones doing the good work every day to support research, create new knowledge, and apply evidence in the service of better decision-making. Even though many interviewees were willing to be quoted by name throughout the book, I decided, out of respect for their privacy and opinions, not to use the names of individuals with the quotations that have been shared throughout the book. This is a practice I have long followed. In instances where names are provided, those quotations or authored materials were already available in the public domain. As always, any errors, omissions, or inadvertent mischaracterizations are my own and bear no reflection on any of the individuals or institutions mentioned, or those participating as interviewees in this research project.

Third, this book would not have been possible without the support of my friends and colleagues at the Alfred P. Sloan Foundation. Many thanks especially to Sloan Foundation President Adam Falk for supporting my writing of this book from the very beginning. I greatly appreciate it. To be clear: I have written this book fully in my personal capacity, and any views expressed here are wholly my own and do not reflect those of the Alfred P. Sloan Foundation or any of its grantees or partners.

Fourth, thanks go to the two publication outlets that have graciously granted me permission to reuse and adapt content included in Chapter 5 that I previously published in other venues. Thank you to the Emerald Group and my article co-author Claudia Juech for granting permission to reuse and adapt material related to The Rockefeller Foundation's Searchlight network, previously published in the following article: Claudia Juech and Evan S. Michelson, "Innovation in Horizon Scanning for the Social Sector: An Introduction to the Searchlight Function," *Foresight*, 14 (6), 2012, pp. 439–449. Additionally, many thanks to the Science Philanthropy Alliance for their permission to reuse material I authored and helped to develop related to the Sloan Digital Sky Survey, previously published in: "Taking to the Stars: the Sloan Foundation's 25-year Partnership with the Sloan Digital Sky Survey," December 11, 2017, available on the Science Philanthropy Alliance website at www.sciencephilanthropyalliance.org/wp-content/uploads/2017/12/Sloan-SDSS-philanthropy-story-pdf-for-web.pdf.

Finally, all the credit in the world goes to my friends and family. Without them, none of this would have been possible. Thank you to Haila and David Kimball for all your love over the years and, in particular, for allowing me the use of your home as a writing base. My extended family Daniel, Marion, Noah, and Nathaniel Kimball are as fantastic as anyone could want. Love you all!

My mother, Lolly Michelson, has provided all the love and support a son could hope for. You have cheered me on every step of the way and have been my biggest supporter. Thank you for everything you have done for me, Mom! *Je t'aime et merci pour tout!* Heather and Eric Tosches, my sister and brother-in-law, are so important to our family and we all love you deeply. You are the best aunt and uncle in the world, and we are so happy to share our lives with you. Can't wait to see what the future brings and celebrate many more wonderful occasions together!

My wife, Ilysa, is truly the best person I know and makes me better every moment I am with her. Ilysa: you are the reason for our happiness, and I couldn't do any of this without you. I love you more than you can imagine and I can't wait for many more wonderful moments to cherish as we journey through life together, especially now that this book is done. And, an additional small thank you for all your copyediting expertise. I wouldn't be here without you. I love you, love you madly!

We couldn't ask for anything better than Mira and Seth. Mira and Seth: you have the world in your hands and joy in your hearts. Always work hard, be kind, help others, and fill those buckets! You bring light to our eyes and love in our souls. You make us proud, now and always. We love you more than all the grains of sand, stars in the sky, and atoms in the universe!

List of acronyms

AAAS	American Association for the Advancement of Science
BIA	BRAIN Initiative Alliance
BRAIN	Brain Research through Advancing Innovative Neurotechnologies
CCST	California Council on Science and Technology
COINS	Committee on Inclusiveness in SDSS
CSE	community and stakeholder engagement
CZI	Chan Zuckerberg Initiative
DAFs	donor advised funds
DEI	diversity, equity, and inclusion
DOE	Department of Energy
EC	European Commission
ECAST	Expert and Citizen Assessment of Science and Technology
EDIS	Equality, Diversity and Inclusion in Science and Health
EPSRC	Engineering and Physical Sciences Research Council
EUFORI	European Foundations for Research and Innovation
FAST	Faculty and Student Team
FOREMAP	Foundations Research Mapping
GDP	gross domestic product
HBCUs	historically black colleges and universities
HHMI	Howard Hughes Medical Institute
IDRC	International Development Research Centre
IFTF	Institute for the Future
IRB	Institutional Review Board
LLCs	limited liability companies
MSIs	mission related investments
NAKFI	National Academies Keck Futures Initiative
NAS	National Academy of Sciences
NASA	National Aeronautics and Space Administration
NBER	National Bureau of Economic Research
NGOs	non-governmental organizations
NIH	National Institutes of Health
NRC	National Research Council

NSF	National Science Foundation
PIT–UN	Public Interest Technology University Network
PRIs	program related investments
R&D	research and development
RCSA	Research Corporation for Science Advancement
RoRI	Research on Research Institute
RQ+	Research Quality Plus
RRI	responsible research and innovation
SDSS	Sloan Digital Sky Survey
SSRC	Social Science Research Council

1 Renewed giving for science

The re-emergence of philanthropic support for the scientific enterprise

Two editorials, twenty years apart

Consider two editorials in the journal *Science* published just under 20 years apart from one another, in time periods rather different with respect to federal funding of science and technology research in the United States. The first editorial, published on August 1, 1997, arrived during a time when substantial government resources were going toward basic science, helping to advance endeavors like the Human Genome Project, the Hubble Space Telescope, nanotechnology research, and other advances across multiple fields of science. The editorial was prescient, however, noting that more than just federal dollars were needed to keep the scientific enterprise moving forward and able to flourish over the coming years. Both retrospective and prospective, the editorial foresaw a need for increased financial resources for scientific research to be provided by foundations and other donors. It highlighted the impact that previous well-known philanthropists had in shaping the direction of science—the likes of Rockefeller, Carnegie, and others—and argued that philanthropy needed to refocus on supporting science efforts going forward. "The transition from the 20th to the 21st century provides American philanthropy with an opportunity to review its history and to renew its commitment to science," wrote the editorial authors Susan Fitzpatrick and John Bruer (Fitzpatrick & Bruer, 1997, p. 621). Instead of going alone, though, they imagined a more collaborative, interactive mode of funding and giving. "Private foundations can best accomplish this by joining in partnerships with other foundations, federal agencies, corporations, and individuals," they wrote (p. 621). "In the new century, support for science must become a national, rather than federal, responsibility" (p. 621).

Fast forward nearly two decades. Scientific research experienced both gains and losses in the intervening years. In the early years of the 20th Century, funding for the National Institutes of Health (NIH) roughly doubled (Johnson & Sekar, 2018). As part of the United States government response to the Great Recession, spending on non-defense research and development (R&D) spiked by nearly $20 billion over fiscal years 2009 and 2010 (Yamaner, 2012). This growth was then followed by nearly eight years of stagnant or even falling resources in aggregate, especially at agencies like the National Science Foundation (NSF). Even more telling is that federally funded R&D spending as a percentage of Gross Domestic Product (GDP) and as a percentage of the total federal budget has also been declining or stagnant. For example, since 2010 all federal R&D spending has fallen well below 1% of total GDP, a key benchmark figure that countries use to measure the intensity of support for science and technology.

On September 30, 2016, a *Science* editorial, written by David Baltimore, renewed a call for more philanthropic resources to go toward basic research to augment and complement funds provided from the public sector. "To solve some of our greatest societal problems, we not only need to focus on basic science research—we also need sufficient resources and new approaches," he wrote (Baltimore, 2016, p. 1473). He continued by emphasizing that philanthropic grantmaking provides the potential to spur new lines of inquiry and take risks that government funders might be hard-pressed to pursue. Foundations, he said, "can initiate research thrusts into unproven directions, which generally do not draw government funding" (p. 1473).

Renewing attention on the philanthropy-science interface

Similar pieces have also appeared in popular and trade press outlets, identifying the need for increased philanthropic involvement in and support for science and technology. For instance, general interest articles describing the rise of philanthropy in science and technology have been published in *Physics Today* (Kramer, 2018) and *The Scientist* (Grant, 2017), in addition to publications focused on the philanthropic sector, including articles in *Philanthropy* magazine (Zinsmeister, 2016), *The Chronicle of Philanthropy* (Anft, 2015), and the website Inside Philanthropy (Williams, 2016). Newspapers like *The Washington Post* (Aldrich, 2014) and *The New York Times* (Broad, 2014), and magazines like *The New Yorker* (Max, 2017), have all published blog posts and articles covering similar ground, both describing the trend of increased philanthropic giving for science and in profiling high-net-worth individuals who have focused their giving in this area.

But why, and why now? Why has there been seemingly more attention paid to the role of foundations in the scientific enterprise? What can be learned about how contemporary foundations are responding to these challenges? What do these responses signal about the future of philanthropic engagement with science and technology going forward? How do foundations shape the way fields of science and technology progress over time? How do foundations think about the societal implications of science and technology? How could science philanthropies support research while simultaneously realizing more societally oriented goals?

The purpose of this book is to investigate these questions and develop a better understanding of the role that philanthropies play in setting the direction of science and technology research and illuminating how these organizations can better account for considerations of societal responsibility with the funding they provide. In an era where other sources of support for science and technology are more tentative or even on the decline, there is a need to examine the role science philanthropies play in this ecosystem. By examining the societal responsibility of science philanthropy, the expectation is that those in leadership positions at foundations can become more intentional about the work that they do and that this investigation might open new avenues for further research and scholarship by those in the academy.

An important point on terminology. The terms "philanthropies" and "foundations" tend to be used interchangeably to denote non-profit, independent grantmaking institutions, which will be the case throughout this book. Similarly, while there are many philosophical debates about the boundaries between and the relationship among terms like "science and technology" and "research and innovation," these too will tend to be used in a comparable mode throughout this book to denote the full scale of the scientific enterprise, from basic research through technological development to innovation.

Even as coverage of these issues in the popular and trade literature has begun to grow in recent years, the gap in the academic literature on this subject is particularly telling and is evident across many fields. Much of the analysis has focused on how government agencies use their funds to inform the direction of different areas of science or how industry fostered technological innovation in a diverse range of fields. To be sure, government funding has a critical role to play not only in advancing basic research but also in fostering technological innovation (Fleming, Greene, Li, Marx, & Yao, 2019; Mazzucato, 2015; Weinberg, et al., 2014). The overwhelming attention paid to the government's role in advancing science and technology can be seen, for instance, in the extent of analysis that has looked at the impact of the National Science Foundation on different fields of study (Kleinman, 1995; Appel, 2000; Solovey, 2013). More recently, there have been a raft of popular histories tracing the influence of entities like the Defense Advanced Research Projects Agency (Jacobsen, 2016; Weinberger, 2017) or profiles of the innovations emerging from industrial sites like Bell Labs (Gertner, 2013) or Xerox's renowned PARC laboratory site (Hiltzik, 2000).

There are few, if any, recent book-length treatments in science and technology policy, science and technology studies, political science, or public policy that examine philanthropy's role in science and technology, let alone speak to the role foundations might play in considering the societal implications of the research that is funded. What research there does exist on the topic is mostly limited to historical considerations from the history of science, either covering more distant donor-scientist relationships from centuries earlier or documenting the early decades of the 20th Century, when many of the major foundations that exist today in the United States got their start (Kohler, R. E., 1976). Even studies that chart the wider history of foundations often have minimal attention on science and technology. For instance, out of 100 examples profiled in a series of philanthropy case studies, only a small number (less than 10%, not including medicine) featured instances of philanthropic funding for science and technology research (Fleishman, Kohler, & Schindler, 2007). An updated, searchable, online version of this philanthropy case study database, maintained by the Center for Strategic Philanthropy & Civil Society at Duke University, contains close to 600 entries of philanthropy examples. However, a search of this database indicates how little attention and study philanthropic giving for science and technology has received. A keyword search of the site only returns three case study examples using the search term "science," zero using the search term "technology," and only 23 examples using the search term "health" (Center for Strategic Philanthropy & Civil Society, n.d.). Furthermore, recent scholarship on the subject mostly tends to be limited or narrowly focused, examining the role foundations played in spurring the evolution of specific scientific disciplines or projects, such as molecular biology (Abir-Am, 2002), the social sciences (Richardson & Fisher, 1999; Fisher, 1993), or specific research projects in fields such as astronomy (Finkbeiner, 2010; Science Philanthropy Alliance, 2017).

Moreover, little attention has been paid to how foundations and philanthropic activity fits within leading, contemporary conceptual frameworks in science and technology policy or science and technology studies. It is only more recently that scholars have turned their attention more deliberately to the role that non-governmental and civil society organizations play with respect to these theories (Michelson, 2016; Ahrweiler, Gilbert, Schrempf, Grimpe, & Jirotka, 2018). As scholars have developed new theoretical constructs about the broader role of science in society, understanding how foundations fit within conceptual frameworks such as anticipatory governance (Barben, Fisher, Selin, & Guston, 2008) and responsible research and innovation (RRI) (Stilgoe, Owen, & Macnaghten, 2013) is critical on multiple fronts. First, there is a need to gain a more well-rounded view as to the range of applicability of these frameworks. Second, this kind of analysis helps philanthropic institutions think about their own role with respect to the societal implications of science and technology. In fact, discussions related to anticipatory governance and RRI, especially in the United States, have not focused much on the role played by funders (in general) and philanthropies (in particular). One modest indicator of this point is that a keyword search of the word "philanthropy," and related variations on the term, conducted in January 2019 in articles published in the *Journal of Responsible Innovation*, a leading journal in the field, returned only four results. None of these articles explicitly addressed the role of philanthropies with respect to these theories and mainly just referred to philanthropies in passing. In short, science philanthropy's relationship with responsible innovation has received insufficient attention (Kundu & Matthews, 2019).

This is not to say that philanthropies have been wholly ignored in the scholarly literature related to research and innovation (European Commission, 2014). Large-scale research projects focused on understanding philanthropic giving in these areas across Europe took place, first, as part of the Foundations

Research Mapping (FOREMAP) study (European Foundation Centre, 2009) and, subsequently, in the European Foundations for Research and Innovation (EUFORI) study (European Commission, 2015). These studies charted giving trends, compared grantmaking size, and analyzed strategic priorities of different donors. While much of the country-by-country analyses focused on philanthropic funding for scientific research and technological innovation, there was some analysis about how certain European foundations engage with the RRI concept. It should be noted, however, that the specific definition and use of the terms "philanthropy" and "foundation" can differ widely across these country contexts, and these institutions vary considerably in terms of their resource base, mode of operation, and other related factors. Moreover, these studies, while highly informative about philanthropic grantmaking for science and technology across Europe, by definition did not cover science and technology philanthropies based in the United States.

Beyond the decline or stagnation of federal funding for scientific research and the retrenchment by the private sector in support of basic research, another key reason for examining the role that American philanthropies play in science and technology is the sheer scale of funding these institutions provide. While the numbers fall well short of the resources provided by government, they remain substantial. One survey found that nearly 50 research institutions in the United States received over $2.3 billion in private funding from philanthropies, individual donors, and other sources in 2017 (Science Philanthropy Alliance, 2018). In one of the first rigorous empirical research studies on philanthropic giving for science and technology, economist Fiona Murray found that philanthropy contributes on the order of $4 billion annually toward academic research, rising to $7 billion annually when income from philanthropy-provided endowments is included (Murray, 2013). Another analysis puts that collected total of philanthropic support for science even higher, finding that a combination of direct philanthropic giving for research projects, coupled with more indirect forms of giving by philanthropy and other sources to university endowments, accounted for a total of $22.7 billion, or 44%, of funding for basic scientific research, when both this direct support and endowment funding are added together (Kastner, 2018). A search conducted in early 2019 of a publicly available database on foundation giving managed by the Foundation Center indicates that in fiscal year 2012, the largest 1,000 foundations in the United States gave over $1.15 billion in funding for science and engineering purposes, plus more than $700 million in additional funding for work in the social sciences (Foundation Center, 2013). While it is impossible to gain a complete accounting of all philanthropic funding for scientific research, these numbers indicate the sizable contribution that private foundations make to the endeavor of science and technology research. With that said, the percentage of total philanthropic giving that goes toward science and technology remains small. In the data provided by the Foundation Center, out of the nearly $51 billion in grantmaking provided by the largest 1,000 foundations in the United States in 2012, science and engineering funding alone accounted for only 2.2% of the total grantmaking and, when adding in funding for social science, this percentage barely moves up to 3.6% (Foundation Center, 2013).

In addition to financial matters, the need to better understand the societal role of philanthropies when it comes to funding science and technology also emerges from a desire to better understand institutional dynamics. A number of foundations have worked in these areas for decades, while a host of new philanthropic institutions have emerged in more recent years, all with a mission toward helping advance state-of-the-art scientific and technological research. For example, well-known philanthropies like The Rockefeller Foundation, founded in 1913, and its affiliated institutions historically played a key role in funding science and technology research and shaping the direction of a wide array of scientific fields (Kohler, R. E., 1991), such as building new telescopes (Florence, 1995) or creating new fields like molecular biology (Kohler, R. E., 1976). Smaller philanthropies also formed during that period have worked to shape the direction of new scientific fields. The Research Corporation for Science Advancement, formed in 1912, concentrates on "providing catalytic and opportunistic funding for innovative scientific research and the development of academic scientists advancing American competitiveness in science and technology" (Research Corporation for Science Advancement, 2017). Similarly, the Alfred P. Sloan Foundation, founded in 1934, has a long history in funding science and technology research, with a mission dedicated to supporting "original research and education related to science, technology, engineering, mathematics, and economics" (Alfred P. Sloan Foundation, 2019). The Howard Hughes Medical Institute, established in 1953, focuses on advancing biomedical research through the provision of prestigious fellowships.

In recent years and decades, newer philanthropies with an orientation toward funding science and technology have emerged, creating a more extensive ecosystem. Consider just a few examples. The Kavli Foundation, formed in 2000, is "dedicated to advancing science for the benefit of humanity, promoting public understanding of scientific research, and supporting scientists and their work" (The Kavli Foundation, 2019). The Simons Foundation, founded in 2009, and expanded later on to include an in-house scientific research organization called the Flatiron Institute, aims to "advance the frontiers of research in mathematics and the basic sciences" (Simons Foundation, n.d.). Other philanthropies may focus their grantmaking on a handful of specific areas in science and technology. For instance, the Gordon and Betty Moore Foundation, created in 2000, provides support to create a next-generation, large-scale telescope in addition to funding marine conservation activities. Similarly, the Heising-Simons Foundation, established in 2007, supports research in physics, astronomy, and climate change science. Additionally, as a response to the decrease in federal funding of basic science research, the Science Philanthropy Alliance was founded in 2013 by six of the leading science philanthropies in the United States. The purpose of the Science Philanthropy Alliance is to help "increase philanthropic support for basic scientific research" by advising and providing guidance to other high-net-worth individuals in how best to support scientific research (Science Philanthropy Alliance, 2019a). The Science Philanthropy Alliance, a membership organization, includes 30 philanthropic institutions (as of November 2019) that provide some degree of support for scientific research. As Table 1.1 shows, participating foundations are divided into three groups of membership types, including member institutions (eight philanthropies), benefactors (four philanthropies), and associate members (16 philanthropies), with two philanthropies preferring to remain anonymous. The Science Philanthropy Alliance draws on the collective experience of these established and emerging science philanthropies—from "youngster" family foundations to "teenager" funders to "grown-up" institutions—to provide guidance to new donors interested in funding science and to facilitate collaborations among science philanthropies interested in working with one another (Science Philanthropy Alliance, 2019b).

Philanthropy, RRI, and societal responsibility: opportunities, challenges, and critiques

While at the most basic level the role of foundations within society is relatively straightforward, there are many questions and uncertainties that arise when considering the sector as a whole. One article even points out a number of pervasive, often under-explored "myths" that characterize how philanthropy is typically conceptualized and understood, noting that there is much analysis to undertake as "we are in the early stages of mapping the generative power of human generosity and both the intended and unintended consequences that result from its expression and motivation" (Faculty of the Lilly Family School of Philanthropy, 2019, p. 33). In his comprehensive overview of how foundations operate, Joel Fleishman succinctly summarizes in *The Foundation* what foundations do: "The leaders of a foundation—usually a staff of professionals guided by a board of trustees—provide funds from the foundation's income or endowment to support not-for-profit organizations, charities, or other programs and organizations in accordance with the mission designated by the founder" (Fleishman, 2007, p. 3). Fleishman (2007) describes that in doing so, foundations can act as a "driver" to achieve a certain specified end-goal, a "partner" that helps to shape how an issue evolves, or a "catalyst" to help found other institutions or initiate work in an area (pp. 3–4). While the specifics of foundation finances are complicated, in the United States these institutions are considered tax-exempt entities, absolving them from paying most taxes on their endowment earnings, as long as they disburse approximately five percent of its value each year toward such societally oriented purposes. This social compact exchange, donating a portion of earnings in order to receive tax breaks, is grounded in the view that foundations work to better society and that their grantmaking efforts are designed to achieve beneficial outcomes.

Table 1.1 Science Philanthropy Alliance: members, benefactors, and associate members

Philanthropy[1]	Year Founded[2]	Headquarters Location	Approximate Total Assets[3] (2017)	Approximate Annual Grantmaking[4] (2017)
Members (8)				
Rita Allen Foundation	1953	Princeton, NJ	$174 million	$5.5 million
Heising-Simons Foundation	2007	Los Altos, CA	$505 million	$62.6 million
The Kavli Foundation*	2000	Los Angeles, CA	$652 million	$26 million
Albert and Mary Lasker Foundation	1942	New York, NY	$81 million	$2.76 million[5]
Gordon and Betty Moore Foundation*	2000	Palo Alto, CA	$6.8 billion	$288 million
Research Corporation for Science Advancement*	1912	Tucson, AZ	$174 million	$4 million
Simons Foundation*	1994	New York, NY	$3.3 billion	$272 million
Alfred P. Sloan Foundation*	1934	New York, NY	$1.9 billion	$85 million
Benefactors (4)				
Howard Hughes Medical Institute*[6]	1953	Chevy Chase, MD	$19 billion	$779 million
The David and Lucile Packard Foundation	1964	Los Altos, CA	$7.8 billion	$335 million
John Templeton Foundation	1987	West Conshohocken, PA	$3.4 billion	$129 million
Wellcome Trust[7]	1936	London, United Kingdom	$28 billion	$1.5 billion

Associate Members (16)

Sergey Brin Family Foundation, The Brinson Foundation, Ross M. Brown Family Foundation, Chan Zuckerberg Initiative, The Shurl and Kay Curci Foundation, Dalio Philanthropies, The Leona M. and Harry B. Helmsley Charitable Trust, Lyda Hill Philanthropies, The Klarman Family Foundation, Leon Levy Foundation, Open Philanthropy Project, The Page Family, The Rockefeller Foundation, Eric and Wendy Schmidt Fund for Strategic Innovation, Winn Family Foundation, Winton Philanthropies

Notes: Table reflects Science Philanthropy Alliance membership status as of November 2019 and does not include two anonymous institutions. Membership category information available at www.sciencephilanthropyalliance.org/who-we-are/members. Information on individual philanthropies as indicated on IRS Form 990-PF, available on Guidestar by Candid, www.guidestar.org. * – Denotes founding member of the Science Philanthropy Alliance; [1] – Organizations listed in alphabetical order, by last name; [2] – Year founded as indicated on philanthropy's website; [3] – Approximate total assets as of 2017, as reported on IRS Form 990-PF, Part II, Line 31, Column B; [4] – Approximate total annual grantmaking as of 2017, as reported on IRS Form 990-PF, Part I, Line 25, Column D; [5] – Information on Lasker Foundation annual grantmaking from IRS Form 990-PF, Section IX-A; [6] – Howard Hughes Medical Institute financial information from the foundation's website; [7] – Information available from Wellcome Trust 2017 Annual Report and using a $1.30 pound to dollar exchange rate.

It is difficult to identify the exact number of grantmaking foundations in the United States. Publicly available data from the Foundation Center—a non-profit organization that studies the field and which recently merged with Guidestar, an organization that tracks philanthropic and non-profit finances, and recently took the name Candid—shows that in 2012 there were over 86,000 independent, corporate, community, and operating foundations that reported giving (Foundation Center, 2014). Collectively, these institutions oversaw approximately $715 billion in assets and nearly $52 billion in giving (Foundation Center, 2014). As noted above, the scale of grantmaking provided for natural science and social science research by these institutions is a mere sliver of this total. Part of the reason why it is so challenging to understand how foundations function, even when examining a narrow set of institutions involved in science and technology, is that the way each foundation operates and approaches grantmaking is unique, making generalizations tough to reach. As one historical overview of foundations summarized, "more numerous and more varied than ever, American foundations respond in individual and idiosyncratic ways to the challenges, opportunities, and constraints posed by today's realities" and that, collectively, these institutions might "defy precise evaluation" (Hammack & Anheier, 2013, p. 118). Writing in the context of philanthropy's involvement in climate change issues, Edouard Morena summarizes the scattered nature of the philanthropic landscape by observing that, "the influence, organization, goals and prerogatives of philanthropic foundations vary greatly from one country and historical epoch to the next" (Morena, 2016, pp. 10–11). Put simply, "foundations do not constitute a monolithic block" (p. 14).

Perhaps it is exactly because of the challenge in assessing how this disparate group of organizations operate that there have always been questions about the role that foundations play in society. Morena summarizes that these critiques often derive from the view that "foundations have no legal obligation to justify their actions to any given stakeholder. A foundation's priorities are more often than not those of an individual or small group of individuals who are accountable to no one" (p. 12). He continues by discussing how these concerns feed into bigger-picture questions about how contemporary economic systems function and the differing responsibilities between public, private, and philanthropic organizations to address societal problems. "The debate on foundation legitimacy and accountability," he reflects, "is often framed in terms of foundations' broader functions under capitalism" (p. 13). Elsewhere, Bishop and Green (2008) have pointed out that today's high-net-worth, socially oriented "philanthrocapitalist" donors see themselves as particularly adept and uniquely positioned to address the complex, long-term, intertwined challenges facing society today. They write, "philanthrocapitalists are developing a new (if familiar-sounding) language to describe their businesslike approach," and "as entrepreneurial 'philanthropreneurs,' they love to back social entrepreneurs who offer innovative solutions to society's problems" (p. 6). Some worry that this introduction of venture-like funding mentalities to the philanthropic sector, which tend to prefer market-based solutions to societal problems, will have disproportionately negative effects on the non-profit sector as a whole. In particular, this new mode of philanthropy may unduly influence what kinds of societal interventions are viewed as most promising, potentially disfavoring support for scientific research, given that it can be slow to proceed, have uncertain payoffs, and be difficult to manage. Writing in the context of the role of philanthropy in addressing global development challenges, some science and technology policy experts at the STEPS Centre at the University of Sussex who have accentuated the core of this argument, highlighting that "a more immediate concern may be the extent to which the logic models underlying the new philanthropy, by advancing particular understandings of social change, leverage and scale, is focusing disproportionate attention (and resources) towards certain types of development problems and solutions and not others" (Brooks, Leach, Lucas, & Millstone, 2009, p. 12).

Additional questions have been raised in recent years, as economic inequality has grown and as the promise of interventions championed by billionaire donors has sometimes failed to live up to lofty expectations that accompany the rhetoric associated with bringing private-sector practices into the philanthropic arena. Most centrally, there are fears that the increase in private interests in philanthropy has hindered the ability of these institutions to achieve their societal and public missions (Giridharadas, 2018). There are also apprehensions about the ways in which foundations invest their substantial endowments, especially given the societally oriented focus of these organizations (Piller, 2018). Beyond raising concerns about the role of private sector approaches and interests in the philanthropic sector, there are other strands of critique that ask whether foundations are too risk averse or too limited in the interventions they are willing to pursue in order to achieve the goals they set out to accomplish. Such critiques question whether groupthink or a herd mentality has interfered with the effectiveness of philanthropic giving in particularly complex or hard-to-address topic areas, such as with respect to climate change or environmental degradation (Nisbet, 2018). In a book examining the difficulties foundations face in responding to a wide range of social problems, Ekkehard Thumler summarizes this overarching challenge by noting that, "foundations face a serious dilemma. They are confronted with external demands and their own ambitions to solve major social problems, and they thrive due to the hopes they mobilize in this regard" (Thumler, 2017, p. 3).

A host of other questions center on the relationship between philanthropic accountability, pluralist democracy, and moral obligations (Reich, 2018; Reich, Cordelli, & Bernholz, 2016). There are few ways for society to have a direct say about philanthropic practices, and there are no "familiar checks and balances" mechanisms akin to elections (Callahan, 2017, p. 9). The lack of democratic accountability implies that a small number of philanthropic actors have the potential for outsized influences in particular issue areas. In discussing the role of foundations in funding climate change research and policy interventions, Matthew Nisbet puts it thusly, "we are heading toward a future in which a few hundred unelected trustees, families, and individuals seek to exercise global power in a manner that is accountable to no one" (Nisbet, 2019, p. 35). Further problematic is that unequal power dynamics can implicitly or explicitly impact foundation relationships with other stakeholders, especially those seeking funding. Power imbalances inevitably arise when a grant-seeking institution interacts with a grant-maker, leading non-profit organizations in all subject areas, including in science and technology, to feel beholden to their philanthropic or individual donors for their financial well-being. If not addressed directly, this "unexamined power and privilege can harm our ability to create social good and improve society," writes Kathleen Enright, and in turn, can reinforce problematic hierarchies that hinders overall philanthropy effectiveness (Enright, 2018). Perhaps indicative of this zeitgeist, an entire season of the Future Perfect podcast series produced by the news website Vox is devoted to examining the various tensions that exists between philanthropy and democracy (Vox, 2019).

While there are many dimensions and gradations to these broader critiques of philanthropy, in general they signal a need to rethink the relationship between philanthropy and society. A September 2019 report from Rockefeller Philanthropy Advisors encapsulates the pressures facing foundations of all types. The report identifies the need to rethink and define the "social compact" between philanthropy and society, which "encompasses concepts such as accountability, legitimacy, transparency, and public trust" (Berman, Karibi-Whyte, & Taraso, 2019, p. 5). It asserts that as philanthropy and its constituent institutions are "coming under more intense scrutiny," there is a need to clarify the collective "value it will create in society," with each organization needing to manifest its "legitimacy (or license to operate) in the eyes of those stakeholders and the public, as well as how it approaches the transparency and accountability that underpin its legitimacy" (p. 10). In fact, one of the report's key conclusions closely parallels the central tenets of RRI, in that the sector as a whole needs to adopt processes and approaches that are geared toward making "more inclusive decisions" and toward better leveraging "the views and experience of a wide range of stakeholders to increase the impact and effectiveness of philanthropic dollars, recognizing that such bottom-up approaches can yield better knowledge, relationships, and decision-making" (p. 21). There are many factors that determine whether or not foundations are imbued with such a social license to operate. As Heydemann and Toepler (2006) write in their book chapter on this subject: "Location, sector, funding, institutional form and identity, the scope and priorities of programming—all of these contribute to the particular context in which legitimacy challenges play out, as does the broader social and political environment in which foundations work" (p. 18). Lastly on this front, it is important to note that these concerns about the societal legitimacy of foundations are not just confined to the United States. Debates surrounding philanthropic legitimacy have emerged over the years in Europe (Prewitt, Dogan, Heydemann, & Toepler, 2006), Canada (Pearson, 2019), Australia (Seibert, 2019), and in other locales where there is a strong tradition of institutionalized philanthropy, with ongoing debates across countries unlikely to be fully resolved anytime soon.

Determining how that larger transformation of the relationship between philanthropy and society can be achieved remains beyond the scope of this book. However, the presence of these field-wide questions create a backdrop against which science and technology foundations are operating. In some ways, science philanthropies are potentially facing a second layer of difficulty in the wider culture given rising distrust in expertise and scientific knowledge. Much has been written on this subject from various disciplinary perspectives (Collins & Evans, 2007; Funtowicz & Ravetz, 1993; Jasanoff, 1998). The public is increasingly skeptical about the role of scientists in decision-making processes (Pew Research Center, 2019). Moreover, there is a growing recognition among policymakers in both the United States and Europe that substantial steps need to be taken to improve the relationship between science and society (Science Advice for Policy by European Academies, 2019; American Academy of Arts & Sciences, 2014).

A key reason why the principles and perspective of RRI can serve as helpful guideposts for science philanthropies is that foundations, especially in the United States, have substantial freedom when it comes to their activities, as was discussed on p. 9. Except for the strictures put in place by mandated payout rules and oversight by their respective governing boards, foundations can have significant and almost unbounded flexibility when it comes to deciding on topics to address and grants to make. Within these spending and legal boundaries, foundations can fund almost any non-profit (and sometimes for-profit) organization to examine almost any issue for any charitable purpose. Even when limiting focus on foundations that fund science, the choices they face are seemingly limitless. Science philanthropies can focus on stimulating new fields, advancing existing ones, or spurring interdisciplinary research. Strategies can focus on supporting up-and-coming scholars, students, or esteemed researchers. The focus can be domestic or international, present- or future-oriented, aimed at immediate or longer-term impact. Grants can be oriented toward helping individual researchers, fostering research teams, growing centers or institutes, or creating organizations from scratch. Foundations can choose to spread out their funding, making many small grants to lots of awardees, or concentrating on supporting a few large bets. Funding can be of short or limited duration to help spur creativity and provide a brief infusion of funds to initiate a research effort. Alternatively, funding can be provided over multiple years to ensure that grantees have a solid financial infrastructure upon which to build their activities. Risks can be taken or avoided. Resources can be directed at specific projects or used for general support purposes.

How those choices are made are informed by an inordinate number of factors, including a philanthropy's mission, institutional history, guidance from governing boards, staff interests and experience, needs of the research community, and so on. Most large, independent philanthropies spend significant time and attention on identifying strategic intervention opportunities and determining the best approach to realizing their missions in order to achieve societal impact. An influential *Harvard Business Review* article from 1999 written by

Michael Porter and Mark Kramer emphasized the need for foundations to develop more coherent strategies in order to better identify their societal value that justifies the preferential tax status that these institutions enjoy, especially in the United States (Porter & Kramer, 1999). The concept of "strategic philanthropy" (Brest, 2012; Kania, Kramer, & Russell, 2014) has been championed in recent years, arguing in favor of "outcome-oriented, result-oriented, and effective philanthropy" that emphasizes the pursuit of "evidence-based strategies" to achieve stated goals, monitoring stated metrics and progress over time, and undertaking rigorous evaluations to promote learning (Brest, 2015).

Other strategists have called for the development of a broader "theory of the foundation" that can "give the sector a way to compare and analyze models, assess how it allocates resources, and seek links between how a foundation operates and what results it achieves" (Berman, M. A., 2016). This analysis calls on foundations to "address urgent questions, explore fundamental beliefs or implicit assumptions about their work, and more effectively align foundation purpose, public benefit, and action" (Berman, Major, & Franklin, 2017, p. 5). Under this framework, foundations are encouraged to examine their formative charter, which encompasses the institution's mission, values, and origins; social compact, including relationships with partners, external stakeholders, and other modes of accountability; and operating capabilities, such as decision-making processes, grantmaking practices, and organizational elements. Doing so will help foundations and their leaders more comprehensively understand the role these organizations play within social systems.

There are evidently many synergies linking these notions about how the philanthropic sector might be more responsive to societal concerns with the framework of responsible research and innovation. First defined in 2011, RRI has evolved from multiple ideas that aim to describe the relationship between science and society, particularly drawing on thinking about how to anticipate the current and future societal implications of emerging technologies. The concept's flexibility, adaptability, and relevance in a wide array of contexts has helped maintain its value and make it useful for a variety of purposes. While presenting a full history of the evolution of the RRI concept is outside the scope of this book, the core components of the idea have remained relatively steady as it has been refined in recent years and applied in more contexts. The first, canonical working definition of RRI described this concept as "a transparent, interactive process by which societal actors and innovators become mutually responsive to each other with a view on the (ethical) acceptability, sustainability and societal desirability of the innovation process and its marketable products (in order to allow a proper embedding of scientific and technological advances in our society)" (von Schomberg, 2011, p. 9). Later on, in a 2013 article written by scholars Jack Stilgoe, Richard Owen, and Phil Macnaghten, RRI is defined as "taking care of the future through collective stewardship of science and innovation in the present" (Stilgoe, Owen, & Macnaghten, 2013, p. 1570). This article also presents a high-level categorization scheme for the RRI concept, which helps to illuminate how RRI might be applied in the real world. The general contours of that structure will be used to help guide the discussion of specific examples throughout this book. The four dimensions of the RRI framework outlined in that article include: anticipation, reflexivity, inclusion, and responsiveness. A book chapter published that same year, with an additional set of co-authors in Michael Gorman, Erik Fisher, and David Guston, provides a similar structure to organize the primary dimensions of the RRI framework, this time using the following headline descriptor terms: anticipatory, reflective, deliberative, and responsive (Owen, et al., 2013, p. 38).

The intention here is not to parse these minor differences between the two presentations of the RRI frameworks. Both versions of the RRI framework either map exactly (the first and fourth) or rather directly (second and third) to one another. The article and the book chapter describe the second component, involving reflexivity, as the need for individuals and institutions to interrogate their underlying assumptions, practices, and desired outcomes from the standpoint of how they want their research efforts to influence society. The third dimension, associated with the inclusion and deliberative dimensions of RRI, makes evident the need to engage a wider range of stakeholders and members of the public when it comes to making decisions about societal impacts of science and technology. The book chapter authors further describe this component as "inclusively *opening up* visions, purposes, questions, and dilemmas to broad, collective deliberation through processes of dialogue, engagement, and debate, inviting and listening to wider perspectives from publics and diverse stakeholder" [italics in original] (Owen, et al., 2013, p. 38). These various presentations of the RRI framework make clear its interpretive flexibility and usefulness in multiple circumstances. One recent article that has charted the progression of RRI as a valuable heuristic tool notes as much, concluding that the "multiple labels, approaches and genealogies alluded to in different areas of the responsible research and innovation literature make this subject difficult to characterize in any definitive way. What is clear is that an expanding body of analysis and policy practice has built up over the last decade around notions of 'responsibility' in this area" (Genus & Stirling, 2018, p. 62).

The role that science philanthropies might play in adopting, applying, and implementing the perspective suggested in each RRI dimension will be explored in greater detail in subsequent chapters. The RRI framework is indispensable in this context for multiple reasons. First, as shown on p. 4, even among the vast and growing literature on RRI, science philanthropies remain under-examined and under-appreciated sites for attention and action. Second, the dimensions of RRI can serve as an interpretative guide for understanding how science philanthropies operate, even if philanthropic institutions have not explicitly utilized RRI terminology as part of their grantmaking or strategic processes. Third, it is clear from these touchstone definitions that adopting the RRI lens can help guide science philanthropies in thinking more critically about their role in the ecosystem of scientific research. In other words, the RRI framework can provide useful criteria to aid science-oriented foundations in their decision-making processes going forward. Finally, and perhaps most importantly, the application of the RRI framework to the philanthropic sector helps uncover where gaps might lie in current practice and suggests new pathways for funders to pursue.

As the examples explored in subsequent chapters indicate, there is a wide range of actions and interventions that can be pursued to build out a robust portfolio RRI-oriented science philanthropy at all levels, from changing how projects for funding are identified, to adjusting how grant proposals are reviewed and assessed, to updating how projects create impact. In these ways, the RRI framework can lead to demonstrable and tangible improvements in understanding how science philanthropies operate. This book will thereby provide funders, researchers, and practitioners interested in science philanthropy with a set of examples, perspectives, and lessons learned that can help each of these stakeholder groups chart their own course in thinking about how to apply principles from the RRI framework to their own particular institutional context.

Motivation and methodological approach: multi-modal qualitative research to illuminate the practice of science philanthropy

A central goal of this book is to combine the RRI theoretical framework with a detailed investigation of the role that foundations play in shaping science and technology. To do so, it will crosswalk the three main RRI dimensions (anticipation, deliberation and inclusion, reflexivity and responsiveness) with a typology of three primary approaches, or modes of support, that characterize how foundations typically tend to work within science and technology systems. The first mode of support is funding for *individuals*, often in the form of funding for fellowships or primary investigator-led research projects. The second mode of support is funding for *institutions*, often in the form of establishing new organizations or helping to sustain institutions or research centers once they have been created. The third mode of support is funding for *networks*, activities that aim to link together researchers or institutions different disciplines, fields, or sectors. By interacting the RRI dimensions with these modes of support, the qualities and characteristics of different philanthropic interventions can be elucidated. Of course, foundations do not operate in a vacuum. There are modes of collaboration with other funders from government and industry, and examples and perspectives presented throughout the book that will touch on some of the salient details of these cross-sectoral partnerships and relationships.

I have employed a variety of qualitative methodological approaches to study these questions and examine issues related to societal responsibility across the landscape of philanthropic funding of science and technology. Qualitative methodologies are particularly valuable in this context, as they allow for the investigation of institutional practices and participant perspectives by utilizing a wide range of data sources (Yanow, 1996; Creswell, 2007). Qualitative research puts the researcher at the center of data collection and interpretive analysis (Yanow & Schwartz-Shea, 2006). Qualitative studies have become increasingly valuable in science and technology policy contexts (Mitcham, 2007), especially case studies that allow for the drawing out of lessons learned across different institutions operating in different contexts. Case studies are particularly effective at illuminating nuances and understanding the underlying motivations behind decision-making that are otherwise difficult to understand using other methodologies (Flyvbjerg, 2006; Yin, 2003).

As noted earlier, it is surprising that there are few case studies directly focused on understanding how foundations work to shape the future direction of different areas of science and technology and how they go about determining which grantmaking opportunities to pursue. Moreover, little attention has been paid to how foundations determine whether to support more basic research that may be more disconnected from societal outcomes or to fund research that has a closer connection to societal purposes. Earlier, I mentioned that a few brief case studies focused on science and technology grantmaking have been published in the *Casebook for The Foundation*, a compendium of short examples accompanying Joel Fleishman's *The Foundation*. Each vignette is relatively brief, at about one or two pages long, and is similarly structured into three or four parts, presenting the background of a particular topic or challenges, describing the strategy behind a foundation's decision to provide support, highlighting the resulting outcomes, and then discussing the more widespread impact resulting from this provision of funds.

For instance, a good example is the description of The Rockefeller Foundation's decision to fund the Hale Telescope on Mount Palomar in California in the early decades of the 20th Century. The capsule description begins by introducing the astronomer George Ellery Hale and his desire to build "a massive new telescope" that "would be a worthy investment in scientific progress" (Kohler, S., 2007, p. 38). The example continues by noting that Hale solicited funding from the International Education Board, then affiliated with The Rockefeller Foundation, which subsequently approved the request and led to the construction of the new instrument. The telescope would be the largest built in the world to that date, and as the case study notes, it was "not built for 'practical' uses" yet was envisioned as "an instrument of discovery for discovery's own sake" (Kohler, S., 2007, p. 39). It concludes by noting that, "the exploration, research, and discovery that it has enabled certainly owe something…to the Rockefeller Foundation, which brought it forth from Hale's imagination onto the slopes of Mount Palomar" (Kohler, S., 2007, p. 39). In the context of discussions of RRI, these last points are rather telling. First, it is the anticipatory or future-oriented nature of Hale's vision that contributed to the foundation's decision to provide support. As with many discussions as to what scientific research foundations choose to fund, the stated rationale for funding the Hale Telescope, at least in this telling, is solely reliant on its ability to advance basic knowledge in the fields of astronomy and astrophysics. This is a laudable goal, and the scientific breakthroughs that this telescope, among others, ushered in transformed these fields. Yet, as with other examples to be discussed throughout this book, there are many other elements of broader social responsibility that science philanthropies can and should take better account of in order to contribute more fully to societal well-being.

The dearth of case studies examining the ways in which foundations support science and technology research is compounded by the fact that there are very few foundations, and perhaps only one, that explicitly have adopted the RRI framework to guide the work they do. The lone example is the Bassetti Foundation, based in Milan, which has adopted the mission "to promote responsibility in innovation within both the national and international setting, helping institutional, private and associational actors to orient their aims and goals, in considering them a factor of interest for the entire society; both in the techno-scientific field and regarding governance models" (Fondazione Giannino Bassetti, 2016). In an endnote published in the 2013 book *Responsible Innovation*, the point of view of the Bassetti Foundation is further described as being grounded "in the belief that *responsibility must lie within the innovation process*" [italics in original] (Hankins, 2013, p. 271). That chapter goes on to describe the funding the foundation provided to conduct public perception surveys on science, technology, and innovation governance issues in Italy and efforts supported to integrate language related to public participation in innovation processes in regional policy-making documents.

As these short descriptions of philanthropic practice show, there is substantial value in using various qualitative resources to examine these institutions in depth. The methods utilized for this book follow this approach, drawing on examples and in-depth case studies culled from a wide range of publicly available published materials, my own personal experience in the area of science philanthropy, and numerous interviews with various subject matter experts designed to elucidate their views and perspectives on the topic. I conducted over 20 interviews with individuals from a variety of sectors—including philanthropy, non-governmental organizations, and academia—to solicit a range of perspectives from those involved in a variety of different roles with respect to the science and technology enterprise. Many interviewees have had experience in multiple kinds of organizations throughout their career, also including government and the private sector, thereby situating them well to provide rich insight from a deep base of knowledge and experience. Approximately half of the interviewees are based at foundations involved in science, technology, or innovation broadly construed. These interviewees from the philanthropic sector reflect a wide range of foundation roles and responsibilities, including strategy development, program design and management, grantmaking implementation and oversight, executive and board relations, and communications. Interviewees from outside philanthropy were individuals that conduct research, analyze the scientific research process, or who have received or regularly sought foundation funding. While most of the perspectives provided were oriented toward the United States, views from those outside the United States were also presented, and many respondents have had extensive experience working in the global science and technology research ecosystem.

Interviews took place over the course of 2018 and 2019, with the majority of interviews occurring by phone—given that most interviewees were busy professionals, that was the most expedient modality—and a handful taking place in-person. Interviews generally lasted less than an hour and most were audio recorded and then subsequently professionally transcribed. Key quotations and themes that emerged were then identified through a review of the interview transcripts. In every instance, interviewees clearly indicated their permission to participate in the project. Since the interviewer serves as the "instrument" of data collection in qualitative research (Stake, 2010), I was sure to make clear to all interviewees my current and previous professional roles in the field, especially given the research topic focused on philanthropy. I also stated to the interviewees that I was undertaking this research in my personal capacity and that all conclusions would be my own and not representative of any foundation where I work now or where I have been affiliated in the past.

In addition to conducting interviews, a wide array of foundation-related documents, reports, and other materials were examined as part of the research process. Many foundations publicly share grantmaking and strategy-related information through their websites, in annual reports, and via other outputs and mechanisms such as press releases and blog posts that provide a glimpse into how these institutions approach their grantmaking. While these publicly available materials rarely tell the whole story, they serve as the interface between a foundation, their set of grantees, and the broader public, providing important signals as to what themes and topics the foundation views as important. Newspaper, magazine, and other media coverage about foundations also were examined to get a sense of how these institutions are perceived externally. These materials serve as useful sources of information for analysis. Utilizing these multiple sources—interviews, public strategy documents, website material, and other documents—allows for the triangulation of findings and helps ensure the development of a well-rounded perspective about how these institutions operate (Tracy, 2013). Where possible throughout the book, material from these different information streams is presented and discussed to help ensure the rigor of analysis, credibility of findings, and significance of contributions (Tracy, 2010).

Book structure

Following this introductory chapter, the second chapter will provide a brief historical overview that will cover examples of how foundations and wealthy individual donors have previously supported and shaped the direction of science and technology research in the past. Many of the tactics adopted by science philanthropies today can trace their origins back to ways of working that were developed and refined by foundations in the early and middle decades of the 20th Century. In particular, this chapter will focus on detailing the historical origins of many of the grantmaking and operational practices that contemporary science philanthropies employ today.

The third chapter outlines the analytic framework that will guide the remainder of the book. This chapter will link together the ways in which science philanthropies contribute to research, guided by canonical versions of the RRI framework. Examining these intersections produces nine types of grantmaking that characterize how foundations can influence the direction of science and technology research.

The fourth chapter will draw on examples from multiple philanthropies to illuminate the nuances of this framework in greater depth. It examines different types of philanthropic grantmaking to individuals, institutions, and networks, featuring instances of philanthropic efforts that reflect qualities of anticipation, deliberation and inclusion, and reflexivity and responsiveness. Some of the examples presented in this chapter will also highlight collaborative funding arrangements that bring together resources from multiple foundations and those that combine funding from multiple sources across different sectors, including philanthropy, government, and industry. The relationship between philanthropic, public, and private funding for science and technology is complex. Funders rarely act alone and are often aware of what one another is undertaking. It is therefore important to understand the synergies that can be gained from these partnerships, appreciate the factors that lead to success, and pay attention to challenges that may arise along the way.

Having covered a wide variety of science philanthropy examples in the fourth chapter, the fifth chapter will then dive into two case studies in greater detail. These case studies will explore how different science philanthropies have supported and cultivated two different kinds of research networks. The first case study will focus on The Rockefeller Foundation's Searchlight network, a multiyear program that consisted of a global group of forward-looking research organizations tasked by the foundation with identifying future trends related to a broad range of topics, one of which was science and technology. The second case study will be the Sloan Digital Sky Survey, a larger-scale, externally oriented research network that has worked over decades to transform the way that astronomy utilizes and leverages sophisticated data science tools and analytic techniques. Operating at different sizes, scales, and strategic purposes, an examination of what can be learned from these two research networks in light of the RRI framework will help show different ways that science philanthropies can operationalize key dimensions of societal responsibility.

The sixth chapter will analyze reflections from individuals involved in the field of science philanthropy, assessing perspectives provided by interviewees on an array of strategic topics related to how science philanthropy operates today and where it may be headed in the future. Despite the substantial variations within the sector, interviewees raised a number of common points that illuminate crucial challenges and opportunities that science philanthropies are likely to face as the field evolves. Among other points, these include the need to broadly scan for ideas, develop new ways of identifying and funding research that may be high-risk yet high-reward, better link research to address global problems, and ensure that foundations continue to take the long view when it comes to investing in research.

The seventh chapter will then study alternative forms of science philanthropy that are on the ascent and consider them in connection to the RRI framework. These developments include, but are not limited to, science philanthropies establishing in-house research centers within their own organizations, the rise of crowdfunding as a tool for supporting science and technology research, and increased interest in foundations utilizing for-profit funding strategies and investments to enhance the impact of their grantmaking. Moreover, this chapter will point to ways in which science philanthropy may be evolving to the point where traditional notions of philanthropic institutions are morphing, dissolving, or being wholly reimagined. This chapter demonstrates both the broad usefulness of the RRI framework as an interpretative schematic for understanding how science philanthropy operates today, as well as showing where some of the boundary cases and limitations may lie.

Finally, the eighth and concluding chapter will both highlight a number of lessons learned that arise from this analysis and lay out a series of hypothetical scenarios that suggest different, alternative futures for the relationship between science philanthropy and societal responsibility. The intention of presenting these imaginary scenarios is to shed light on the idea that while the exact future of science philanthropy is not knowable, it is possible to think through alternative possibilities productively and in a way that can be preparatory for whatever developments do arise. In the end, I hope that this book deepens the conversation about the role that science philanthropies can play in society and provides a roadmap for how to navigate this environment in the years ahead.

Bibliography

Abir-Am, P. G. (2002). The Rockefeller Foundation and the Rise of Molecular Biology. *Nature Reviews Molecular Cell Biology*, 3(1), 65–70.

Ahrweiler, P., Gilbert, N., Schrempf, B., Grimpe, B., & Jirotka, M. (2018). The Role of Civil Society Organizations in European Responsible Research and Innovation. *Journal of Responsible Innovation*, 6(1), 25–49.

Aldrich, J. (2014, March 20). Why Scientific Research Needs Both Public and Private Support. Retrieved January 2019, from *The Washington Post*: www.washingtonpost.com/news/monkey-cage/wp/2014/03/20/why-scientific-research-needs-both-public-and-private-support/?utm_term=.0add4bd01796.

Alfred P. Sloan Foundation. (2019). About. Retrieved January 2019, from Alfred P. Sloan Foundation: https://sloan.org/about#mission.

American Academy of Arts & Sciences. (2014). *Restoring the Foundation: The Vital Role of Research in Preserving the American Dream*. Cambridge, MA: American Academy of Arts & Sciences.

Anft, M. (2015, February 8). When Scientific Research Can't Get Federal Funds, Private Money Steps In. Retrieved January 2019, from *The Chronicle of Philanthropy*: www.philanthropy.com/article/When-Scientific-Research/151777.

Appel, T. A. (2000). *Shaping Biology: The National Science Foundation and American Biological Research, 1945–1975*. Baltimore, MD: Johns Hopkins University Press.

Baltimore, D. (2016, September 21). The Boldness of Philanthropists. *Science*, 353 (6307), 1473.

Barben, D., Fisher, E., Selin, C., & Guston, D. H. (2008). Anticipatory Governance of Nanotechnology: Foresight, Engagement, Integration. In E. J. Hackett, O. Amsterdamska, M. Lynch, & J. Wajcman, eds., *The Handbook of Science and Technology Studies: Third Edition* (pp. 979–1000). Cambridge, MA: MIT Press.

Berman, M. A. (2016, March 21). The Theory of the Foundation. Retrieved February 2019, from *Stanford Social Innovation Review*: https://ssir.org/articles/entry/the_ theory_of_the_foundation.

Berman, M. A., Karibi-Whyte, R., & Taraso, O. (2019). *Social Compact in a Changing World: How Philanthropies are Grappling with Growing Scrutiny and Critique*. New York, NY: Rockfeller Philanthropy Advisors.

Berman, M., Major, D., & Franklin, J. (2017). *Frameworks for Private Foundations: A New Model for Impact*. New York, NY: Foundation Center and Rockefeller Philanthropy Advisors, Inc.

Bishop, M., & Green, M. (2008). *Philanthrocapitalism: How the Rich Can Save the World*. New York, NY: Bloomsbury Press.

Brest, P. (2012, Spring). A Decade of Outcome-Oriented Philanthropy. Retrieved January 2019, from *Stanford Social Innovation Review*: https://ssir.org/articles/entry/a_ decade_of_outcome_oriented_philanthropy.

Brest, P. (2015, April 27). Strategic Philanthropy and Its Discontents. Retrieved January 2019, from *Stanford Social Innovation Review*: https://ssir.org/up_for_debate/article/ strategic_philanthropy_and_its_discontents.

Broad, W. J. (2014, March 15). Billionaires with Big Ideas are Privatizing American Science. Retrieved January 2019, from *The New York Times*: www.nytimes.com/2014/03/ 16/science/billionaires-with-big-ideas-are-privatizing-american-science.html.

Brooks, S., Leach, M., Lucas, H., & Millstone, E. (2009). *Silver Bullets, Grand Challenges and the New Philanthropy*. Brighton, United Kingdom: STEPS Centre, University of Sussex.

Callahan, D. (2017). *The Givers: Wealth, Power, and Philanthropy in a New Gilded Age*. New York, NY: Alfred A. Knopf.

Center for Strategic Philanthropy & Civil Society. (n.d.). Case Study Database. Retrieved February 2019, from http://cspcs.sanford.duke.edu/learning-resources/ca se-study-database.

Collins, H., & Evans, R. (2007). *Rethinking Expertise*. Chicago, IL: The University of Chicago Press.

Creswell, J. W. (2007). *Qualitative Inquiry and Research Design: Choosing Among Five Approaches*. Thousand Oaks, CA: SAGE Publications.

Enright, K. P. (2018, October 1). Power, Privilege, and Effectiveness: Are Funders Connecting the Dots? Retrieved January 2019, from *Stanford Social Innovation Review*: https://ssir. org/articles/entry/power_privilege_and_effectiveness_are_funders_connecting_the_dots.

European Commission. (2014). *The Role of Philanthropy in the Promotion of Responsible Research and Innovation*. Brussels, Belgium: European Commission.

European Commission. (2015). *Synthesis Report – EUFORI Study: European Foundations for Research and Innovation*. Brussels, Belgium: European Commission.

European Foundation Centre. (2009). *Understanding European Research Foundations: Findings from the FOREMAP Project*. London, UK: Alliance Publishing Trust.

Faculty of the Lilly Family School of Philanthropy. (2019, Fall). Eight Myths of US Philanthropy. *Stanford Social Innovation Review*, 17(4), 26–33.

Finkbeiner, A. (2010). *A Grand and Bold Thing: An Extraordinary New Map of the Universe Ushering in a New Era of Discovery*. New York, NY: Free Press.

Fisher, D. (1993). *Fundamental Development of the Social Sciences: Rockefeller Philanthropy and the United States Social Science Research Council*. Ann Arbor, MI: The University of Michigan Press.

Fitzpatrick, S. M., & Bruer, J. T. (1997, August 1). Science Funding and Private Philanthropy. *Science*, 277(5326), 621.

Fleishman, J. L. (2007). *The Foundation: A Great American Secret*. New York, NY: PublicAffairs.

Fleishman, J. L., Kohler, J. S., & Schindler, S. (2007). *Casebook for The Foundation: A Great American Secret*. New York, NY: PublicAffairs.

Fleming, L., Greene, H., Li, G., Marx, M., & Yao, D. (2019, June 21). Government-Funded Research Increasingly Fuels Innovation. *Science*, 364(6446), 1139–1141.

Florence, R. (1995). *The Perfect Machine: Building the Palomar Telescope*. New York, NY: Harper Perennial.

Flyvbjerg, B. (2006). Five Misunderstandings About Case-Study Research. *Qualitative Inquiry*, 12(2), 219–245.

Fondazione Giannino Bassetti. (2016, May 29). Fondazione Giannino Bassetti. Retrieved February 2019, from What is FGB: www.fondazionebassetti.org/en/pages/2016/05/fondazione_giannino_bassetti.html#sede.

Foundation Center. (2013, October). Distribution of Grants from FC 1000 Foundations by Subject Area, 2012. Retrieved January 2019, from Foundation Stats: http://data.foundationcenter.org/#/fc1000/subject:all/all/total/bar:amount/2012.

Foundation Center. (2014). *Key Facts on U.S. Foundations: 2014 Edition*. New York, NY: Foundation Center.

Funtowicz, S. O., & Ravetz, J. R. (1993, September). Science the Post-Normal Age. *Futures*, 25(7), 739–755.

Genus, A., & Stirling, A. (2018). Collingridge and the Dilemma of Control: Towards Responsible and Accountable Innovation. *Research Policy*, 47(1), 61–69.

Gertner, J. (2013). *The Idea Factory: Bell Labs and the Great Age of American Innovation*. London, UK: Penguin Books.

Giridharadas, A. (2018). *Winners Take All: The Elite Charade of Changing the World*. New York, NY: Alfred A. Knopf.

Grant, B. (2017, December). Can Philanthropy Save Science? *The Scientist*, pp. 61–63.

Hammack, D. C., & Anheier, H. K. (2013). *A Versatile American Institution: The Changing Ideals and Realities of Philanthropic Foundations*. Washington, DC: Brookings Institution Press.

Hankins, J. (2013). Building Capacity for Responsible Innovation. In R. Owen, J. Bessant, & M. Heintz, eds., *Responsible Innovation: Managing the Responsible Emergence of Science and Innovation in Society* (pp. 269–273). West Sussex, UK: John Wiley & Sons.

Heydemann, S., & Toepler, S. (2006). Foundations and the Challenge of Legitimacy in Comparative Perspective. In K. Prewitt, M. Dogan, S. Heydemann, & S. Toepler, eds., *The Legitimacy of Philanthropic Foundations: U.S. and European Perspectives* (pp. 3–26). New York, NY: Russell Sage Foundation.

Hiltzik, M. A. (2000). *Dealers of Lightning: Xerox PARC and the Dawn of the Computer Age*. New York, NY: Harper Business.

Jacobsen, A. (2016). *The Pentagon's Brain: An Uncensored History of DARPA, America's Top-Secret Military Research Agency*. New York, NY: Little, Brown.

Jasanoff, S. (1998). *The Fifth Branch: Science Advisors as Policymakers*. Cambridge, MA: Harvard University Press.

Johnson, J. A., & Sekar, K. (2018). *NIH Funding: FY1999-FY2019.* Washington, DC: Congressional Research Service.

Kania, J., Kramer, M., & Russell, P. (2014, Summer). Strategic Philanthropy for a Complex World. Retrieved January 2019, from *Stanford Social Innovation Review*: https://ssir.org/up_for_debate/article/strategic_philanthropy.

Kastner, M. (2018, December 14). Philanthropy: A Critical Player in Supporting Scientific Research. Retrieved June 2019, from *Science Philanthropy Alliance*: www.sciencephilanthropyalliance.org/philanthropy-a-critical-player-in-supporting-scientific-research-alliance-blog/.

Kleinman, D. L. (1995). *Politics on the Endless Frontier: Postwar Research Policy in the United States.* Durham, NC: Duke University Press.

Kohler, R. E. (1976). The Management of Science: The Experience of Warren Weaver and the Rockefeller Foundation Programme in Molecular Biology. *Minerva*, 14(3), 279–306.

Kohler, R. E. (1991). *Partners in Science: Foundations and Natural Scientists, 1900–1945.* Chicago, IL: Chicago University Press.

Kohler, S. (2007). Mount Palomar "Hale" Telescope. In J. L. Fleishman, J. S. Kohler, & S. Schindler, eds., *Casebook for The Foundation: A Great American Secret* (pp. 38–39). New York, NY: PublicAffairs.

Kramer, D. (2018, June). Foundations Play a Supporting Role in Basic Science. *Physics Today*, pp. 26–29.

Kundu, O., & Matthews, N. E. (2019). The Role of Charitable Funding in University Research. *Science and Public Policy*, 46(4), 611–619.

Max, D. T. (2017, December 18 and 25). The Numbers King. Retrieved January 2019, from *The New Yorker*: www.newyorker.com/magazine/2017/12/18/jim-simons-the-numbers-king.

Mazzucato, M. (2015). *The Entrepreneurial State: Debunking Public vs. Private Sector Myths.* New York, NY: PublicAffairs.

Michelson, E. S. (2016). *Assessing the Societal Implications of Emerging Technologies: Anticipatory Governance in Practice.* Oxford, UK: Routledge.

Mitcham, C. (2007). Qualitative Science Policy. *Qualitative Health Research*, 17(10), 1434–1441.

Morena, E. (2016). *The Price of Climate Action: Philanthropic Foundations in the International Climate Debate.* New York, NY: Palgrave Macmillan.

Murray, F. (2013). Evaluating the Role of Science Philanthropy in American Research Universities. In J. Lerner & S. Stern, eds., *Innovation Policy and the Economy, Volume 13* (pp. 23–60). Chicago, IL: University of Chicago Press.

Nisbet, M. (2018). Strategic Philanthropy in the Post-Cap-and-Trade Years: Reviewing U.S. Climate and Energy Foundation Funding. *WIREs Climate Change*, 524, 1–17.

Nisbet, M. C. (2019, Winter). Sciences, Publics, Politics: Climate Philanthropy and the Four Billion (Dollars, That Is). *Issues in Science and Technology*, 35(2), 34–36.

Owen, R., Stilgoe, J., Macnaghten, P., Gorman, M., Fisher, E., & Guston, D. (2013). A Framework for Responsible Innovation. In R. Owen, J. Bessant, & M. Heintz, eds., *Responsible Innovation: Managing the Responsible Emergence of Science and Innovation in Society* (pp. 27–50). Chichester, UK: John Wiley & Sons.

Pearson, H. (2019, October 27). Private Philanthropy and Public Legitimacy. Retrieved January 2020, from *Alliance*: www.alliancemagazine.org/blog/private-philanthropy-and-public-legitimacy/.

Pew Research Center. (2019). *Trust and Mistrust in Americans' Views of Scientific Experts.* Washington, DC: Pew Research Center.

Piller, C. (2018, December 7). At Arm's Length. *Science*, 362(6419), 1100–1103.

Porter, M. E., & Kramer, M. R. (1999, November–December). Philanthropy's New Agenda: Creating Value. *Harvard Business Review.*

Prewitt, K., Dogan, M., Heydemann, S., & Toepler, S. (2006). *The Legitimacy of Philanthropic Foundations: U.S. and European Perspectives.* New York, NY: Russell Sage Foundation.

Reich, R. (2018). *Just Giving: Why Philanthropy Is Failing Democracy and How It Can Do Better.* Princeton, NJ: Princeton University Press.

Reich, R., Cordelli, C., & Bernholz, L. (2016). *Philanthropy in Democratic Societies: History, Institutions, Values.* Chicago, IL: The University of Chicago Press.

Research Corporation for Science Advancement. (2017). About RCSA. Retrieved January 2019, from Research Corporation for Science Advancement: http://rescorp. org/about-rcsa.

Richardson, T. & Fisher, D., eds. (1999). *The Development of the Social Sciences in the United States and Canada: The Role of Philanthropy.* Stamford, CT: Ablex Publishing Corporation.

Science Advice for Policy by European Academies. (2019). *Making Sense of Science for Policy Under Conditions of Complexity and Uncertainty.* Berlin, Germany: Science Advice for Policy by European Academies.

Science Philanthropy Alliance. (2017, December 11). Science Philanthropy Alliance. Retrieved February 2019, from Taking to the Stars: The Alfred P. Sloan Foundation's 25-year Partnership with the Sloan Digital Sky Survey: www.sciencephilanthropyallia nce.org/science-philanthropy-success-story-the-sloan-foundations-25-year-partnership-with-the-sloan-digital-sky-survey/.

Science Philanthropy Alliance. (2018, June 7). U.S. Research Institutions Received Over $2.3 Billion in Private Funding for Basic Science in 2017. Retrieved January 2019, from Science Philanthropy Alliance: www.sciencephilanthropyalliance.org/u-s-research-institutions-received-over-2-3-billion-in-private-funding-for-basic-science-in-2017-alliance-news/.

Science Philanthropy Alliance. (2019a). Our Mission. Retrieved January 2019, from Science Philanthropy Alliance: www.sciencephilanthropyalliance.org/our-mission/.

Science Philanthropy Alliance. (2019b, June 19). Models for Basic Science Philanthropy. Retrieved October 2019, from Science Philanthropy Alliance: www.sciencephila nthropyalliance.org/models-for-basic-science-philanthropy-alliance-blog-post/.

Seibert, K. (2019). Giving Under the Microscope: Philanthropy, Legitimacy, and a New Era of Scrutiny. *Third Sector Review*, 25(1), 123–141.

Simons Foundation. (n.d.). Mission and Model. Retrieved January 2019, from Simons Foundation: www.simonsfoundation.org/about/.

Solovey, M. (2013). *Shaky Foundations: The Politics-Patronage-Social Science Nexus in Cold War America.* New Brunswick, NJ: Rutgers University Press.

Stake, R. E. (2010). *Qualitative Research: Studying How Things Work.* New York, NY: The Guilford Press.

Stilgoe, J., Owen, R., & Macnaghten, P. (2013). Developing a Framework for Responsible Innovation. *Research Policy*, 42(9), 1568–1580.

The Kavli Foundation. (2019). About the Foundation. Retrieved January 2019, from The Kavli Foundation: www.kavlifoundation.org/about-foundation.

Thumler, E. (2017). *Philanthropy in Practice: Pragmatism and the Impact of Philanthropic Action*. Oxon, UK: Routledge.

Tracy, S. J. (2010). Qualitative Quality: Eight "Big-Tent" Criteria for Excellent Qualitative Research. *Qualitative Inquiry*, 16(10), 837–851.

Tracy, S. J. (2013). *Qualitative Research Methods: Collecting Evidence, Crafting Analysis, Communicating Impact*. Hoboken, NJ: Wiley-Blackwell.

von Schomberg, R. (2011). *Towards Responsible Research and Innovation in the Information and Communication Technologies and Security Technologies Field*. Luxembourg: European Commission.

Vox. (2019). Future Perfect Podcast. Retrieved October 2019, from Vox: www.vox.com/future-perfect-podcast.

Weinberg, B. A., Owen-Smith, J., Rosen, R. F., Schwarz, L., Allen, B. M., Weiss, R. E., et al. (2014, April 4). Science Funding and Short-Term Economic Activity. *Science*, 344(6179), 41–43.

Weinberger, S. (2017). *The Imagineers of War: The Untold Story of DARPA, the Pentagon Agency that Changed the World*. New York, NY: Alfred A. Knopf.

Williams, T. (2016, July 6). Help Wanted: A Funders Alliance Rallies Newcomers to Science Philanthropy. Retrieved January 2019, from *Inside Philanthropy*: www.insidephilanthropy.com/home/2016/7/6/help-wanted-a-funders-alliance-rallies-newcomers-to-science.html.

Yamaner, M. (2012). *ARRA Increased Federal Research and Development and R&D Plant Obligations by $19.2 Billion for FY 2009–10*. Arlington, VA: National Science Foundation.

Yanow, D. (1996). *How Does a Policy Mean? Interpreting Policy and Organizational Actions*. Washington, DC: Georgetown University Press.

Yanow, D., &Schwartz-Shea, P. (2006). *Interpretation and Method: Empirical Research Methods and the Interpretive Turn*. Armonk, NY: M. E. Sharpe.

Yin, R. (2003). *Case Study Research: Design and Methods, Third Edition*. Thousand Oaks, CA: SAGE Publications.

Zinsmeister, K. (2016, Summer). The Power of Science Philanthropy. Retrieved January 2019, from *Philanthropy*: https://www.philanthropyroundtable.org/philanthropy-magazine/article/the-power-of-science-philanthrop

2   Tracing the past

The historical role of foundations in science and technology

A long history, easily forgotten: the origins of philanthropic support for science

In light of the rapid scientific and technological change taking place today, it is easy to forget the many contributing factors involved in creating the advancements we now enjoy, especially when it comes to their funding and financial backing. For this reason, the focus of this chapter both looks back and brings us to the present day. The first purpose is to feature the ways in which foundations and private donors have contributed historically to supporting science and technology research, mainly through an exploration of the rise of philanthropic support during the 20th Century. The second goal is to lay the groundwork for integrating the practice of science philanthropy with the RRI framework, connections that will be probed further in subsequent chapters of the book.

However, it is still the case that most studies in science and technology policy have traced the historical role of government support for research (Kaiser, 2019; Lucier, 2019; England, 1982; Kevles, 1977; Kleinman, 1995; Appel, 2000; Mata & Scheiding, 2012), with considerably less attention paid to the history of science philanthropy. Nevertheless, the origins of modern philanthropy in the United States generally go back more than a century. Similarly, giving by wealthy individuals to science and technology dates to the middle of the 19th Century, if not earlier. Much of this giving occurred in a personalized, somewhat ad hoc manner, as universities and independent research institutions undertaking scientific research were in their nascent stages. This was also an active period in terms of the formation of many of the core institutions of science that exist today, a number of which were either established by or with support from key individual philanthropic patrons through the turn of the century. These include the Smithsonian Institution, created in 1836 from a bequest by British scientist James Smithson; the American Association for the Advancement of Science (AAAS), founded in 1848 as the professional scientific society for the United States; The National Academy of Sciences (NAS), founded by government charter in 1863 as the nation's premier science honorary body; what is now the Rockefeller University, originally the Rockefeller Institute for Medical Research, founded in 1901; and the Carnegie Institution of Washington, established in 1902 as one of the first independent scientific institutions dedicated purely to research.

Writing on this topic of patronage in earlier centuries, Miller (1970) notes in *Dollars for Research* that, "private support helped make possible the first steps in the social organization of modern science in America" (p. x). Later on in the book, he continues by highlighting the central importance these wealthy patrons had on the pursuit of scientific research in the United States, noting that this "patronage...contributed significantly to the pace and quality of American scientific enterprise" and that "the scientific schools, the laboratories, and the numerous astronomical observatories that dotted the country by mid-century formed the foundation of a substantial scientific tradition" (pp. 184–185). In her examination of financial support for scientific research presented in *How Economics Shapes Science*, economist Paula Stephan (2012) reinforces the point that foundations played a critical role not only in shaping the conduct of scientific research today, but in many ways, both individual patrons and philanthropic institutions set the scene for later giving by government. Stephan writes, "long before either the federal government of industry has become a ready source of funds for university research, the Carnegie Foundation, the Rockefeller Foundation, and the Guggenheim Foundation were supporting scientific research" (Stephan, 2012, p. 119).

The formalization of the foundation as an organizational form took place early in the 20th Century. The establishment of the first family foundation— the Russell Sage Foundation, which happened to be dedicated to advancing social science research—occurred in 1907. The eventual "mainstreaming of the modern private foundation" took place in 1911 with the establishment of the Carnegie Corporation of New York and in 1913 the formation of The Rockefeller Foundation (Philanthropy New York, 2008). The Rockefeller Foundation was perhaps the most influential science and technology private philanthropy in the early and middle decades of the 20th Century, spurring advancements that led to the eradication of hookworm and the advent of the Green Revolution. As discussed in Chapter 1, other foundations dedicated to supporting science and technology research emerged over that time period as well, including the Research Corporation for Science Advancement in 1912, the Alfred P. Sloan Foundation in 1934, and the Howard Hughes Medical Institute in 1953. As noted in Chapter 1, a host of newer science and technology foundations were created in the first decade of the 21st Century, including the Gordon and Betty Moore Foundation, The Kavli Foundation, Heising-Simons Foundation, and Simons Foundation, among others.

Since comprehensive coverage of the full and detailed history of science and technology philanthropy is not possible in this brief space, and since others have written more extensively on these historically oriented questions (Kohler, R. E., 1978; Kohler, R. E., 1985; Kohler, R. E., 1987; Reingold, 1997), I will cover some of the key types of developments that emerged over that time frame. In general, in the early decades of the 20th Century, when the form of the foundation was first developed, philanthropic giving to science and technology was mainly driven by the personal interests of wealthy benefactors, with their preferences guiding grantmaking to specific individuals or preferred projects, either out of their own funds directly or through their newly institutionalized foundations. A good example of this approach is The Rockefeller Foundation support of the Hale Telescope described in Chapter 1 (Kohler, S., 2007), an investment which set the stage for other foundations to provide private funding for astronomical observations in the future (McCray, 2004). By the middle decades of the century, as these institutions became more professionalized, they tended to fund more deliberately and intentionally, entering fields strategically or looking to create new ones. A third phase, which brings us to the present day, not only includes the formation of new foundations with a science and technology orientation, but it also involves the establishment of groups like the Science Philanthropy Alliance to help advise newer donors on how to approach the funding of research (Science Philanthropy Alliance, 2019a). Over the past century, some of this giving has resulted in truly transformational improvements in society, what one writer has called "philanthropic moonshots," that has led to everything from figuring out how nature works on a fundamental level, to curing disease, to feeding those in need (Gunther, 2019).

Of course, there is a long and influential history linking scientists with wealthy patrons, influential state actors, and government policymaking going back centuries and across the continents of Europe, North America, and beyond (Westfall, 1985; Andersen, Bek-Thomsen & Kjoergaard, 2012; Moran, 1991). A vast academic literature in the history of science has made evident that the heralded scientists and scientific discoveries of the past would not have been possible without this backing. One thing was plainly clear to those undertaking scientific research: "the certainty that money mattered" (Andersen, Bek-Thomsen, & Kjoergaard, 2012, p. 311). While this point certainly is not new, nor is its relevance limited just to science and technology, this statement underscores that one needs to understand how and why scientific and technological research is funded to get a full picture of how different fields of research evolve and progress over time. Andersen, Bek-Thomsen and Kjoergaard (2012) continue by further describing *why* this funding mattered, expounding that, "money and the need for it kept networks together, cultivated new generations of scientists, opened some doors and closed others, drove people toward topics and places, guided public debates, determined publication patterns, and influenced educational discussions" (p. 311).

The pressing need to consider the funding dimension of science is ever more important today, as the conduct of science becomes more expensive, time frames for reporting findings and results become elongated, research teams get larger, collaborations involve more partners in more countries, debates over intellectual property become more intense, and potential risks increase due to the ability to manipulate natural and human-made systems at both finer and larger scales. Reflecting on these overlapping challenges, Andersen, Bek-Thomsen and Kjoergaard (2012) summarize this point by noting, "with the rise of big science, industrial production, and corporate research and the emergence of a new professional elite of technical experts in the twentieth century, in addition to the increasing demand for external research funding in twenty-first-century universities, the question of how to get what you want always returns to the question of money" (p. 312). As Caroline Wagner has shown, the globalization of science—larger teams, located in different parts of the world, working virtually and collaboratively in a "new invisible college"—creates network effects that not only link together the production and dissemination of knowledge, but in my view, also link together (whether implicitly or explicitly) funding decisions and financial support in ways that are not yet fully understood (Wagner, 2018; Wagner, 2008). This changing nature of the research enterprise has also coincided with the increased interaction of private sector and venture capital money with philanthropic and public sector funding in academic science.

A brief overview of 20th Century science philanthropy

While the contours of contemporary science and technology philanthropy have not been well covered in the academic and public literature, the historical emergence of these wealthy individuals and the early years of these philanthropic institutions has been better documented. Over the course of the 20th Century, high-net-worth individuals' spending from their own coffers and the titular donors headlining these institutions took personal interest in many science-oriented causes that came to bear their name. A number of these examples can be found in *The Almanac of American Philanthropy* that has compiled and catalogued many of these historical reference points in a series of short case studies (Zinsmeister, 2016). To take just three from the many examples included in this collection, the Scripps Institution of Oceanography was funded early in the last century, taking on the name of the donating family and becoming one of the key research centers studying oceanography and marine biology. Later on, the wealthy donor Alfred Loomis funded the famous Loomis Laboratory at the Massachusetts Institute of Technology that resulted in the invention of radar, which significantly contributed to the United States' ability to win World War II. Fast forwarding to the beginning of the 21st Century, Zinsmeister's *The Almanac* also profiles how Microsoft's Paul Allen's interest in neuroscience lead to the founding of the Allen Institute for Brain Science that aims to better understand how the brain functions.

Beyond just putting their names on research institutions, these individual and institutional philanthropic efforts have historically been geared toward creating new fields of science and technology investigation and shaping new directions for existing fields. Morena (2016) portrays this field-building role as one of the most critical contributions that foundations can make to a particular area of inquiry. "Foundations act as field-builders and stewards by providing the vital resources to evaluate field potential, map prospective participants, build collaboration and consensus, encourage public participation, mobilize other foundations and, where necessary, launch new organizations to fill an identified gap," he concludes (p. 15). The Rockefeller Foundation is among the most prominent and visible philanthropies whose early years and decades were focused on giving to both the natural and social sciences, being involved in creating and shaping fields as diverse as physics, oceanography, biology, public health, and agriculture, just to name a few. Beyond just funding science, historical documents indicate The Rockefeller Foundation was interested in applying the principles of scientific inquiry to how the foundation made decisions about programs and grants to pursue. The adoption of "scientific giving" as a key guiding idea throughout its early decades included the now-common practices of gathering data on the scope of a problem, identifying research needs, and identifying metrics to aid in evaluation (The Rockefeller Foundation, n.d.b).

Over time, this perspective would lead The Rockefeller Foundation to create and transform a number of fields and institutions in both the natural and social sciences, both in the United States and abroad (Gemelli, 2001). For instance, The Rockefeller Foundation was instrumental in systematically working to create the fields of cellular and molecular biology from the 1930s through the 1960s (Abir-Am, 2002; Kay, 1993; Kay, 1997). It led the fight to eradicate hookworm and yellow fever, built research laboratories, funded the development of vaccines, sprayed for mosquitoes to remove disease vectors, and created new schools of public health. In doing so, The Rockefeller Foundation created what one author describes as "an attempt to build up what today would be called a public health infrastructure" (Farley, 2004, p. 2). Similarly, The Rockefeller Foundation became an indispensable funder of professionalizing and modernizing medical education, following up on the recommendations of the Flexner Report, produced in 1910 and itself commissioned by a foundation, the Carnegie Foundation for the Advancement of Teaching, to assess the need and challenge improving medical education in the United States and further grounding medical education in emerging science (Duffy, 2011; Gallin, Franko, & Bond, 2018).

Along with other donors, The Rockefeller Foundation also played a critical role in shaping the direction of the physical sciences and mathematics. The foundation supported the establishment of research laboratories and entire university physics departments in both the United States and Europe (The Rockefeller Foundation, n.d.c). Perhaps most notable is their systematic effort to provide a safe haven for physicists, engineers, and mathematicians before, during, and after World War II, giving fellowships and securing placements at universities around the world (Aaserud, 1990; Siegmund-Schultze, 2001). It emphasized interdisciplinary research by connecting scholars in physics, biology, and chemistry, having established a Division of Natural Sciences in the late 1920s to house its grantmaking for scientific research (The Rockefeller Foundation, n.d.b). Furthermore, The Rockefeller Foundation was a key player in promoting the fields of computer science, spurring research that resulted in the formation of research fields focused on advancing machine learning and artificial intelligence. It supported the development of an analog computer by researcher and science policy originator Vannevar Bush, dedicated as the Rockefeller Differential Analyzer, and subsequently turned to supporting digital computing, both as its own field and in combination with other scientific fields like biology and mathematics (The Rockefeller Foundation, n.d.a). In 1956, The Rockefeller Foundation supported what would become a pivotal gathering of researchers in computer science, called the Dartmouth Conference on Artificial Intelligence, in which the leading minds of the field came together to set the pathway forward for research in this area. In fact, it turns out that "the field was so new that mathematician John McCarthy had to invent a new term to help explain the concept of machine learning. In fact, the first known use of the term, 'artificial intelligence,' was in the proposal that McCarthy (with co-authors [Claude E.] Shannon, [Marvin] Minsky, and [Nathan] Rochester) submitted to" The Rockefeller Foundation (The Rockefeller Foundation, n.d.a).

Beyond funding individual scientists and creating new fields of science and technology, foundations like The Rockefeller Foundation, Carnegie Corporation, and others were instrumental in establishing a series of key complementary institutions central to the scientific enterprise that built on and expanded the institutions of science that had their origins in the 19th Century. For instance, the Carnegie Corporation was one of the key foundations that played a central role in providing funding to establish the National Research Council (NRC) in 1916 at the National Academy of Sciences, with the NRC now serving as the operating research arm to conduct research studies in the public interest (Lagemann, 1989; Dupree, 1979). The Carnegie Institution of Washington expanded in the decades since its founding as well, growing to include research in astronomy, geoscience, molecular biology, and other fields that deeply influenced the direction of many scientific disciplines (Reingold, 1979; Good, 1994).

Similar advancements in the early decades of the 20th Century took place with the social sciences, with the Russell Sage Foundation being the first foundation interested in advancing research in the social sciences (Hammack & Wheeler, 1994). The view that better decisions could be made in response to challenging social policy questions through the adoption of rigorous analysis was just beginning to emerge. As Alice O'Connor (2007) writes, the creation of this new foundation near the turn of the last century was one indicator of this growing "conviction that rational, scientific understanding of society and its problems is both a sign and an instrument of purposeful social advance" and that "the role of scientific research, as envisioned at the Russell Sage Foundation, would be to transcend personal bias, ideology, and partisan political interest to shape and inform reasoned public debate" (p. 1). As the 20th

Century progressed, additional social science research foundations and research centers were established, including the Wenner-Gren Foundation for Anthropological Research in the early 1940s (Lindee & Radin, 2016); the Richard Lounsbery Foundation in the late 1950s, which is now focused on supporting work related to United States science policy (Richard Lounsbery Foundation, 2020); and many other social science institutions that were backed by Rockefeller family funding and by The Rockefeller Foundation. In particular, there is substantial literature debating the ways in which philanthropic money in general, and Rockefeller family money in particular, shaped the course of social science inquiry, the emergence and development of different fields, and the structure of academic disciplines and departments (Fisher, 1993; Seim, 2015; Richardson & Fisher, 1999; Aldrich, 2014). Though the purpose here is not to adjudicate these debates, there is no denying that philanthropic funding for the social sciences professionalized, systematized, and codified these modes of thought and research. A particularly important watershed moment was the creation by the Laura Spellman Rockefeller Memorial Fund of the Social Science Research Council (SSRC) in 1923, the first national, independent social science research institution (The Rockefeller Foundation, n.d.d). Fisher (1993) writes that, "the creation of the SSRC was the most important indicator of the dramatic shift in the social science disciplines toward a more scientific and systematic approach," trying "to coordinate the now separate disciplines into a supradiscipline—a new science of society" (p. 5).

This was an era that also saw the creation of the National Bureau of Economic Research (NBER) in 1920, an independent organization designed to help coordinate, collect, and share economic research. Fabricant (1984) describes the purpose of NBER as creating "a firmer basis of economic policy" by substantiating economic research in empirical analytic methods and by being carried out with the greatest degree of objectivity and impartiality (p. 1). One book examining the history of the development of economics research institutions emphasizes the importance of philanthropy in creating entities like the SSRC and NBER, stating that "private foundations played a crucial role in the founding of the NBER," noting that the Laura Spellman Rockefeller Memorial Fund "was responsible for much of the fortyfold increase in philanthropic support for the social sciences that occurred during this period" (Fogel, Fogel, Guglielmo, & Grotte, 2013, p. 45). Without this funding from the philanthropic community that existed at the time, it is unlikely that these institutions that are so essential and indispensable to many fields in the social sciences would have been as influential as they are today.

Over the decades, as additional foundations and federal agencies began to move into funding science, debates ensued about which pathways were appropriate for funders and researchers to pursue in the social sciences. These included disagreements about which specific social science disciplines warranted philanthropic support, whether foundations should fund more basic or applied social science efforts, how closely researchers should engage or interact with stakeholders from industry or government, and where the study of, and involvement in, politics began and ended. Many of these debates continue to this day, signaling the importance of questions associated with how philanthropic funding—its sources, interests, and contingencies—might impact the results of academic research that studies human behavior. As Solovey (2013) concludes in his book on this topic, "understanding how we have gotten to this polyvalent and even deeply confusing historical juncture requires careful consideration of the changing funding landscape" (p. 203).

Beyond all the disciplinary field-building and provision of direct support for natural and social science research, foundations in the United States also had a considerable role to play in laying the groundwork for later efforts to advance diversity in science and in establishing cross-cutting fields like science and technology policy. There is little academic scholarship on either topic about the historical role that philanthropies played in advancing diversity, equity, and inclusion in science or on the early relationship between philanthropy and development of the field of science and technology policy. On the issue of addressing diversity and inclusion, a book chapter written by Percy Pierre documents the role that the Alfred P. Sloan Foundation played in the 1970s in helping to advance training for under-represented minority doctoral students in science and engineering, particularly at historically black colleges and universities (HBCUs) and other minority serving institutions (Pierre, 2015). There is some analysis to indicate that foundations were quite central in helping to advance the field of science and technology policy. In a monograph covering the history of the field, science policy scholar Albert Teich (2018) offers various examples in which philanthropies have played an essential role in an array of science and technology policy matters. In addition to noting that "private foundations have contributed in a major way to the development of higher educational institutions in the United States," he points to examples drawn from the history of the Sloan Foundation in which philanthropic funding has been instrumental in contributing to advances in science and technology policy (Teich, 2018, p. 119). Teich describes the Sloan Foundation as having an "outsized impact on academic science policy as well as on engineering education and research on societal aspects of science and technology," underlining grants the Sloan Foundation made to organize a series of touchstone workshops and programs at both the NAS and AAAS all the way back to the 1960s that served as foundational developments in the field. This includes the support for a "Symposium on Basic Research" at the AAAS and funds in 1968 to help establish a "Science and Public Policy Studies Group," a community-building effort that helped to crystallize the field through participation of leading academic researchers, government science administrators, and other influential stakeholders (p. 119–120).

The contemporary impact of foundations in the area of science and technology policy is most evident in the establishment of the Science Philanthropy Alliance, formed in 2013, as one mechanism by which the leading science foundations of today could help further advance philanthropic giving toward science and technology. An essay prepared by the presidents of the six founding members at that time—Howard Hughes Medical Institute, The Kavli Foundation, Gordon and Betty Moore Foundation, Simons Foundation, Alfred P. Sloan Foundation, and Research Corporation for Science Advancement—describes the pressing need for this kind of effort. "Our premise is that building bridges within and among government, universities, and philanthropy, the three great American pillars that support and carry out basic research, is critical to ensuring our nation's science and innovation leadership," write the authors of this brief essay (Conn, et al., 2013, p. 1). This document notes that the first two goals of the organization were "to create via a targeted effort a greater appreciation among philanthropists and foundations (both current and new) of the importance of scientific research to all aspects of our society" and "to increase substantially philanthropic funding for basic research, with the specific goal of increasing that support by at least $1 billion annually within five years" (Conn, et al., 2013, p. 1). As of October 2019, the Science Philanthropy Alliance indicated that it has largely accomplished this goal and "estimates it has influenced more than $1 billion in new funding to basic science" (Science Philanthropy Alliance, 2019c).

A third goal, which has become the cornerstone of Science Philanthropy Alliance efforts in more recent years, was encouraging and facilitating partnerships between science and technology philanthropies and helping to advise new philanthropists and their foundations eager to provide more funding to the sciences. The aforementioned essay continues by highlighting that the very flexibility foundations enjoy in their operations, as I noted in Chapter 1, is one of the core reasons as to why foundations should not only direct more of their resources toward science and technology, but that these institutions should do so in a collaborative and collective manner. The authors of this essay, the leaders of some of the most well-known science-oriented funders in the country, summarize this point as follows:

> Philanthropic institutions and philanthropists themselves often have more freedom to operate than do the science funding agencies of government, permitting them to be more flexible and nimble. We believe now is the time that they should take advantage of that flexibility by directing an increased fraction of their giving to support bold and innovative research in basic science. Moreover, we believe that these dollars can go further if funders can find new ways to collaborate in areas of shared interest.
>
> (Conn, et al., 2013, p. 3)

Coverage and commentary on the establishment of the Science Philanthropy Alliance emphasized similar points. For instance, a 2015 *Science* article about the appointment of the organization's inaugural president Marc Kastner describes the organization's intent as "getting more people and organizations to emulate what they are already doing: giving money to the nation's universities for basic science" (Mervis, 2015). A similar article in *Nature* from 2016 frames the

Science Philanthropy Alliance's motivation as a response to uneven federal funding for research, noting that "uncertain government funding drives efforts to increase private support for research" (Hayden, 2016, p. 302).

From patronage to professionalization in science philanthropy

As philanthropies became increasingly engaged in funding and guiding science and technology, it is evident from this discussion of philanthropy in the 20th Century that a new model for how foundations would come to operate began to come into focus. The various contributing factors to this new mode, what one might call the professionalization of science philanthropy, is discussed in perhaps that most comprehensive historical account of how science philanthropy arose, *Partners in Science: Foundations and Natural Scientists, 1900–1945*, written by Robert E. Kohler (1991). In this book, Kohler describes why understanding how the professionalization of science philanthropy came to be is vitally important for gaining insight about how science is done today. He notes that while "the practice of science has meant a more complex social relationship with extramural sponsors," often the practicalities of this arrangement garner less attention, since "grant-getting and the organizational work of science seem far less interesting and important than the production of knowledge as such" (Kohler, R. E., 1991, p. 1) Kohler's extensive study of the early decades of science philanthropy identifies the ways in which many of the practices that guide science philanthropy today were established in the first half of the 20th Century.

Kohler points out the three key components of this "new system of science patronage" that persist to this day (p. 265). The first is the "the belief that it was necessary and proper for sponsors to identify specific disciplines or research specialties in which to invest," indicating that foundations began to make deliberate choices between fields as they selected where to give their money (p. 265). The second element Kohler identifies, and "most crucial" in his formulation, is the emergence of "the activist program manager, who knew enough science to devise a program, select fields of concentration, and make informed judgments about individuals and their projects" (p. 265). What Kohler is describing here is the professionalization of program management positions in foundations, with a new set of individuals filling these roles that combine a degree of knowledge in a topic area with expertise in program oversight, budgeting, strategy, and other related characteristics. The third element is the development of the "project grant, a vehicle of funding that made an activist, programmatic style of patronage practicable, and that gave individual grants a larger institutional purpose" (p. 265). Science historian Philip Mirowski has pointed out that these core characteristics that have come to be closely associated with science philanthropy were very much drawn from the industrial routines of the day. One of the downsides that Mirowski (2011) suggests in his book *Science-Mart* is that these traits were one of the factors that, in the early years, tended to concentrate grantmaking for science to a small number of elite universities. "In everything from recasting the research grant as a contract that imposed certain standards of bureaucratic accountability, to imposing the line- and division-managerial structure on university administrations and departments, to encouraging the creation of hierarchical teams of researchers, the corporate officers who staffed the large foundations tended to foster the standards and practices of the large American corporation within their targeted flagship research universities," writes Mirowski (Mirowski, 2011, pp. 102–103).

Perhaps the most iconic personification of this new practitioner role in the early years of science philanthropy was Warren Weaver, the head of The Rockefeller Foundation's natural science division and later the vice president at the Sloan-Kettering Institute for Cancer Research. In this model, science and technology funders like Weaver developed a new approach to overseeing science philanthropy grantmaking. In an earlier article on the impact of Weaver's approach on the relationship between science and philanthropy, titled "The Management of Science," Kohler describes an emerging mode in which projects were selected "according to an elaborate plan" and that individual program leads were "active in formulating specific schemes of research which flowed from that plan and in finding competent scientists to carry them out" (Kohler, R. E., 1976, p. 280). In this article, Kohler continues by noting that in the early decades of the 20th Century, "the large foundations espoused the idea that science was a cultural 'resource' to be managed in the interests of the country as a whole" (p. 304). Kohler further describes this period as one in which "the emergence of a new social role, the 'scientist-entrepreneur'" took hold, signaling the establishment of a new type of professional involved in the scientific enterprise: one that had "an understanding of both the academic scientist and the practical needs of the institution in which they worked" and, because of this dual expertise, was capable of "bringing together groups with quite different conceptions of science and its social use" (p. 305).

In both *Partners in Science* and "The Management of Science" article, Kohler evocatively describes the role of this new institutional role that characterized the grantmaking approach of numerous programmatic leads like Weaver; Wickliffe Rose and H. J. Thorkelson of the General Education Board, affiliated with The Rockefeller Foundation; Augustus Trowbridge of The Rockefeller Foundation's International Education Board; and others like them. This new breed of philanthropy professional brought themselves "into the inner sanctum of scientific careers, laboratory practices, and community organizations," creating "a cycle of visits, proposals, conferences, reports, and renewals [that] was the social machinery of an active, working partnership" (Kohler, R. E., 1991, p. 395). "The science programs of the Carnegie, Rockefeller, and other foundations were an evolving social system," writes Kohler (p. 395). It is this history that foreshadowed how new institutions would operate, and created a new model that would forever link philanthropic donors with research scientists across almost all areas of science and technology.

The mechanisms described by Kohler, developed by philanthropies decades earlier to inform decision-making, continue to be relevant today. The leading science philanthropies of the 21st Century regularly use these processes to set institutional priorities. A 2018 blog post from the Science Philanthropy Alliance reporting on the themes emerging from a discussion among the presidents of the The Kavli Foundation, Research Corporation for Science Advancement, and the Alfred P. Sloan Foundation illustrates that these institutions draw on many of the same procedures to determine their direction. These leaders note that science philanthropies still make "extensive use of scientific advisory boards, meet with scientists, and convene meetings and workshops. The input of the scientific community is an important part of their decision-making" (Conn, 2018). A subsequent 2019 blog post reporting on a panel discussion that included the leaders of the Heising-Simons Foundation, The Shurl and Kay Curci Foundation, and the Gordon and Betty Moore Foundation accentuated similar points (Science Philanthropy Alliance, 2019b). The discussion highlighted that foundations across various stages of development, from early formation to being more established, rely on the operational styles that were first pioneered by those at The Rockefeller Foundation and other foundations in the previous century. This included not only relying on statements of donor intent to guide grantmaking, but also developing clearly-worded mission statements to set funding priorities, assessing research fields to understand the funding landscape, and engaging external expert advisory committees to help inform how grantmaking should proceed.

Science philanthropy in the complex ecosystem of research support

As evidenced by the examples discussed throughout this chapter, philanthropy played a fundamental role in generating and advancing much science and technology research throughout the 20th Century. That role not only remains today, but I argue that within the context of the contemporary science and technology enterprise, the role of philanthropy has become even more multi-faceted and complex as the resources needed to undertake large-scale research projects multiply, as institutional priorities change, and as new organizations form. In her study of contemporary philanthropy's role in science and technology, economist Fiona Murray usefully expresses this perspective as follows: "science's modern-day patrons play a unique, significant, and underappreciated role in US scientific competitiveness. Compared to government funding, however, whose purpose is broadly understood, and industrial funding sources, which usually drive near-term applications, the distribution of today's philanthropic funding cannot easily be theorized" (Murray, 2013, p. 26). Murray's research shows science philanthropy warrants more examination given the role that it plays in setting the direction of science and technology. "While much attention has been paid to the impact of rising industry funding, philanthropists constitute a much bigger contributor to fundamental and translational research taking place in academia," she argues (p. 53). Murray continues by noting that the relationship between these various entities changes over time and often is in flux, concluding "with regard to the relationship between federal and philanthropic funding, their interaction is complex, and the missions, orientations, and approaches of these sources are not always complementary" (p. 54).

Yet, the growing complexity of the funding landscape has also led to changes in how scientists look to secure support for their work. Consider again what Kohler and others, like Steven Shapin (2008) in *The Scientific Life*, have termed the "scientist entrepreneur." This is the emergence of a kind of researcher who looks to bring in and balance funding from multiple sources, having to "sell" their research, as one article put it, in order to stand out in an increasingly crowded and competitive landscape that sees more applications by more investigators for funding each year (Ledford, 2012, p. 254). Sociologist David Johnson has studied the ways in which scientists increasingly face this new "commercialist reward system," which has added profit-seeking motivation and product commercialization to accompany more traditional markers of academic success, such as publication of peer-reviewed papers or tenure promotion (Johnson, 2017, p. 2). As Johnson writes, "the traditional role of universities as committed to a disinterested search for truth now exists alongside a new institutional goal of science that emphasizes the creation of technologies that have a concrete societal impact" (Johnson, 2017, pp. 2–3).

This mode of conducting science oriented more toward industry has grown in stature, especially as traditional government and philanthropic funding is joined by a wide range of private sector sources of capital for research. To this point, Johnson describes that the increasing role of corporate funding for academic science is changing traditional professional norms. He notes that these changes can create frictions that are not easily resolved by those who view entrepreneurial science as being a boon for the research enterprise and those who see this kind of funding as potentially tarnishing scientific pursuits. There are benefits and drawbacks to the presence of both kinds of funding in the academic science ecosystem. Some might argue that the presence of increased private money for science might help steer the academic research enterprise in addressing societal challenges because private funding might have the effect of focusing researcher attention on addressing more applied questions. Others might say that private money comes with a potentially corrupting influence on the science that is done, as it could threaten academic independence and either implicitly or explicitly introduce bias if a researcher looks to shade the conclusions of their studies in favor of their corporate funder. Johnson concludes his assessment of this potentially fraught tension between corporate and public funding by painting a picture of how these two sources of financial support can coexist. "The fruits of science contain both natural and societal applications, but the quest to extract such fruits by any logic that undermines the advance of knowledge could surely be to the detriment of society by severing the meanings, norms, and identity that make academe an integrated, rather than a fractured, profession," he writes (Johnson, 2017, p. 146). Johnson concludes, "science's status in society and what universities do will continue to be shaped by both the relatively old and the relatively new reward systems" (p. 146).

Other research and commentary pieces have reflected on the relationship between public, private, and philanthropic funding, and how the three relate to one another. For instance, commenting on the state of funding for biomedical research in particular, one editorial in *Nature Methods* pointed out that researchers increasingly need to combine support from these different funding sources, even if doing so has its challenges and involves operating in a more entrepreneurial style. "With federal funding for life science becoming increasingly competitive in the United States, it would be a mistake, particularly for young investigators, not to carefully consider money from private sources," it finds (Nature Methods, 2016, p. 537). Similarly, a 2018 workshop organized by the National Academies addressed this topic of how research is increasingly being funded by a variety of different actors across multiple sectors. A key tenet emerging from this meeting is that "how these partnerships are established and maintained, how effective they are in supporting science and innovation, and how to assess their overall impact on the U.S. research enterprise are increasingly relevant questions for leaders in both science and policy" (National Academies of Sciences, Engineering, and Medicine, 2018, p. 1).

Understanding the emerging relationship between different sources of support for science and technology innovation is critical, especially as a growing body of research has shown that science funded by government often plays a disproportionate role in accelerating technological innovation that can improve society (Bonvillian, 2014; Bonvillian, 2018; Fleming, Greene, Li, Marx, & Yao, 2019; Mazzucato, 2015; Mazzucato, 2018). Nevertheless, funds from these other sources of support can have a bolstering and magnifying effect, filling in gaps where government funding is scarce, offering resiliency in times of government funding scarcity, providing additional resources when needed, strengthening researcher networks, and demonstrating widespread interest in an idea that can lead to further knowledge diffusion. In this way, a researcher's ability to combine public, private, and philanthropic dollars can have a multiplicative effect that can boost the chances of a particular research project in having more extensive influence. Additionally, given the flexibility enjoyed by foundations in deciding what research to fund, there is the potential that adding philanthropic sources of support to a research project can add momentum toward a push for ensuring broader societal impact. To this end, based on a study of disclosure rules used by different types of funders when providing support for research, Gans and Murray (2012) find that philanthropic funders have asked for a more explicit attention to be paid to these societal considerations. They determine that, "while public funding organizations have paid attention to the impact of funding conditions on the outcomes of specific projects they fund, very little attention is paid to broader outcomes on the innovation system per se… In contrast, the growing not-for-profit foundation sector, in an attempt to differentiate themselves from purely public funders, has increased their emphasis on social impact" (Gans & Murray, 2012, pp. 98–99).

The inaugural President of the Science Philanthropy Alliance, Marc Kastner, made this case in a blog post published at the end of 2018. In considering the roles "that various funders, including government, industry, academia, and philanthropy play in funding scientific research," Kastner argues that, "I believe that science philanthropy plays a critical role in funding science, one that is distinct from, yet complementary to, the government's role" (Kastner, 2018). While not necessarily using language that directly refers to RRI, Kastner contends that science philanthropy—both in terms of direct giving to research and indirect support provided to university endowments—has a particular role to play in providing funding that responds to the tenets of RRI. For instance, he notes that philanthropic funding can more easily go to support early career scientists who "do not yet have the track record needed to compete for scarce federal funds," can "place bets on scientific research which may be riskier than the science that the government funds," and "can help fund those explorations that would otherwise languish on the idea shelf" (Kastner, 2018).

However, the increasing presence of philanthropy and other kinds of funders in the conduct of science and technology can introduce its own set of risks and potential downsides. For one, the examples above make evident that philanthropic giving in science and technology has always involved a combination of merit review and personal relationships. This potentially creates and reinforces the dynamics of inequality and concentration of funding that critics of philanthropy, discussed in Chapter 1, have raised. Murray's empirical research has shown this to be the case. She finds the majority of funding for science and technology from both federal and philanthropic sources is directed at biomedical research that has already garnered support. Her research also shows that, "philanthropists are more concentrated in their giving to specific (translational) fields than the government, suggesting that with few exceptions…patrons add support to already well-funded wealthy fields instead of filling gaps (p. 54). Stephan has also noted that philanthropy's ability to complement and supplement federal support for scientific research can be hindered by a number of factors, in addition to those that Murray raises. In her book, Stephan points out that philanthropies are subject to market forces, with the rise-and-fall of endowments impacting how much foundations can give away at any particular time. She writes, "nonprofit-foundations support for research can suffer from the same ups and downs related to the business cycle as does government funding and industrial support" (Stephan, 2012, p. 120). Elsewhere, Stephan comments on the concentration of philanthropic funding at a small number of elite research institutions, leading to inequalities among organizations that can be hard, if not impossible, to overcome. Stephan stresses this point by noting, "the philanthropy 'answer' is less readily available to publicly funded and nonelite institutions, whose endowments have grown at a considerably slower pace than those at elite private and top-tier research institutions" (Stephan, 2015, p. 360).

In the end, it is clear that the ways science and technology philanthropies operate today are directly influenced by the intertwined histories of how philanthropy and the scientific research enterprise evolved over the preceding decades. As individual wealthy patrons established formal grantmaking institutions to house their giving for science and technology, many features of the relationship between science and philanthropy took form. This includes the identification of and support for leading researchers, the focus on establishing new fields of inquiry, the creation of new institutions and research centers, and encouraging the combination of resources from multiple sectors. Additionally, the professionalization of the philanthropic program manager role all have their roots in the philanthropies that trace their origins back to the early years of the 20th Century. Yet for all the attention that has been paid to the history of these organizations, contemporary philanthropic practice related to science and technology remains just as rich to explore and understand, especially given the enhanced role these institutions have come to play in the research and innovation system. The next chapter will survey this relationship further, presenting a typology that will serve as the organizing framework for an in-depth examination of these institutions.

Bibliography

Aaserud, F. (1990). *Redirecting Science: Niels Bohr, Philanthropy, and the Rise of Nuclear Physics*. Cambridge, UK: Cambridge University Press.

Abir-Am, P. G. (2002). The Rockefeller Foundation and the Rise of Molecular Biology. *Nature Reviews Molecular Cell Biology, 3*, 65–70.

Aldrich, J. H. (2014). *Interdisciplinarity: Its Role in a Discipline-based Academy*. Oxford, UK: Oxford University Press.

Andersen, C., Bek-Thomsen, J., & Kjoergaard, P. C. (2012). The Money Trail: A New Historiography for Networks, Patronage, and Scientific Career. *Isis, 103*(2), 310–315.

Appel, T. A. (2000). *Shaping Biology: The National Science Foundation and American Biological Research, 1945–1975*. Baltimore, MD: Johns Hopkins University Press.

Bonvillian, W. B. (2014, July). The New Model Innovation Agencies: An Overview. *Science and Public Policy, 41*(4), 425–437.

Bonvillian, W. B. (2018). DARPA and Its ARPA-E and IARPA Clones: A Unique Innovation Organization Model. *Industrial and Corporate Change, 27*(5), 897–914.

Conn, R., Joskow, P., McCormick, S., Pladziewicz, J., Simons, J. A., & Tjian, R. (2013, September). The Science Philanthropy Alliance: Funding Basic Research – The Foundation of Our Future. Retrieved April 2019, from Science Philanthropy Alliance: www.sciencephilanthropyalliance.org/wp-content/uploads/2016/05/Sci-Phil-Alliance-Paper-Sept.-2013.pdf.

Conn, V. (2018, December 6). Leaders in Science Philanthropy Share their Visions. Retrieved July 2019, from Science Philanthropy Alliance: www.sciencephilanthropya lliance.org/leaders-in-science-philanthropy-share-their-visions-alliance-blog/.

Duffy, T. P. (2011). The Flexner Report – 100 Years Later. *Yale Journal of Biology and Medicine, 84*(3), 269–276.

Dupree, A. H. (1979). The National Academy of Sciences and the American Definition of Science. In A. Oleson & J. Voss, eds., *The Organization of Knowledge in Modern America, 1860–1920* (pp. 342–363). Baltimore, MD: The Johns Hopkins University Press.

England, J. M. (1982). *A Patron for Pure Science: The National Science Foundation's Formative Years, 1945–1957*. Washington, DC: National Science Foundation.

Fabricant, S. (1984). Toward a Firmer Basis of Economic Policy: The Founding of the National Bureau of Economic Research. Retrieved March 2019, from National Bureau of Economic Research: www.nber.org/nberhistory/sfabricantrev.pdf.

Farley, J. (2004). *To Cast Out Disease: A History of the International Health Division of Rockefeller Foundation (1913–1951).* Oxford, UK: Oxford University Press.

Fisher, D. (1993). *Fundamental Development of the Social Sciences: Rockefeller Philanthropy and the United States Social Science Research Council.* Ann Arbor, MI: The University of Michigan Press.

Fleming, L., Greene, H., Li, G., Marx, M., & Yao, D. (2019, June 21). Government-Funded Research Increasingly Fuels Innovation. *Science*, 364(6446), 1139–1141.

Fogel, R. W., Fogel, E. M., Guglielmo, M., & Grotte, N. (2013). *Political Arithmetic: Simon Kuznets and the Empirical Tradition in Economics.* Chicago, IL: University of Chicago Press.

Gallin, E. K., Franko, M., & Bond, E. (2018). Philanthropy's Role in Advancing Biomedical Research. In J. I. Gallin, F. P. Ognibene, & L. L. Johnson, eds., *Principles and Practice of Clinical Research, 4th Edition* (pp. 611–630). London, UK: Elsevier.

Gans, J. S., & Murray, F. (2012). Funding Scientific Knowledge: Selection, Disclosure, and the Public-Private Portfolio. In J. Lerner & S. Stern, eds., *The Rate and Direction of Inventive Activity Revisited* (pp. 51–103). Chicago, IL: University of Chicago Press.

Gemelli, G. (2001). *American Foundations and Large-Scale Research: Construction and Transfer of Knowledge.* Bologna, Italy: CLUEB.

Good, G. A. (1994). *The Earth, the Heavens, and the Carnegie Institution of Washington: History of Geophysics, Volume 5.* Washington, DC: American Geophysical Union.

Gunther, M. (2019, July 7). *Philanthropy Lessons.* Retrieved November 2019, from Medium: https://medium.com/the-moonshot-catalog/philanthropy-lessons-7d229aefca16.

Hammack, D. C., & Wheeler, S. (1994). *Social Science in the Making: Essays on the Russell Sage Foundation, 1907–1972.* New York, NY: Russell Sage Foundation.

Hayden, E. C. (2016, October 20). Science Group Guides Silicon Valley Philanthropists. *Nature*, 538(7625), 302.

Johnson, D. R. (2017). *A Fractured Profession: Commercialism and Conflict in Academic Science.* Baltimore, MD: Johns Hopkins University Press.

Kaiser, D. (2019, September 26). Discovery is Always Political. *Nature*, 573(7775), 487–490.

Kastner, M. (2018, December 14). Philanthropy: A Critical Player in Supporting Scientific Research. Retrieved June 2019, from Science Philanthropy Alliance: www.sciencephilanthropyalliance.org/philanthropy-a-critical-player-in-supporting-scientific-research-alliance-blog/.

Kay, L. E. (1993). *The Molecular Vision of Life: Caltech, The Rockefeller Foundation, and the Rise of the New Biology.* New York, NY: Oxford University Press.

Kay, L. E. (1997, September). Rethinking Institutions: Philanthropy as an Historiographic Problem of Knowledge and Power. *Minerva*, 35(3), 283–293.

Kevles, D. J. (1977). The National Science Foundation and the Debate over Postwar Research Policy, 1942–1945: A Political Interpretation of Science – The Endless Frontier. *Isis*, 68(1), 5–26.

Kleinman, D. L. (1995). *Politics on the Endless Frontier: Postwar Research Policy in the United States.* Durham, NC: Duke University Press.

Kohler, R. E. (1976). The Management of Science: The Experience of Warren Weaver and the Rockefeller Foundation Programme in Molecular Biology. *Minerva*, 14(3), 279–306.

Kohler, R. E. (1978, Winter). A Policy for the Advancement of Science: The Rockfeller Foundation, 1924–1929. *Minerva*, 16(4), 480–515.

Kohler, R. E. (1985, March). Philanthropy and Science. *Proceedings of the American Philosophical Society*, 129(1), 9–13.

Kohler, R. E. (1987). Science, Foundations, and American Universities in the 1920s. *Osiris*, 3, 135–164.

Kohler, R. E. (1991). *Partners in Science: Foundations and Natural Scientists, 1900–1945.* Chicago, IL: Chicago University Press.

Kohler, S. (2007). Mount Palomar "Hale" Telescope. In J. L. Fleishman, J. S. Kohler, & S. Schindler, *Casebook for The Foundation: A Great American Secret* (pp. 38–39). New York, NY: PublicAffairs.

Lagemann, E. C. (1989). *The Politics of Knowledge: The Carnegie Corporation, Philanthropy, and Public Policy.* Middletown, CT: Wesleyan University Press.

Ledford, H. (2012, January 18). Alternative Funding: Sponsor My Science. *Nature*, 481 (7381), 254–255.

Lindee, S., & Radin, J. (2016, October). Patrons of the Human Experience: A History of the Wenner-Gren Foundation for Anthropological Research, 1941–2016. *Current Anthropology*, 57(S14), S218–S301.

Lucier, P. (2019, October 24). Can Marketplace Science be Trusted? *Nature*, 574(7779), 481–485.

Mata, T., & Scheiding, T. (2012, December). National Science Foundation Patronage of Social Science, 1970s and 1980s: Congressional Scrutiny, Advocacy Network, and the Prestige of Economics. *Minerva*, 50(4), 423–449.

Mazzucato, M. (2015). *The Entrepreneurial State: Debunking Public vs. Private Sector Myths.* New York, NY: PublicAffairs.

Mazzucato, M. (2018). Mission-Oriented Innovation Policies: Challenges and Opportunities. *Industrial and Corporate Change*, 27(5), 803–815.

McCray, W. P. (2004). *Giant Telescopes: Astronomical Ambition and the Promise of Technology.* Cambridge, MA: Harvard University Press.

Mervis, J. (2015, 27 February). Billionaires for Basic Research. Retrieved April 2019, from *Science*: www.sciencemag.org/news/2015/02/billionaires-basic-research.

Miller, H. S. (1970). *Dollars for Research: Science and Its Patrons in Nineteenth-Century America.* Seattle, WA: University of Washington Press.

Mirowski, P. (2011). *Science-Mart: Privatizing American Science.* Cambridge, MA: Harvard University Press.

Moran, B. T. (1991). *Patronage and Institutions: Science, Technology, and Medicine at the European Court, 1500–1750.* Rochester, NY: Boydell Press.

Morena, E. (2016). *The Price of Climate Action: Philanthropic Foundations in the International Climate Debate.* New York, NY: Palgrave Macmillan.

Murray, F. (2013). Evaluating the Role of Science Philanthropy in American Research Universities. In J. Lerner & S. Stern, eds., *Innovation Policy and the Economy, Volume 13* (pp. 23–60). Chicago, IL: University of Chicago Press.

National Academies of Sciences, Engineering, and Medicine. (2018). *Strategies for Engagement of Non-Traditional Partners in the Research Enterprise: Proceedings of a Workshop.* Washington, DC: The National Academies Press.

Nature Methods. (2016, July). Private Funding for Science. *Nature Methods*, 13(7), 537.

O'Connor, A. (2007). *Social Science for What? Philanthropy and the Social Question in a World Turned Rightside Up.* New York, NY: Russell Sage Foundation.

Philanthropy New York. (2008). History of U.S. Philanthropy. Retrieved March 2019, from Philanthropy New York: https://philanthropynewyork.org/sites/default/files/resources/History%20of%20Philanthropy.pdf.

Pierre, P. A. (2015). A Brief History of the Collaborative Minority Engineering Effort: A Personal Account. In J. B. Slaughter, Y. Tao, & W. Pearson Jr., eds., *Changing the Face of Engineering: The African American Experience* (pp. 13–35). Baltimore, MD: Johns Hopkins University Press.

Reingold, N. (1979). National Science Policy in a Private Foundation: The Carnegie Institution of Washington. In A. Oleson & J. Voss, eds., *The Organization of Knowledge in Modern America, 1860–1920* (pp. 313–341). Baltimore, MD: The Johns Hopkins University Press.

Reingold, N. (1997, September). Form, Function and Fecundity in American Institutions. *Minerva, 35*(3), 221–232.

Richard Lounsbery Foundation. (2020). Richard Lounsbery and the Foundation's Origins. Retrieved January 2020, from Richard Lounsbery Foundation: www.rlounsbery.org/history.

Richardson, T., & Fisher, D. (1999). *The Development of the Social Sciences in the United States and Canada: The Role of Philanthropy.* Stamford, CT: Ablex Publishing Corporation.

Science Philanthropy Alliance. (2019a). Our Mission. Retrieved January 2019, from Science Philanthropy Alliance: www.sciencephilanthropyalliance.org/our-mission/.

Science Philanthropy Alliance. (2019b, June 19). Models for Basic Science Philanthropy. Retrieved October 2019, from Science Philanthropy Alliance: www.sciencephilanthropyalliance.org/models-for-basic-science-philanthropy-alliance-blog-post/.

Science Philanthropy Alliance. (2019c, October 31). Science Philanthropy Alliance Announces Incoming President and Board Chair. Retrieved November 2019, from Science Philanthropy Alliance: www.sciencephilanthropyalliance.org/science-philanthropy-alliance-announces-incoming-president-and-board-chair-alliance-news/.

Seim, D. L. (2015). *Rockefeller Philanthropy and Modern Social Science.* London, UK: Routledge.

Shapin, S. (2008). *The Scientific Life: A Moral History of a Late Modern Vocation.* Chicago, IL: University of Chicago Press.

Siegmund-Schultze, R. (2001). *Rockefeller and the Internationalization of Mathematics Between the Two World Wars.* Basel, Switzerland: Springer Basel AG.

Solovey, M. (2013). *Shaky Foundations: The Politics-Patronage-Social Science Nexus in Cold War America.* New Brunswick, NJ: Rutgers University Press.

Stephan, P. (2012). *How Economics Shapes Science.* Cambridge, MA: Harvard University Press.

Stephan, P. (2015). The Endless Frontier: Reaping What Bush Sowed? In A. B. Jaffe & B. F. Jones, eds., *The Changing Frontier: Rethinking Science and Innovation Policy* (pp. 321–366). Chicago, IL: University of Chicago Press.

Teich, A. H. (2018). In Search of Evidence-based Science Policy: From the Endless Frontier to SciSIP. *Annals of Science and Technology Policy,* 2(2), 75–199.

The Rockefeller Foundation. (n.d.a). Computer Science. Retrieved April 2019, from The Rockefeller Foundation: A Digital History: https://rockfound.rockarch.org/computer-science2/16.

The Rockefeller Foundation. (n.d.b). Natural Sciences. Retrieved March 2019, from The Rockefeller Foundation: A Digital History: https://rockfound.rockarch.org/natural-sciences.

The Rockefeller Foundation. (n.d.c). Physics. Retrieved April 2019, from The Rockefeller Foundation: A Digital History: https://rockfound.rockarch.org/physics.

The Rockefeller Foundation. (n.d.d). Social Science Research Council. Retrieved March 2019, from The Rockefeller Foundation: A Digital History: https://rock found.rockarch.org/social-science-research-council.

Wagner, C. S. (2008). *The New Invisible College: Science for Development*. Washington, DC: Brookings Institution.

Wagner, C. S. (2018). *The Collaborative Era in Science: Governing the Network*. Cham, Switzerland: Palgrave Macmillan.

Westfall, R. S. (1985). Science and Patronage: Galileo and the Telescope. *Isis*, 76(1), 11–30.

Zinsmeister, K. (2016). *The Almanac of American Philanthropy*. Washington, DC: The Philanthropy Roundtable.

3 Typologies of science philanthropy
Linking philanthropic approaches with responsible research and innovation

Philanthropy and the RRI framework: current state of the discussion

The history of science and technology philanthropy, covered in the previous chapter, indicates that foundations play a central and critical role within the scientific endeavor. In fact, as noted in Chapter 1, this ability to operate with few practical restrictions, so long as fiduciary responsibilities are met, is one of the factors that contribute to the wide variety of approaches that science philanthropies have adopted—differences in what to fund, who to fund, where to fund, and when to fund. Making sense of this varied landscape is a challenge. Utilizing a typology to categorize how science and technology philanthropies operate can be helpful to shed light on such varied practices and identify similarities and differences that arise among funding institutions.

There is also little in the existing literature that shines a light on foundations and explicitly links their efforts with the responsible research and innovation (RRI) paradigm. This is a concept that, while crystallizing in recent years, has been deliberately framed in broad terms to allow for flexibility of application and interpretation. One assessment of the many attempts to define RRI found that, "several years after its nominal launch, however, what RRI precisely entails is still under negotiation" (Klaassen, Rijnen, Vermeulen, Kupper, & Broerse, 2019, p. 77). Definitions and characterizations of the concept have morphed over time, but they all bear a clear familial resemblance in terms of how science and technology research relates to society. Owen, et al. (2013) present "an intentionally broad definition of responsible innovation" as follows: "Responsible innovation is a collective commitment of care for the future through responsive stewardship of science and innovation in the present" (p. 36). In the lead chapter of a 2018 book titled *Governance and Sustainability of Responsible Research and Innovation Processes*, a chapter authored by Forsberg, Shelly-Egan, Ladikas, and Owen (2018) emphasizes the interpretive flexibility that allows RRI to be broadly applied in a wide array of contexts. They write, "one needs to take into account the incentives and motivations of actors, the institutional contexts in which RRI practices develop and that promote or constrain the behaviors of actors, and consider the mission and maneuvering space of the organizations and individuals that own the practices" (p. 7).

Surprisingly, then, there has been little overlap among the RRI and philanthropy literatures to date. This is unfortunate given that there is a close relationship between the two. Much of the attention has been paid to the role that government funders have played in promulgating the concept, such as the chapters on this topic included in the recently published book *Responsible Research and Innovation: From Concepts to Practices* (Gianni, Pearson, & Reber, 2019). Like government funders, foundations have the ability to adopt RRI principles to guide their funding as well as encouraging, if not stipulating, that their research grantees do the same. To date, however, there has been less attention in the RRI community on how foundations function and shape the direction of science and technology research. It is evident that philanthropies need to be more centrally considered within the RRI framework, in particular, and within the context of the science and technology innovation system more generally.

Part of the reason why this disconnect between philanthropy and RRI is so surprising is that the RRI concept very much came about in the context of interests by the funding community. The idea was to encourage scientists and engineers to take better account of the societal implications of their research, especially when funded by public research dollars. In reflecting on the emergence of the RRI framework, one of the concept's core developers, Richard Owen, has noted the importance of having funding bodies like the European Commission (EC) and the United Kingdom's Engineering and Physical Sciences Research Council (EPSRC) adopt the concept in the framing of open calls for research (European Commission, 2011; Engineering and Physical Sciences Research Council, n.d.). In 2014, Owen wrote, "I have long felt that Research Councils have an important role to play in RI [responsible innovation]. Since EPSRC had begun to reposition itself less as a 'funder' and more as a 'sponsor' and 'shaper' of research in the engineering and physics sciences, a discussion of its potential role in promoting RI was one they seemed willing to engage with" (Owen, 2014, p. 114). Owen continues by describing how EPSRC's adoption of the dimensions of RRI directly influences the research it supports and the practices its grant recipients must adopt. "In doing so, EPSRC states that it (and others it works with such as universities) will need to promote partnerships with other disciplines and spheres of expertise, and support programs of training, integrated approaches and collaborative research across disciplines and beyond to enable a meaningful commitment to RI to be taken forward," writes Owen (p. 116). Owen makes a similar point about RRI's rise in prominence as being directly connected to the EC's adoption, musing that the attention heaped on RRI from the academic and policy communities is "due to a commitment by the European Commission to Responsible Research and Innovation (RRI) that was announced in 2011 and has continued since" (Owen, 2019, p. ix). Others have begun examining the relationship between RRI and the funding community in other European countries outside of the United Kingdom (Forsberg, Shelley-Egan, Ladika, & Owen, 2018; Guske & Jacob, 2019).

The RRI framework is most often applied in the context of research addressing emerging areas of science and technology, such as nanotechnology, synthetic biology, geoengineering, artificial intelligence, neuroscience, or other novel technologies. Shelley-Egan, Bowman, and Robinson (2018) document how funding agencies have used RRI to steer research in emerging areas of science and technology in a particular direction, putting in place guidelines and requirements for proposals that are designed to improve how researchers address societal responsibility by including more anticipatory, reflective, or deliberative activities within their funding submissions. These authors, writing in the context of applying RRI to nanotechnology research, describe the role of public funder adoption of RRI as a "meso-level" governance approach, in which these "intermediary organizations...exert leverage on developments through their actions, namely by mandating scientists to include broader issues within the funding proposal itself" (p. 1732). Later in that same article, they generalize this idea, concluding that, "funding organizations may refer to RRI in setting funding requirements which may lead to change in actual research practices" (p. 1739).

While these authors do not extend this assessment to the philanthropic communities explicitly, I argue that the same holds true for foundation funding. Practices, procedures, and requirements that philanthropic donors put in place that mirror or draw on the principles of RRI can shape the direction of research fields, institutions, and researchers themselves. Analysis undertaken by Murray (2013) and Stephan (2015) that was discussed in Chapter 2 reinforces this point. In short, they argue that researchers and research institutions do respond to and organize around the interests of funders, whether they be government or philanthropic. A report from 2013 presenting the results of a workshop focused on the role of philanthropy in relation to RRI found that, at the time, there were a small number of efforts in which the philanthropic community has put "the same explicit emphasis on the notion of 'responsibility'" (European Commission, 2014, p. 15). What little attention had been paid to RRI by the philanthropic community at the time of that report's publication was rather diffuse, covering a broad range of topics related to public engagement, youth education, communications, ethics, gender equality, and open access to research results.

This report from the European Commission concludes with two key assertions. The first relates to the point made above: philanthropic funders, leveraging the power of purse-strings, can have substantial influence in how research is conducted by making the themes and tenets of RRI an element of their grantmaking, thereby setting expectations about what they are looking for from their grantees. This report acknowledges as much, stating that "because the majority of researchers, universities and research institutes put their mouths where the money is, these financial sources may function as 'soft persuaders' of RRI, and therefore an additional way to steer the research community toward RRI" (European Commission, 2014, p. 22). A second point raised in this document is that there is a need for a reconceptualization of how various stakeholders within the research enterprise interact with one another, from government to foundations to research institutions to the general public. Foundations fund research, of course, but they also can reflexively apply the principles of RRI to their own institutions. The report calls out this need to rethink these traditional typologies. "A categorization such as 'funders', 'suppliers' and 'consumers' of research results may not be valid anymore," states the report (p. 22). "Philanthropic organizations can be also 'funders' of course but may wish to be 'consumers' for guiding their own choices, or even 'suppliers'…A new taxonomy has therefore to be put in place for better understanding the many interactions among the various stakeholders of the RRI world" (p. 22).

Existing categorization schemes for assessing science philanthropy

Any framework aiming to categorize philanthropic intervention associated with science and technology needs to account for the many ways in which foundations fund different elements of the scientific enterprise and relate to historical antecedents. Models, typologies, and categorization schemes permeate in the science and technology policy literature, arising from particular historical conditions, disciplinary interests, explanatory goals, and reflecting various conceptual trade-offs. Chapter 1 outlined four dimensions of responsible research and innovation that have been presented in Owen, et al. (2013) and Stilgoe, Owen, and Macnaghten (2013) and that serve as core components of the RRI framework: anticipation, reflexivity, deliberation/inclusion, and responsiveness. Scholars like Wickson and Carew (2014), have developed even more elaborate rubrics and quality criteria to assist in evaluating how extensively these dimensions or criteria are reflected in funded research projects.

The one well-known typology of science and technology innovation that has begun to be explicitly linked with philanthropy is the quadrant model of scientific research developed by Donald Stokes (1997) in his book *Pasteur's Quadrant*. The Pasteur's Quadrant model moves away from the linear model of innovation in favor of a two-dimensional model that clusters research as to whether it aims for fundamental understanding of nature (vertical axis) or consideration of practical use (horizontal axis). The resulting four quadrants then represent different types of research, including what Stokes called "pure basic research" (characterized by the desire for fundamental discovery as practiced by physicist Niels Bohr), "pure applied research" (characterized by the desire for practical invention as practiced by engineer Thomas Edison), and "use-inspired basic research" (characterized by dual desire for fundamental discovery and practical application as practiced by biologist Louis Pasteur) (p. 73).

More recently, this model has been extended by scholars in many ways, including tying the Pasteur's Quadrant model directly to philanthropy. Some researchers working to describe the envisioned convergence of scientific and technology fields have added a fifth quadrant to this model to represent "vision-inspired basic research" that reflects a push toward creating new fields of inquiry (Roco, Bainbridge, Tonn, & Whitesides, 2013, p. 16). A subsequent report on the subject of research convergence published by the National Academies describes that this addition of a "vision-inspired basic research" quadrant emphasizes the exploration of "transformative ideas beyond known applications...that can be recombined to generate convergent advances" (National Research Council, 2014, p. 25). Other endeavors have extended the Pasteur's Quadrant model to better represent other actors in the science and technology innovation system. Tijssen (2018) adds an additional axis focused on "end user engagement" to account for the role of technology commercialization and entrepreneurship, extending the framework into what is termed a "Pasteur's Cube model" (p. 1630).

In her 2013 book chapter examining the historical role of science philanthropy in the United States, Fiona Murray utilizes the Pasteur's Quadrant model and applies a version of it to categorizing how different philanthropic funders of science have operated in the past. Murray (2013) adapts the two-dimension axis structure developed by Stokes to categorize funders based on whether they focus on supporting research that is more fundamental or translational (horizontal axis) or whether existing levels of funding are low or high (vertical axis). Doing so creates four types of philanthropic funders for science and innovation research. In domains where there are low levels of existing funding and attention paid to fundamental research, Murray characterizes such philanthropy as a "patron filling gaps in knowledge foundations" (p. 28). She harkens back to the funding of science by the Medici family as a touchstone for this kind of philanthropy, yet I would argue that many contemporary philanthropic institutions today look to operate in this mode. Furthermore, as was articulated in Chapter 1, the Science Philanthropy Alliance formed exactly for this reason: to serve as a gathering mechanism to connect foundations and other new donors interested in supporting basic science research. In situations where funding is low yet the focus is on translational research, Murray portrays this type of science philanthropy as a "mission-driven patron identifying critical gaps in translations," such as the Gates Foundation's focus on disease eradication in which funding is provided for "impact-oriented, translational research that would identify and fill knowledge gaps in order to rapidly advance the field" (p. 28, 30). Where existing levels of funding are high, coupled with an aim to have an impact on fundamental research, the example offered is the Howard Hughes Medical Institute (HHMI), acting as a "patron extending well-funded knowledge" (p. 28). One of HHMI's primary modes of science philanthropy is "providing unrestricted funding for fundamental biological research to promising young scholars" in ways that "reinforce government support...of foundational life science projects" (p. 30).

The final quadrant in Murray's analysis combines areas with high levels of existing funding with an aim for an impact on translational impact. This kind of science philanthropy is depicted as a "mission-driven patron amplifying existing funding to accelerate outcomes" (p. 28). In Murray's model, the goal of this approach to science philanthropy is often characterized as a desire to try out different ways of overseeing and managing the research enterprise. For instance, Daniel Sarewitz (2016) profiles such alternative approaches to funding research that some science philanthropies like the James S. McDonnell Foundation has adopted in their funding of brain science research, approaches that are more outcome- and goal-oriented than traditional public funding schemes. In this mode of funding, philanthropic dollars are not necessarily seeking out to identify unfunded topic areas; instead, they are looking to bolster different ways of conducting science in areas that already have funding as a way to accelerate progress in existing research domains.

While this variation on the Pasteur's Quadrant model is helpful in understanding different kinds of philanthropic support for science and technology research, a different framework is needed to better illuminate how the various dimensions of RRI intersect with the grantmaking practices of science philanthropies. A helpful heuristic in thinking about where and how science philanthropies provide their funding is looking at the different mechanisms that these institutions utilize to achieve a desired end goal. Put differently, it is helpful to think about the "leverage points," where science philanthropies are able to "intervene" in the research enterprise, in the words of systems analyst Donella Meadows (2008, p. 145). Systems thinking is not only a useful approach to help understand the various roles that different institutions play within a particular domain (Williams & Hummelbrunner, 2009; Senge, 2006; Boardman & Sauser, 2008), but the application of this perspective is becoming increasingly prevalent in philanthropic circles as foundations look to further enhance and improve the impact of the work they undertake (Kirsch, Bildner, & Walker, 2016; Walker, 2017). Practitioners and analysts have also observed that philanthropies tend to be in a good position to undertake systemic interventions given the flexibility in operations that they enjoy. One philanthropy leader noted as much in a recent article, writing that, "foundations do seem particularly well-placed to undertake systems work. Their freedom allows them to make choices about entering and exiting systems, and about the role they wish to adopt in relation to them" (Corner, 2019, p. 34). In fact, one article, reporting on the rise of science philanthropy in *Physics Today*, highlighted the breadth of system intervention options that these institutions can follow, noting "philanthropic efforts on behalf of basic research span a range of modalities, from assistance for individual investigators to the establishment of research institutes" and emphasizing that "individual philanthropies use a broad variety of funding mechanisms when they support basic research" (Kramer, 2018, p. 26).

An evolving typology of science philanthropy for the 21st Century

Numerous typologies and categorization schemes drawn from economics, sociology, political science, and other disciplines have characterized the relationship between different actors within innovation systems (Nelson, 1993; Godin, 2017; Etzkowitz, 2008; Gorman, 2010; Gibbons, et al., 1994; Barben, Fisher, Selin, & Guston, 2008; Funtowicz & Ravetz, 1993). While exploring each of these frameworks in depth remains outside the scope of this book, it should be noted that, in most instances, the role played by philanthropies is often ignored or not explicitly called out in these various conceptual frameworks. Many of these categorization schemes focus their attention on government and industrial funders of research, in addition to the role played by universities and other actors within the research enterprise. I contend that not only is it imperative to shine a light on the role played by science philanthropies, but that the RRI framework—with its existing emphasis on understanding how funders might help advance considerations of responsibility—offers an occasion to do so quite substantially. In particular, it is useful to categorize philanthropic approaches to funding scientific research along three main dimensions based upon the mode of intervention within the research enterprise, even as these modes of support often are combined with one another. Dividing them along these lines helps to surface many of the key types of support that foundations currently provide for science and technology research. There are at least two benefits to adopting this approach. The first is that this categorization scheme can be helpful to both scholars and practitioners interested in understanding how different types of giving for science philanthropy relate to one another. Second, it provides a heuristic that can be used going forward to understand how new interventions fit with others already in place.

The first dimension of this framework is support for *individuals*. This funding typically comes in the form of fellowships, scholarships, or prizes that are awarded through a competitive selection process. These fellowships are awarded at a range of career stages, but they typically focus on those earlier in their career, from undergraduates, doctoral students, or post-doctoral fellows to early- or mid-career professors. Awards and prizes for senior scholars also fall under this category, yet a fair amount of attention is increasingly paid by science philanthropies in boosting early-career researchers to examine previously understudied questions. Many times, such fellowships also have an explicit focus on improving the diversity and inclusion of researchers and faculty involved in science and technology.

The second dimension is support for *institutions*. This kind of giving is now typically in the form of establishing new entities or funding research centers, institutes, or even entire schools or departments within universities. Funding to establish entirely new, stand-alone universities or research institutions is less prevalent now than it was in the science philanthropy of the 20th Century, although it still occurs when a foundation or high-net-worth individual is able to amass and dispense the significant resources necessary to make this kind of investment. Moreover, newer versions of this kind of institutional support have emerged in recent years in the form of establishing in-house research centers within a philanthropy, not as a separate grant-receiving organization.

The third dimension is support for *networks*. Building on the first two intervention kinds, establishing and sustaining networks are critical elements of science philanthropy funding that help ensure that the sum of philanthropic investments can be more impactful and longstanding than the constituent parts. Networks supported by science philanthropy can vary in scale, from linking together a small number of faculty or research institutions increasing in size to encompass many organizations and hundreds or thousands of researchers. Network building involves the development and sustainment of multi-institutional collaborations, often with the aim of connecting institutions across multiple sectors or regions. Given the number of institutions and the complexities involved, science philanthropy provided for the purpose of network building is among the most intriguing and impactful kinds of intervention that can help connect research with societal considerations.

While this grouping along the lines of individuals, institutions, and networks is a helpful heuristic to understand the actions of science philanthropies and how they fit within the RRI framework, there are new developments in the field that are forging new avenues and are challenging to categorize. Chapter 2 showed that the history of science philanthropy throughout the 20th Century in the United States is that foundations tend to be structured as non-profit grantmaking institutions, giving money to grantees that are separate organizations. However, as noted above, some foundations are now eschewing a focus on giving grants altogether, establishing research centers in-house, within the philanthropy itself, in order to have more of a direct say in how to advance particular areas of research. In other instances, some foundations funding science are being institutionalized in corporate forms other than as not-for-profit organizations, offering these organizations potentially even more flexibility as to what kind of work is undertaken. For example, in the United States, philanthropies generally are not allowed to provide funds for lobbying efforts, but other institutional arrangements, such as limited liability corporations (LLCs), are permitted to fund such activities. In still other organizational forms, the traditional model of a philanthropic institution funded by a wealthy individual or family is being entirely upended by new funding instruments. Entities are being created that allow funders to pool their resources and turn over grantmaking responsibilities to donor advisory organizations. The rise of crowdfunding and other resource-pooling channels via Internet platforms is allowing anybody with an interest in supporting science and technology to sponsor and underwrite innovative new research, projects, regardless of how much money they have available to give. These alternative modes of giving will be addressed in more detail in Chapter 7. These developments serve as another reminder that the practice of science philanthropy is not static and that novel approaches are regularly being tested and adapted to new situations.

As Table 3.1 shows, the three primary "modalities" (Kramer, 2018, p. 26) or *levels of intervention of science philanthropy*—support for individuals, institutions, and networks—can be crossed with the different dimensions of the RRI framework to provide a useful categorization scheme that helps understand the ways in which philanthropies intervene in and support science and technology. The horizontal rows of the chart present three *groupings of the RRI framework dimensions*: anticipation, deliberation and inclusion, and reflexivity and responsiveness. Considering these dimensions in light of the three philanthropy-oriented dimensions discussed above creates nine categories of interventions that can structure how to think about the relationship between philanthropy and science and technology. It should be noted that given the plethora of programs that science philanthropies are supporting in this day and age, it is not possible to cover every instance in the following pages. Instead, the plan is to highlight not only a wide variety of examples that demonstrate the breadth of activity being undertaken in these domains, to be discussed in this and the following chapters, but to also dive deeper into a handful of specific case studies to unpack the different dimensions of interest.

Following down the first column, the first category relates to philanthropic support for individuals, with an emphasis on anticipating future developments in science and technology. This kind of funding often emerges in the form of support for path-breaking research, often with a focus on funding early career researchers and scholars. This is an extensive area of interest for foundations, so it is not surprising that there are many philanthropic efforts of this kind that span a variety of funding levels and disciplines. These kinds of programs represent a key way in which philanthropies attempt to shape the future

Table 3.1 Typology of philanthropic interventions and RRI dimensions

Typology Dimensions	Individuals	Institutions	Networks
Anticipation	Support for early career researchers pursuing new avenues of science and technology	Creation of research centers focused on advancing new areas of science and technology	Programs that create a cohort of scholars or bring together institutions to undertake collaborative research
Deliberation and Inclusion	Support to improve diversity, equity, and inclusion representation in science and technology, or fellowships to consider broader societal impacts	Support to improve institutional culture change, policies, and practices related to diversity, equity, and inclusion	Efforts to extend deliberation and inclusion practices among multiple stakeholders
Reflexivity and Responsiveness	Application of RRI principles to grantee and investigator selection	Establishment of embedded, in-house, forward-looking research efforts within science philanthropies	Support for, and creation of, multi-institutional collaborative partnerships that reflect a foundation's values and interests

directions of science and technology: by providing funding that simultaneously advances the careers of top investigators and that breaks new ground in terms of discovery.

The second category down this column are philanthropic programs focused on supporting scholarships and fellowships that aim to either improve diversity, equity, and inclusion within science and technology, or that promote consideration of the broader societal implications of science and technology. Many of these programs, focused on funding individuals, inevitably have cross-over elements with other categories, as foundations often look to strengthen institutions as well as integrate elements of network building. Many institutional science philanthropies place a distinctive focus in these areas, yet the next chapter will show that some of the most prominent of these diversity and inclusion programs were seeded by funds from an individual donor.

The final category in this column is where the reflexive and collectively responsive elements of the RRI framework intersect with philanthropic programs that fund individuals. This grouping is characterized by foundations applying RRI principles to their own practices and reflect what is expected from grantees. Ensuring that these principles are reflected in a foundation's own behaviors is key. As program director Barbara Chow writes in a report on the critical role that foundations play in advancing diversity, equity, and inclusion, "perhaps the most important foundation practice to support DEI is ensuring that the individuals who comprise the foundation staff are themselves knowledgeable about the nuances and history of DEI, from academic, societal, and foundation perspectives" (Chow, 2018, p. 9). A number of science philanthropies have made explicit that they work to ensure diversity, equity, and inclusion when it comes to funding of individual fellowships and in awarding grants to institutions. As the next chapter will highlight, many foundations have come to require that prospective grantees submitting full proposals address how they will ensure diversity, equity, and inclusion in research team composition and as a decision-making criterion when selecting a cohort of fellows.

The first category of the second column addresses a highly prominent type of science philanthropy: support for and creation of institutions to advance cutting-edge research. Chapter 2 showcased that this mode of giving was highly prominent in the 20th Century, and it remains a core component of philanthropic support for science today. Science philanthropies provide support for myriads of research projects and research centers across a range of funding scales. Additionally, science philanthropies continue to have an impact in this mode by providing core funding for large science research instruments, harkening back to funding provided decades ago by other leading philanthropies to support earlier generations of scientific equipment.

The second category in the second column reflects efforts by philanthropies to provide funding to institutions to not only advance diversity and inclusion activities, but also to promote deliberation of broader societal impacts of research. Once again, these programs can take many forms, and they are often related to efforts that provide financial support to individuals for similar purposes. By focusing on advancing institutional change, foundations can help foster more systemic change in terms of who is supported to do science and how institutions respond to the needs of a more diverse cohort of researchers.

The final category of this dimension reflects ways in which science philanthropies have pursued new ways of funding institutions that are reflective of the foundation's priorities and, in some instances, represent the adoption of responsiveness to societal considerations as a core component of the institution's purpose upon urging by the foundation. In addition to funding institutions externally, science philanthropies have begun to once again create institutions as stand-alone research centers or, in a new twist, embedding research centers within the organizational structure of the philanthropy itself. The establishment of these kinds of research centers embedded in a foundation is a novel form of support for science philanthropy that has the potential to greatly expand as more donors become interested in supporting science.

The last column of this typology involves philanthropic support for networks and network-building activities. Strengthening networks within a research ecosystem has become one of the more widespread forms of science philanthropy in recent years. In many respects, philanthropic support for the establishment, advancement, and maintenance of research networks are among the most intriguing to study and most relevant when it comes to understanding philanthropy's role in supporting science that has an eye toward societal responsibility. Philanthropic grantmaking initiatives that fall in the first category aim to link together individuals and institutions undertaking forward-looking, cutting edge research for the purpose of filling research gaps and stimulating new investigation. A workshop report from 2019 found that foundations are appropriately situated to "provide proof of principle and push forward ideas that contribute to convergence" (National Academies of Sciences, Engineering, and Medicine, 2019, p. 38). Moreover, since foundations often aim to catalyze new areas of discovery and work in areas where researchers can leverage additional funding from other sources, the report notes the combination of public and philanthropic dollars is critical "when tackling complex challenges and addressing societal issues, the types of projects often associated with convergent collaborations" (National Academies of Sciences, Engineering, and Medicine, 2019, p. 38).

Next in the figure are philanthropic-funded interventions that look to further extend deliberation and inclusion practices by connecting scientists and engineers with other stakeholders to establish a more inclusive and socially responsible framing for research. Many of these network-building activities focused on deliberation and inclusion across sectors are in their nascent stages, having emerged in recent years to address the growing disconnect between those experts involved in the research enterprise and other constituencies that may be able to bring to bear different perspectives. Many of these networking activities are driven by the research community, yet foundations have proven to be critical actors in terms of providing the resources necessary to bring these projects to fruition.

The final category in the table represents undertakings in which a philanthropy reflexively applies the principles of RRI on networks that it establishes and looks to ensconce these values and interests more fully onto the networks it supports externally. Whether established within or outside of the philanthropy, examples of this kind of philanthropic intervention tend to be closely associated with the funding organizations themselves. These network-building activities tend to be multi-year projects that evolve over time, with a centralized management function that coordinates the networks' activities and works to ensure that the impact of the whole is greater than the sum of the network components. Two such foundation-funded research networks will be discussed in greater detail as case studies in Chapter 5.

Analyzing science philanthropy in the age of responsible research

This chapter has shown that while there are a handful of schemes that look to make sense of philanthropic giving for science, none have yet to marry the tenets of RRI with a practical understanding of the ways that foundations intervene in research systems through different kinds of funding approaches. In many respects, RRI takes up the question of what we want science philanthropy to deliver in terms of societal impact. As Rip (2014) writes, "responsible research and innovation implies changing roles for the various actors involved in science and technology development and their embedding in society," a reflection that warrants consideration by all research funders, especially those in the philanthropic community (p. 8). Owen, Macnaghten, and Stilgoe (2012) describe the unique obligation that funders can and should play at the forefront of this re-evaluation of the relationship between science and societal responsibility. "Funders have a leadership role to play in establishing a framework for responsible innovation and its associated expectations, including processes of governance and oversight. But they must also lead by example. They have a role to play in catalyzing the development of capacity for responsible innovation to meet such expectations," they argue (p. 756).

While government funders, especially in Europe, were among the first to take on this mantle, newer efforts have begun to spread the RRI concept to a growing number of other geographic contexts, not just in the United States but in Asia and Africa as well (von Schomberg & Hankins, 2019). For instance, there have even been studies that investigate the private sector's contribution and place in the RRI landscape (Martinuzzi, Blok, Brem, Stahl, & Schonherr, 2018; Dreyer, et al., 2017). Yet, to date, philanthropy has been mostly left out of the RRI conversation. This is particularly problematic, especially given that foundations play particularly critical roles in the funding ecosystem to advance science and technology research. As Rene von Schomberg and Jonathan Hankins (2019) write in their introduction to the recently published *International Handbook on Responsible Innovation*, "market innovations do not automatically deliver societally desirable objectives, and require a broad governance of knowledge coalitions of governmental bodies and industrial and societal actors to address market deficits" (p. 1–2). A report resulting from a workshop organized by the National Academies to highlight opportunities for inter-sectoral funding collaboration summarized a similar point raised by one of the speakers, Daniel Goroff of the Sloan Foundation. Goroff describes the underlying economic rationale for philanthropic funding of sciences, noting that foundations are particularly adept at "resolving externality uncertainty, and public goods problems" (National Academies of Sciences, Engineering, and Medicine, 2018, p. 2). The report continues by noting that foundations can often address these challenges in a more societally oriented way than other funders. "The externality problem in science often prevents companies from investing in discoveries that external parties may use without paying a share of the cost. The uncertainty problem describes the tendency of traditional research funders to be reluctant to support some research because of the unpredictability of pay-off," it states (National Academies of Sciences, Engineering, and Medicine, 2018, p. 2). Foundations can help overcome such challenges. Since they are not financially reliant on profits from research they fund, foundations can encourage or require that discoveries resulting from their dollars enter the public domain. Since many foundations are designed to exist in perpetuity, they can be patient with their funding and more easily invest in individuals, institutions, or networks that may have a bright future ahead (Kastner, 2018).

The RRI framework provides a pathway that science philanthropies can follow beyond funding top-notch research. There are many degrees by which these institutions could incorporate the perspectives provided by RRI into the work that they undertake across a wide spectrum. At one end, there is the potential for these organizations to integrate RRI in ways that suit their institutional, historical, cultural, and strategic characteristics. In this view, not all science philanthropies have to take on the same disposition toward funding research. Since science philanthropies differ across many aspects of their work, these distinctive traits could be reflected in supporting a broad array of research activities that involve differing gradations of consideration toward societal responsibility. Some funders might be better equipped to continue supporting basic research without giving much attention to its eventual societal implications. Others might concern themselves with a limited subset of the components that comprise the RRI framework. Still others might be in a position to set aside or earmark funds for particular projects or programs that integrate societal responsibility to a certain extent. Some institutions may choose to adopt the dimensions of responsibility presented in the RRI framework rather fully, using these criteria to inform decisions on which topic areas to support and in adjudicating between different grant proposals. On the other end of spectrum, there is a stronger version of this conclusion. This view holds that if science philanthropies truly want to take responsibility seriously, as it were, these institutions actually have an imperative to integrate the core principles of societal responsibility into the various aspects of what they do. This stance would lead science philanthropies to adopt the RRI framework as an evaluative screen or as a central decision-making mechanism that guides the entirety of a foundation's direction and helps determine the course an institution might take over the long term. In short, science philanthropies could embrace the notion of societal responsibility as a way of fulfilling their social contract as funders of science.

There are many examples that demonstrate how science philanthropies can make societal responsibility a component of what they do. The following chapters will explore a wide array of these real-world examples and case studies, while also presenting perspectives from a range of stakeholders involved in science philanthropy about the different ways that science philanthropies have shaped the direction of where research is headed and the process by which it gets there. Doing so will both highlight the richness of what is already happening and sketch out what may lay ahead in terms of how science philanthropies can contribute to advancing responsibility—a core element of their giving for science.

Bibliography

Barben, D., Fisher, E., Selin, C., & Guston, D. H. (2008). Anticipatory Governance of Nanotechnology: Foresight, Engagement, Integration. In E. J. Hackett, O. Amsterdamska, M. Lynch, & J. Wajcman, eds., *The Handbook of Science and Technology Studies: Third Edition* (pp. 979–1000). Cambridge, MA: MIT Press.

Boardman, J., & Sauser, B. (2008). *Systems Thinking: Coping with 21st Century Problems.* Boca Raton, FL: CRC Press.

Chow, B. (2018). *From Words to Action: A Practical Philanthropic Guide to Diversity, Equity, and Inclusion.* New York, NY: Foundation Center.

Corner, J. (2019, March). Systems Change and Philanthropy. *Alliance*, 24(1), 32–38.

Dreyer, M., Chefneux, L., Goldberg, A., Von Heimburg, J., Patrignani, N., Schofield, M., et al. (2017). Responsible Innovation: A Complementary View from Industry with Proposals for Bridging Different Perspectives. *Sustainability*, 9(1719), 1–25.

Engineering and Physical Sciences Research Council. (n.d.). Framework for Responsible Innovation. Retrieved April 2019, from Engineering and Physical Sciences Research Council: https://epsrc.ukri.org/research/framework/.

Etzkowitz, H. (2008). *The Triple Helix: University-Industry-Government Innovation in Action.* New York, NY: Routledge.

European Commission. (2011, November 30). Horizion 2020 – The Framework Programme for Research and Innovation. Retrieved April 2019, from European Commission: http://ec.europa.eu/research/horizon2020/pdf/proposals/communication_from_the_commission_-_horizon_2020_-_the_framework_programme_for_research_and_innovation.pdf.

European Commission. (2014). *The Role of Philanthropy in the Promotion of Responsible Research and Innovation.* Brussels, Belgium: European Commission.

Forsberg, E.-M., Shelley-Egan, C., Ladika, M., & Owen, R. (2018). Implementing Responsible Research and Innovation in Research Funding and Research Conducting Organizations—What Have We Learned so Far? In F. Ferri, N. Dwyer, S. Raicevich, P. Grifonia, H. Altiok, H. T. Andersen, et al., eds., *Governance and Sustainability of Responsible Research and Innovation Processes: Cases and Experiences* (pp. 3–11). Cham, Switzerland: Springer.

Funtowicz, S. O., & Ravetz, J. R. (1993, September). Science for the Post-Normal Age. *Futures*, 25(7), 739–755.

Gianni, R., Pearson, J., & Reber, B., eds. (2019). *Responsible Research and Innovation: From Concepts to Practices*. Oxon, United Kingdom: Routledge.

Gibbons, M., Limoges, C., Nowotny, H., Schwartzman, S., Scott, P., & Trow, M. (1994). *The New Production of Knowledge: The Dynamics of Science and Research in Contemporary Societies*. London, United Kingdom: SAGE Publications.

Godin, B. (2017). *Models of Innovation: The History of an Idea*. Cambridge, MA: The MIT Press.

Gorman, M. (2010). *Trading Zones and Interaction Expertise: Creating New Kinds of Collaboration*. Cambridge, MA: The MIT Press.

Guske, A.-L., & Jacob, K. (2019). Policy Relevance and the Concept of Responsible Research and Innovation. In R. Gianni, J. Pearson, & B. Reber, eds., *Responsible Research and Innovation: From Concepts to Practices* (pp. 129–149). Oxon, UK: Routledge.

Kastner, M. (2018, December 14). Philanthropy: A Critical Player in Supporting Scientific Research. Retrieved June 2019, from Science Philanthropy Alliance: https://www.sciencephilanthropyalliance.org/philanthropy-a-critical-player-in-supporting-scientific-research-alliance-blog/.

Kirsch, V., Bildner, J., & Walker, J. (2016, July 25). Why Social Ventures Need Systems Thinking. Retrieved July 2019, from *Harvard Business Review*: https://hbr.org/2016/07/why-social-ventures-need-systems-thinking.

Klaassen, P., Rijnen, M., Vermeulen, S., Kupper, F., & Broerse, J. (2019). Technocracy versus Experimental Learning in RRI: On Making the Most of RRI's Interpretive Flexibility. In R. Gianni, J. Pearson, & B. Reber, eds., *Responsible Research and Innovation: From Concepts to Practices* (pp. 77–98). Oxon, United Kingdom: Routledge.

Kramer, D. (2018, June 1). Foundations Play a Supporting Role in Basic Science. *Physics Today*, 71(6), 26–29.

Martinuzzi, A., Blok, V., Brem, A., Stahl, B., & Schonherr, N. (2018). Responsible Research and Innovation in Industry—Challenges, Insights and Perspectives. *Sustainability*, 10(702), 1–9.

Meadows, D. H. (2008). *Thinking in Systems: A Primer*. Oxon, United Kingdom: Earthscan.

Murray, F. (2013). Evaluating the Role of Science Philanthropy in American Research Universities. In J. Lerner & S. Stern, eds., *Innovation Policy and the Economy, Volume 13* (pp. 23–60). Chicago, IL: University of Chicago Press.

National Academies of Sciences, Engineering, and Medicine. (2018). *Strategies for Engagement of Non-Traditional Partners in the Research Enterprise: Proceedings of a Workshop*. Washington, DC: The National Academies Press.

National Academies of Sciences, Engineering, and Medicine. (2019). *Fostering the Culture of Convergence in Research: Proceedings of a Workshop*. Washington, DC: The National Academies Press.

National Research Council. (2014). *Convergence: Facilitating Transdisciplinary Integration of Life Sciences, Physical Sciences, Engineering, and Beyond*. Washington, DC: The National Academies Press.

Nelson, R. R. (1993). *National Innovation Systems: A Comparative Analysis*. Oxford, United Kingdom: Oxford University Press.

Owen, R. (2014). The UK Engineering and Physical Sciences Research Council's Commitment to a Framework for Responsible Innovation. *Journal of Responsible Innovation*, 1(1), 113–117.

Owen, R. (2019). Foreword: From Responsible Innovation to Responsible Innovation Systems. In R. Gianni, J. Pearson, & B. Reber, eds., *Responsible Research and Innovation: From Concepts to Practices* (pp. ix–xiv). Oxon, UK: Routledge.

Owen, R., Macnaghten, P., & Stilgoe, J. (2012). Responsible Research and Innovation: From Science in Society to Science for Society, with Society. *Science and Public Policy*, 39(6), 751–760.

Owen, R., Stilgoe, J., Macnaghten, P., Gorman, M., Fisher, E., & Guston, D. (2013). A Framework for Responsible Innovation. In R. Owen, J. Bessant, & M. Heintz, eds., *Responsible Innovation: Managing the Responsible Emergence of Science and Innovation in Society* (pp. 27–50). Chichester, UK: John Wiley & Sons.

Rip, A. (2014). The Past and Future of RRI. *Life Sciences, Society and Policy*, 10(17), 1–15.

Roco, M. C., Bainbridge, W. S., Tonn, B., & Whitesides, G., eds. (2013). *Convergence of Knowledge, Technology, and Society: Beyond Convergence of Nano-Bio-Info-Cognitive Technologies*. Dordrecht, The Netherlands: Springer.

Sarewitz, D. (2016, Spring/Summer). Saving Science. *The New Atlantis*, 5–40.

Senge, P. M. (2006). *The Fifth Discipline: The Art & Practice of the Learning Organization*. New York, NY: Doubleday.

Shelley-Egan, C., Bowman, D. M., & Robinson, D. K. (2018). Devices of Responsibility: Over a Decade of Responsible Research and Innovation Initiatives for Nanotechnologies. *Science and Engineering Ethics*, 24(6), 1719–1746.

Stephan, P. (2015). The Endless Frontier: Reaping What Bush Sowed? In A. B. Jaffe & B. F. Jones, eds., *The Changing Frontier: Rethinking Science and Innovation Policy* (pp. 321–366). Chicago, IL: University of Chicago Press.

Stilgoe, J., Owen, R., & Macnaghten, P. (2013). Developing a Framework for Responsible Innovation. *Research Policy*, 42(9), 1568–1580.

Stokes, D. (1997). *Pasteur's Quadrant: Basic Science and Technological Innovation*. Washington, DC: Brookings Institution Press.

Tijssen, R. J. (2018, November). Anatomy of Use-Inspired Researchers: From Pasteur's Quadrant to Pasteur's Cube Model. *Research Policy*, 47(9), 1626–1638.

von Schomberg, R., & Hankins, J. (2019). Introduction to the International Handbook on Responsible Innovation. In R. von Schomberg & J. Hankins, eds., *International Handbook on Responsible Innovation: A Global Resource* (pp. 1–11). Cheltenham, UK: Edward Elgar.

Walker, J. C. (2017, April 5). Solving the World's Biggest Problems: Better Philanthropy Through Systems Change. Retrieved July 2019, from *Stanford Social Innovation Review*: https://ssir.org/articles/entry/better_philanthropy_through_systems_change.

Wickson, F., & Carew, A. L. (2014). Quality Criteria and Indicators for Responsible Research and Innovation: Learning from Transdisciplinarity. *Journal of Responsible Innovation*, 1(3), 254–273.

Williams, B., & Hummelbrunner, R. (2009). *Systems Concepts in Action: A Practitioner's Toolkit*. Stanford, CA: Stanford University Press.

4 Individuals, institutions, and networks

Contemporary examples of science philanthropy

The previous chapter outlined a categorization scheme that frames how science philanthropies have an impact on the research enterprise and do so in ways that relate to the principles of RRI. This and the following chapters apply this framework empirically in order to illuminate the relevant features of the new and ongoing grantmaking efforts supported by these institutions. By examining how this conceptual model relates to real-world examples of science philanthropy, it becomes easier to make sense of the many overlapping philanthropic interventions that take place related to science and technology. It also helps to extract some of the salient characteristics of this grantmaking that point to how the RRI dimensions may be more evident than they may first appear. As previous chapters noted, it is not that foundations are explicitly utilizing the principles in the RRI rubric to guide their grantmaking; that kind of explicit reliance on the theory occurs rarely, if ever. Instead, it is more that foundations tend to share a commitment to many of the underlying values and standards that serve as the impetus for much of the RRI endeavor. Therefore, it is more accurate to think of philanthropies as implicitly demonstrating and advancing these characteristics within their grantmaking even if the RRI categorization scheme is not referenced directly.

Table 4.1 builds on the framework presented in Chapter 3, fleshing out the categorization scheme by indicating a few of the examples discussed throughout this chapter and in subsequent chapters as a way to illustrate each type of philanthropic activity. As a reminder, the columns include the three primary levels of intervention of science philanthropy (individuals, institutions, and networks) and the rows contain three groupings of the RRI framework dimensions (anticipation, deliberation and inclusion, and reflexivity and responsiveness). Based on the intersection of these components, this three by three matrix presents at least nine different kinds of science philanthropy, each of which is evidenced by multiple examples taking place today.

Of course, the reality of these projects and programs is that many inevitably combine elements from more than one category and they each may have attributes that do not neatly fall within the bounds of this system. Many foundations will aim to achieve multiple goals simultaneously within a single program, if not across programs, merging together elements that might combine

Table 4.1 Examples of philanthropic interventions and RRI dimensions

Typology Dimensions	Individuals	Institutions	Networks
Anticipation	Support for early career researchers pursuing new avenues of science and technology. *Examples: Howard Hughes Medical Institute Investigator Program, Schmidt Science Fellows, Moore Inventor Fellows*	Creation of research centers focused on advancing new areas of science and technology. *Examples: The Kavli Foundation Institutes, Sainsbury Wellcome Centre*	Programs that create a cohort of scholars or bring together institutions to undertake collaborative research. *Examples: BRAIN Initiative, Research Corporation for Science Advancement Scialog program, National Academies Keck Futures Initiative*
Deliberation and Inclusion	Support to improve diversity, equity, and inclusion representation in science and technology, or fellowships to consider broader societal impacts. *Examples: Meyerhoff Scholars Program, Moore Foundation support of California Council on Science and Technology Science Fellows program*	Support to improve institutional culture change, policies, and practices related to diversity, equity, and inclusion. *Examples: Wellcome Trust Review of PhD Training in Biomedical Research, HHMI Inclusive Excellence Initiative, Sloan Foundation Minority PhD Program and Sloan Indigenous Graduate Partnership*	Efforts to extend deliberation and inclusion practices among multiple stakeholders. *Examples: Ford Foundation and Hewlett Foundation supported Public Interest Technology University Network; philanthropic support for Expert and Citizen Assessment of Science and Technology network activities*
Reflexivity and Responsiveness	Application of RRI principles to grantee and investigator selection. *Examples: philanthropy diversity statements, Heising-Simons Foundation 51 Pegasi b Fellowship in Planetary Astronomy*	Establishment of embedded, in-house, forward-looking research efforts within science philanthropies. *Examples: Allen Institute, Simons Foundation Flatiron Institute, Schmidt Ocean Institute*	Support for, and creation of, multi-institutional collaborative partnerships that reflect a foundation's values and interests. *Examples: Wellcome supported Research on Research Institute, Sloan Digital Sky Survey, Rockefeller Foundation Searchlight network*

aspects of anticipation, deliberation, inclusion, and even reflexivity. There is also an inherent tension that can arise when applying a standard framework to make sense of a diverse and disparate setting of organizations that exist within the realm of science philanthropy.

However, despite this recognition, utilizing this scheme to gain insight in the practices of contemporary science philanthropy provides a variety of benefits. First, it helps to bring some clarity to the sometimes idiosyncratic and seemingly bespoke ways in which science philanthropies go about their grantmaking. In fact, the large number of examples examined here and in the following chapters suggest that there may be more underlying commonalities that exist among these institutions than is typically thought, illuminating similarities that often get less attention. Second, using a standard lens drawn from the RRI dimensions can help to highlight connections across projects and programs, establishing common linkages across disparate efforts that might not seem to share common traits on the surface. Third, it can also show how the same foundation might aim to achieve different goals and objectives in different program areas or types of intervention, demonstrating that foundations often look to utilize multiple kinds of grantmaking strategies. Finally, the hope is that, by demonstrating how philanthropic efforts related to science and technology fit under a modified version of the RRI framework that is geared toward foundations, these institutions might begin to employ these concepts more deliberately and explicitly going forward, thereby seeding this perspective more widely in the science philanthropy community.

It is evidently not possible to discuss and identify every high-profile science philanthropy effort that reflects elements of anticipation, deliberation and inclusion, or reflexivity and responsiveness. For that reason, the examples presented here are deliberately drawn from a wide range of institutions and science philanthropies located in both the United States and Europe. The examples were selected to cover multiple scales, from efforts that may be a few million dollars in size over a short period of time to those that are large-scale, flagship science philanthropy interventions that might be in the order of hundreds of millions of dollars awarded over decades. Both existing and new efforts are covered as a way to explore how these principles might be reflected in newer or more established activities. In fact, it is sometimes the less well-known or more nascent examples that can be most illuminating in this context.

Most importantly, it is critical to note that this analysis is intended to serve mainly as an initial substantive foray into these questions, not as the last word in their development. As the field is dynamic and regularly changing, with new projects beginning and existing ones closing, this analysis only purports to function as a snapshot of the science philanthropy landscape in a particular point in time. In the end, the discussions that follow look to illustrate how the relationship between the RRI framework and science philanthropy is starting to present itself in practice and therefore enrich the burgeoning interactions between these two communities.

Science philanthropy for individuals: fellowships exploring new areas of research

Anticipating and bolstering the talent of the future: support for early career scholars conducting cutting-edge research

Philanthropic support for individual researchers in the form of scholarships and fellowships is among the oldest and most common form of foundation funding for science, reflecting a desire that many of these institutions have, to support cutting-edge research that breaks new ground. Many of these programs typically focus on supporting early- and mid- career researchers, either students at the graduate or post-doctoral level, or faculty that are rising through the ranks. The purpose of many of these fellowship programs is to bolster the research prospects of promising scholars and help launch their careers at the outset. Foundations also provide honorific awards and prizes for more senior scholars that recognize their life-long achievements. Yet it is the support for early- and mid-career scientists that many foundations view as being critical to their missions of supporting the next generation of emerging investigators. There is the view that researchers at the beginning of their upward trajectory bring to bear the newest ideas, cutting-edge tools and technologies, and most novel and innovative perspectives on addressing thorny problems in the sciences. Directing fellowship money at the beginning and middle stages of a researcher's career is one implicit way that foundations attempt to look toward where a field is headed and demonstrate an anticipatory disposition. Operating in this mode of providing fellowships and scholarships is a rather straightforward way of funding a diverse array of scholars. Foundations often make a particular point to accentuate their desire for having a diverse array of candidates apply for these prestigious fellowship positions, serving as a signal to the fields in which they work the importance of diversity and inclusion.

To be sure, this is also a crowded space, with numerous philanthropies holding competitive fellowship solicitation processes in the fields and disciplines in which they work. This kind of intervention is also not solely the purview of philanthropy. An array of government science funding agencies provide similar kinds of fellowships and scholarship opportunities as part of their annual funding cycles. Even when the lens is broadened beyond the provision of individual fellowship competitions, governments and foundations often focus project support grants on early career investigators. One recent analysis found that many doctoral students in the sciences often are being supported by more than one such award, either provided directly to them or indirectly through a more senior primary investigator (Chang, Cheng, Lane, & Weinberg, 2019). There is even emerging evidence that philanthropic and government funders can shape the direction of fields not just through the awardees that are selected but simply through holding such competitions in the first place. New analysis has found that it is not just the winners of these funding competitions who benefit. Instead, even those who undertake the extensive effort to apply and, in the end, do not receive funding from government or philanthropic funding competitions might still come out ahead. Part of the reason why this may be the case is that "the efforts provided to put together the project and set the research agenda boost the level of advancement and the quality of applicant's research, hence positively stimulating the subsequent number of scientific publications and the average impact factor of the journals where they are published" (Ayoubi, Pezzoni, & Visentin, 2019, p. 91). The authors of this study discover that, "when applying for grants, scientists design projects and create work ties with co-applicants. We find that they build on these ties afterward regardless of the result of the grant competition. Applicants are exposed to the knowledge of their co-applicants and spillovers are likely to occur" (Ayoubi, Pezzoni, & Visentin, 2019, p. 91). Findings such as these indicate that there are many pathways by which a philanthropic funder can influence the direction of a researcher's career and speak to the multiple benefits that may arise from these individual level grantmaking interventions.

Perhaps the most well-known philanthropic-supported fellowship in science and technology is the Howard Hughes Medical Institute (HHMI) Investigator Program, which currently supports nearly 300 researchers in fields related to biomedical research. The stated goal of the prestigious HHMI Investigator Program is catalyzing "discovery science by investing in outstanding researchers with generous and flexible funding for significant periods of time," going on to note quite succinctly that "HHMI selects people, not projects" (Howard Hughes Medical Institute, n.d.). Quite large in size, HHMI awardees tend to receive roughly $8 million over a seven-year period, with approximately 20 newly funded investigators supported each year. In a strategic planning document released in 2017, HHMI expands on the underlying rationale as to why it has taken this approach of providing large scale funding to early career investigators. "Significant new knowledge cannot be supplied on demand—it unfolds over time, through exploration, experimentation, and rigorous debate," it states (Howard Hughes Medical Institute, 2017, p. 3). To facilitate this process, HHMI has decided to "place big bets on curious and ambitious researchers, supporting them with generous and flexible funding for significant periods of time, subject to rigorous periodic scientific review" (Howard Hughes Medical Institute, 2017, p. 3). Like many of these philanthropic fellowship funding programs, HHMI and other funders will often track and tout the number of their early career awardees who have gone on to win prestigious prizes later in their career, like the Nobel Prize and the National Medal of Science in various science disciplines, the Fields Medal in mathematics, and the John Bates Clark Medal in economics. In this strategy document, HHMI points out that as of 2017, 28 of its current or former funded scientists have won the Nobel Prize.

Similarly, the Moore Foundation has held a number of these kinds of fellowship programs, often in newer areas of science. In 2014, it selected 14 researchers as Moore Investigators in Data-Driven Discovery, each of whom received $1.5 million in unrestricted funds to "enable the recipients to make a profound impact on scientific research by unlocking new types of knowledge and advancing new data science methods across a wide spectrum of disciplines" (Gordon and Betty Moore Foundation, 2014). Furthermore, the explicit purpose of these individual awards was to stimulate novel, interdisciplinary science collaborations. The announcement of these awards goes on to articulate this catalytic purpose, stating that "these new awards will strengthen incentives for data scientists in academia and create greater rewards for working between disciplines. The awards will support sustained collaborations among data science researchers to build on one another's work, capitalize on the best practices and tools, and create solutions that can be used more broadly by others" (Gordon and Betty Moore Foundation, 2014). The Moore Foundation has also held competitive fellowship programs to support a cohort of investigators in their Emergent Phenomena in Quantum Systems Initiative, with the aim of providing "the freedom and flexibility to pursue challenging and novel research directions, which often take time to result in tangible results and may produce surprising discoveries. Many investigators work on development of novel experimental techniques to solve outstanding problems in the field" (Gordon and Betty Moore Foundation, 2019a). To date, 19 scientists have been awarded these five-year Experimental Investigators awards, with an ongoing competition in 2019 to make a similar number of awards that will total $34 million, amount to approximately $1.8 million per grantee.

Another example of this kind of intervention from the Moore Foundation is their Moore Inventor Program. As its name suggests, this fellowship program focuses on advancing more application-oriented discoveries than those in the basic sciences. This program emphasizes supporting "early-career scientist-inventors who create new tools and technologies with a high potential to accelerate progress in the foundation's areas of interest: scientific research, environmental conservation and patient care" (Gordon and Betty Moore Foundation, 2019c). In a blog post, the lead of the Moore Foundation science effort described how the philanthropy will fund five "scientist-inventor–problem solvers" a year for ten years (totaling 50), giving each $825,000 over a three-year period, noting in a blog post that a key reason for doing so is that, "philanthropic funding serves society by creating the right conditions in areas where imagination, scientific thinking, and intellectual freedom can create something new" (Kirshner, 2016). Here the goal is to bridge the gap between more basic and applied discoveries and help in the translation of fundamental science to more technologically oriented inventions.

A third example of an effort to support top rising scientists is the Sloan Research Fellowship program. The Sloan Research Fellowships provide $75,000 of support over two years to 126 early career scientists "in recognition of distinguished performance and a unique potential to make substantial contributions to their field" (Alfred P. Sloan Foundation, 2019a). As of 2019, Sloan Research Fellowships were awarded in eight categories that span the natural and social sciences, including chemistry, physics, mathematics, neuroscience, ocean science, computer science, computational and evolutionary molecular biology, and economics. Having begun in 1955, the Sloan Research Fellowships are the foundation's longest-running program area and include over 5,000 alumni awardees. As tracked by the Sloan Foundation, numerous fellowship winners have gone on to win highly visible prizes later on in their career, after being awarded a Sloan Research Fellowship, including, as of October 2019, 50 Nobel Prize recipients, 69 National Medal of Science recipients, 17 Fields Medal recipients, and 19 John Bates Clark Medal recipients.

The Rita Allen Foundation provides fellowships at a similar budgetary scale, specifically geared toward early career scientists in biomedical fields such as neuroscience or immunology, with scholars chosen from a set of preselected eligible institutions. These grants of $110,000 per year for up to five years are aimed at helping these rising researchers "establish labs and pursue research directions with above-average risk and promise" (Rita Allen Foundation, 2019a). In their description of the program, they too tout the accomplishments of award recipients, noting that scholars funded in this program "have gone on to make transformative contributions to their fields of study, and have won recognition including the Nobel Prize in Physiology or Medicine, the National Medal of Science, the Wolf Prize in Medicine, and the Breakthrough Prize in Life Sciences" (Rita Allen Foundation, 2019a). There are other foundation-funded fellowships in the biomedical sciences of this kind as well, where fellows are selected among a set of applicants who are put forward from a select number of nominating institutions. For instance, The Pew Charitable Trusts has its longstanding Pew Biomedical Scholars in which top assistant professors in health and biomedical research from a predetermined set of participating universities are nominated to compete for a set of $300,000 awards over a four-year time frame. Competitive nominees must "demonstrate outstanding promise as contributors in science relevant to human health" and proposed research projects must "incorporate particularly creative and pioneering approaches" (The Pew Charitable Trusts, n.d.).

A final example in this model of giving comes from a new science philanthropy entity called Schmidt Futures, established by Eric and Wendy Schmidt, the former who was previously Chief Executive Officer at Google. The Schmidt Science Fellows is one of their flagship programs that "aims to develop the next generation of science leaders to transcend disciplines, advance discovery, and solve the world's most pressing problems" (Schmidt Science Fellows, 2019). This program provides a cohort of early career scholars with the opportunity to undertake post-doctoral fellowship research, coupled with a series of organized group activities, that are deliberately focused on developing a wider perspective about how their scientific research could be most productively utilized and directed at improving society. The language of RRI and societal responsibility is used throughout the description of what the Schmidt Science Fellows program is for. The program's purpose is articulated as such, stating that "the best scientists should draw insights from across numerous different disciplines, be able to apply new techniques, and possess a broad worldview informed by the intersections between science and the rest of society" (Schmidt Futures, 2019a). It continues by affirming that "our goal is to give the world's best aspiring scientific minds a broader perspective, the ability to engage in an interdisciplinary way, and the opportunity to make a lasting impact in society" (Schmidt Futures, 2019a).

Diversity, equity, inclusion, and deliberation: fellowships that introduce new voices, change the face of science, and expand the conversation about science in society

The second category in this column involves support provided to individual scientists with the aim of helping to make progress on diversity, equity, and inclusion. Also included in this category are awards to researchers with the aim of strengthening deliberation on and engagement with the broader societal implications of science and technology. In the United States, progress in terms of diversity and inclusion in science and technology is critical and has been difficult to achieve in recent years. A key 2011 consensus study on this topic from the National Academy of Sciences bluntly summarizes the challenge that is faced, declaring that, "America faces a demographic challenge with regard to its S&E [science and engineering] workforce: Minorities are seriously under-represented in science and engineering" and that "the United States stands again at the crossroads: A national effort to sustain and strengthen S&E must also include a strategy for ensuring that we draw on the minds and talents of all Americans, including minorities who are under-represented in S&E and currently embody a vastly underused resource and a lost opportunity for meeting our nation's technology needs" (National Academy of Sciences, National Academy of Engineering, and Institute of Medicine, 2011, pp. 1–2).

While there are certainly no easy fixes to these long-standing challenges, this report highlights that the provision of fellowships and scholarships specifically geared toward supporting under-represented minority students can serve as one effective and necessary response. Foundations in particular are called out as having the ability to make an impact in this regard, with the report recommending that, "with relative freedom to explore new program approaches, foundations should develop and/or fund programs that employ innovative strategies or target particular niches in undergraduate and graduate STEM education for under-represented minorities" (National Academy of Sciences, National Academy of Engineering, and Institute of Medicine, 2011, p. 180). Of course, this is not only true in the American context. Philanthropic and government funders in countries like the United Kingdom and others around the world are increasingly recognizing that there is an intensive need to improve the diversity of scientists that are supported at all stages of the research enterprise, especially in terms of fellowships received, grants awarded, and hires made (Chambers, et al., 2017; Jones & Wilsdon, 2018). Moreover, a recent editorial in *Nature* highlights that supporting a diverse cohort of scholars is not just ethical and the "right thing" to do, but providing this kind of funding empirically leads to better and more societally responsible science being done (Nature, 2018, p. 5). This piece continues by stating the crucial point that, "a more representative workforce is more likely to pursue questions and problems that go beyond the narrow slice of humanity that much of science (biomedical science in particular) is currently set up to serve. Widening the focus is essential if publicly funded research is to protect and preserve its mandate to work to improve society" (Nature, 2018, p. 5).

Although less grand in scale in terms of the scope of the problem, there is also a need to foster deliberation and closer connections between scientists, decision-makers, and the public. While considering these two dimensions of deliberation and inclusion in the same grouping may seem odd at first, there is a natural synergy between the two. Both reflect an impulse toward considering the wider societal implications of science and technology, one in terms of which groups are able to contribute and participate in the scientific enterprise and the other in terms of more directly considering how the results of scientific research might result in broader impacts. A 2017 report from the American Association for the Advancement of Science (AAAS) that provided a landscape analysis of various mechanisms connecting scientists and policymakers—itself the result of a year-and-a-half long research effort funded by the Moore Foundation—describes how critical these arrangements are to promote broader deliberation about science's impact on society. "As science and technology drive change in society, and society drives change in governance," begins the report, "there is an increasing need and demand for mechanisms that build relationships among scientists, engineers, and policymakers to support evidence-based policy and practice" (American Association for the Advancement of Science, 2017, p. 3). The very first example provided in the report's typology of science advisory mechanisms are fellowships, which can help bring technical knowledge and expertise to better inform policy decisions. As the report notes, all of these science, policy, and society interactive and connecting mechanisms can serve a range of purposes, "including building future leadership for science policy positions in government, providing career paths beyond academia and industry, cultivating more effective means of communicating science, or influencing applied research to address societal concerns" (American Association for the Advancement of Science, 2017, p. 40). The report observes that philanthropies often serve as critical sources of support for these efforts, augmenting funding from government, non-governmental organizations, and even private donors.

Perhaps the foremost example of success of a science philanthropy effort focused on providing fellowships that help to diversify the scientific enterprise is the Meyerhoff Scholars Program. Initiated by Robert and Jane Meyerhoff in 1988, the Meyerhoff Scholars Program provides fellowship support at the undergraduate level "to increase diversity among future leaders in science, engineering, and related fields" at the University of Maryland, Baltimore County, which by now has included over 1,400 participants, among which

1,100 have completed the program (University of Maryland, Baltimore County, n.d.a). The Meyerhoff Scholars Program has developed a more inclusive model of training and support to help advance under-represented minority students in science and engineering. The program has thirteen components that combine financial support with the promotion of more collaborative learning environments, a summer training session to improve student preparation, study group formation, tutoring, summer research internships, and extensive faculty mentoring and administrative involvement, among other elements (University of Maryland, Baltimore County, n.d.b). The program has been so successful that it is being replicated at The Pennsylvania State University and the University of North Carolina at Chapel Hill with funding from HHMI. The Chan Zuckerberg Initiative awarded $6.9 million in April 2019 to replicate the Meyerhoff Scholars Program model at two additional institutions, the University of California, San Diego and the University of California, Berkeley (Hansen, 2019; Hrabowski III & Henderson, 2019). In late 2019, HHMI announced it will provide additional resources to further expand the Meyerhoff model, funding six additional universities at up to $2.5 million over five years to implement a version of this program on their campuses (Mervis, 2019a).

Clearly, the Meyerhoff Scholars Program is a good example of a type of individual-level philanthropic intervention that blends together elements of institutional and network-building support. "The key elements of the Meyerhoff program focus on values, financial support, academic success, social integration, and professional development," write Hrabowski III and Henderson (2017), who have been central to the ongoing implementation of the Meyerhoff Program. "The strategy is to deliberately form a sense of belonging and community that nurtures the students," they share (Hrabowski III & Henderson, 2017). Research has begun to show that the success demonstrated by the Meyerhoff Scholars Program in graduating and placing under-represented minorities in the sciences and engineering is transferrable and is evident in other programs that have adopted this model (Domingo, et al., 2019).

There are other fellowship programs focused on advancing diversity supported by science philanthropies. HHMI began the Hanna H. Gray Fellows Program in 2017 to "increase diversity in the biomedical research community" by providing fellows with financial support both through their post-doctoral training period and as they enter the professoriate (Howard Hughes Medical Institute, 2019). The program provides awardees $80,000 in annual support for two to four years during their post-doctoral stage, rising to $270,000 over four years when participants become faculty. This sustained financial backing of a diverse array of scholars as they move through multiple early phases of their careers is designed to help awardees "become leaders in academic research and inspire future generations of scientists from America's diverse talent pool" (Howard Hughes Medical Institute, 2019). Beyond just providing direct funding, this fellowship program also includes mentoring and networking components to help bolster the prospects of participating scientists. Similarly, the Heising-Simons Foundation has established a grantmaking emphasis centered on supporting women in physics and astronomy as a way to make these fields more inclusive, providing funding that looks to "empower individuals," "improve institutional climate," and "build networks and support systems," unmistakably noting the need for interventions targeted at providing assistance at the individual, institutional, and network levels (Heising-Simons Foundation, 2019).

As noted above, in addition to providing individuals with scholarships focused on addressing diversity, equity, and inclusion considerations, foundations have also funded individual fellowship for the purpose of engaging scientists with policy and the societal consideration of science and technology. The 2017 report from AAAS documents a number of examples related to how these connections could be made. For instance, it states that "programs in the U.S. legislative branch funded by private foundations include the Robert Wood Johnson Foundation Health Policy Fellows program. In addition, the Atlantic Philanthropy's Health and Aging Policy Fellows Program supports assignments in the U.S. federal executive and legislative branches, as well as in state and local government" (American Association for the Advancement of Science, 2017, p. 41). The most visible program of this type is the AAAS Science & Technology Policy Fellowship program, which places scientists in staff positions in the executive branch (in federal agencies), legislative branch (congressional offices or committees), or sometimes in the judicial branch. These are typically one-year fellowship positions that are renewable for a second year. Foundations have provided support for some of the individuals participating in this program in the past, either directly to AAAS or through specific disciplinary societies. In a similar vein, AAAS recently begun a new state-based effort, called the Local Science Engagement Network, with the assistance of philanthropic support. This program looks "to integrate scientists with local and state policy-makers, community stakeholders, and the public to leverage scientific evidence and inform efforts to address varied local impacts of climate change," such as by providing technical input to inform policy responses and by becoming more involved in public engagement activities (Hoy, 2019). First piloted in Missouri and Colorado, these efforts are expected to expand going forward.

Less well known, however, is an effort supported by the Moore Foundation to reproduce this program at the state level. In 2008, the Moore Foundation provided support for the California Council on Science and Technology (CCST) to create a California-oriented version of the AAAS science policy fellowship program. Moore Foundation President Harvey Fineberg noted in a blog post that these kinds of federal and state programs strengthen the relationship between science and society by providing the "opportunity to tap staff scientists and engineers provides a clear advantage and a path to sounder, evidence-based policy making" (Fineberg, 2016). The Moore Foundation and the Simons Foundation have since made additional planning grants to build on and spread the CCST science policy fellowship model to nine other states, providing small amounts of pilot funding to determine if this model could spread to other locations across the country (Williams, 2017; California Council on Science & Technology, 2017). This giving has allowed participating states across the country to conduct "landscape analyses, feasibility studies, and other strategic steps towards creating their own state-based, immersive science and technology policy fellowship" (California Council on Science and Technology, 2018). Relatedly, the Moore Foundation supported the launch of a new initiative at the National Academy of Sciences designed to offer early- and mid- career researchers the opportunity to gain experience working at the interface of science and public policy. Called New Voices in Science, Engineering, and Medicine, this program aims "to help identify and try out activities designed to expand the diversity of expertise that is engaged in the convening and advisory functions of the National Academies" (National Academies of Sciences, Engineering, and Medicine, 2019a; Alisic & Hilgenkamp, 2018). There are even newer efforts to help diversify the next generation of science journalists to ensure that these roles are more inclusive and filled by reporters who are more representative of the country as a whole (Chan Zuckerberg Initiative, 2019).

Similarly, foundations are also increasingly focused on providing opportunities for individual scientists to engage directly with communities and other stakeholders impacted by research that is conducted, especially when that research has a substantial field work component. An article on this subject by James Lavery has emphasized the need for engagement between scientists and community members. "There is increasing recognition that substantive community and stakeholder engagement (CSE) can improve the performance, and even make or break the success, of some science programs by providing a means of navigating, and responding to, the complex social, economic, cultural, and political settings in which science programs are conducted," he writes (Lavery, 2018, p. 554). This article continues by pointing out that, "a number of major funders of science programs have already made substantial investments in research on CSE, including the Wellcome Trust, the National Institutes of Health, and the Bill & Melinda Gates Foundation" (Lavery, 2018, p. 556). In fact, Lavery describes how funders can demonstrate the importance of these kinds of science, technology, and society interactions by the ways in which they frame their programs and set expectations among the research community they support. "Funders have a unique power to reframe this narrative, and better justify investments in evidence about CSE, by emphasizing its potential to improve the performance, as well as the ethics, of science programs" (Lavery, 2018, p. 556).

To this end, the Rita Allen Foundation has made "civic science" a primary programmatic focal point, looking "to foster a culture of civic science, in which broad engagement with science and evidence helps to inform solutions to society's most pressing problems" (Rita Allen Foundation, 2019b). It is partnering with other funders, including The Kavli Foundation and other members of the Science Philanthropy Alliance, to establish a Civic Science Fellowship program that will achieve this goal by "embed[ding] emerging leaders from diverse backgrounds in organizations working at the many interfaces of science and society" in order to "create connections and shared resources to strengthen the development of a culture of civic science across many types of networks" (Rita Allen Foundation, 2019b). Other foundations support similar activities within their grantmaking portfolios as well. For instance, Schmidt Futures has framed one of its core funding pillars around the theme of "advancing society through technology," providing support across all three dimensions of individuals, institutions, and networks toward the goal of "harnessing the power of science and technology to solve some of our toughest societal challenges" (Schmidt Futures, 2019b).

A *Stanford Social Innovation Review* article describing the virtues of civic science—co-written by an academic researcher and representatives of the Rita Allen Foundation and The Kavli Foundation—outlines a number of different ways in which these links between science and society can be fostered. Effective strategies to promote these connections include the ability to "capitalize on the strength of diverse coalitions," "build capacity to deal with moving targets," and "build trusting relationships through applied research and feedback loops" (Christopherson, Scheufele, & Smith, 2018, pp. 49–51). The article provides suggestions about how such principles can be operationalized. For instance, the authors write that "grantmakers should be willing to see projects change based on new circumstances and understanding, provide funding that isn't earmarked for particular uses, open routes to funding for new ideas and organizations, and speed up review processes when necessary to meet timely opportunities" (p. 50). The article also describes other ways of advancing "a civic science system that is resilient and responsive," such as "helping equip scientists to speak about their own work as it develops; supporting intermediary organizations to build relationships among scientists, journalists, and policy makers; and creating lifelong learning opportunities to improve the public's ability to assess the quality of new scientific information" (p. 50).

Reflexivity and responsiveness: applying RRI principles as criteria for grant selection

In many ways, these examples speak to the internalization of these RRI principles within science philanthropies themselves, moving to the last cell in this first column, which involves the reflexive application of RRI principles by foundations in terms of the practices, procedures, and principles they adopt when making decisions about funding of individuals through fellowships and scholarships. The need for these changes is becoming increasingly evident, especially as more attention is being paid throughout the research enterprise to addressing issues of bias, harassment, and other forms of misconduct (National Academies of Sciences, Engineering, and Medicine, 2018b). There are growing calls on research funding bodies of all kinds to respond more forcefully to these matters and require that individuals and institutions directly address such questions as a standard component of all grant proposal application processes (Greider, et al., 2019).

In addition to concerns about harassment and misconduct, research also shows that various forms of implicit bias can arise in a number of other unexpected ways throughout the funding process. Consider, for instance, the results of a recently conducted social science research project examining grant award decisions across thousands of proposals submitted for consideration by the Gates Foundation over a period of a decade. Researchers found that, "despite blinded review, female applicants receive significantly lower scores, which cannot be explained by reviewer characteristics, proposal topics, or ex-ante measures of applicant quality" (Kolev, Fuentes-Medel, & Murray, 2019, p. 1). Proposals submitted by men tend to use "broader terms" in their grant applications, yet the study found that "funded applications that contained many broad words didn't result in work that led to more publications and future grants, the researchers found. And when women secured funding, they generally outperformed men on these measures" (Else, 2019). Results such as these indicate that funders need to reflexively apply the principles of the RRI framework to themselves and begin to change how they evaluate proposals, oversee programs, and set grant metrics to allow for this kind of societally oriented science research to flourish. Lavery makes this very suggestion in his article as well. "Funders could substantially advance the mutual value of CSE for researchers and stakeholders," he writes, "by experimenting with more flexible and responsive management strategies, including innovations in protocol and budget processes, and studying the implications for various aspects of program performance" (Lavery, 2018, p. 556).

Many examples on this front abound in the world of science philanthropy, as foundations have gone through a period of reflection, often in the public sphere, to describe the updating and changing of their grantmaking requirements to reflect these perspectives. Consider the Science program at the Heising-Simons Foundation, which recently adjusted its own practices when reviewing and selecting applicants for a prestigious fellowship program in the field of astronomy, called the 51 Pegasi b Fellowship in Planetary Astronomy. In announcing the fellowship class for 2019 in a blog post, the Heising-Simons Foundation highlighted a number of self-reflexive practices that the foundation adopted. The adoption of these practices has led to "improvements…to move the application, review, and award processes towards more inclusive and equitable practices" (Atherton, 2019). These changes included, among others, "changing to an open application process," "adding a diversity, equity, and inclusion (DEI) statement to the application requirements," and making this required diversity statement "one of six parts of the scoring rubric on which each candidate was evaluated," (Atherton, 2019). The fellowship selection process also involved "revamping the panel review, including having the in-person review facilitated by a nationally recognized STEM [science, technology, engineering, and mathematics] diversity, equity, and inclusion expert" and adopting "multiple techniques to address the panel reviewers' bias literacy, avoid decision fatigue and unconscious biases, and base decisions on evidence" (Atherton, 2019). The sum-total effect of these and other changes led to the selection of a more diverse fellowship class once these practices were implemented. Joyce Yen, who helped to develop and implement these practices, writes that it is of utmost importance that science philanthropies and other funders "interrogate evaluation processes and actively embrace research-based effective practices" in order to "improve decision-making processes, reset evaluation norms, and foster greater diversity, equity, and inclusion" (Yen, 2019, p. 1042). She concludes by noting that, "rather than waiting for an external demand for change, organizations can proactively adopt better, more equitable processes that expand who is included, recognized, and rewarded in science" (p. 1042).

Many other science philanthropies have taken steps to make similar changes and improvements to their grantmaking strategies. At the Sloan Foundation, every proposal submitted for consideration is required to include an Attention to Diversity appendix, which discusses the proposer's "current and planned efforts to ensure racial and gender diversity in the project," with the guidance that is provided stating that "proposers should strive for diversity when drafting their proposals, constructing research teams, creating advisory panels, and assigning leadership and management responsibilities on a project" (Alfred P. Sloan Foundation, 2019c, p. 9). The President's Letter included in the Sloan Foundation's 2015 annual report directly addressed the institution's commitment to diversity and inclusion, noting that an increase emphasis had been placed to "unsilo" these considerations across the foundation (Alfred P. Sloan Foundation, 2016, p. xxi). "Diversity goals should be pursued in all of our programs in all of their dimensions," writes former Sloan Foundation President Paul Joskow (p. xxi). "All of Sloan's grantmaking programs are now required to take both racial and gender diversity into account, working with grantees to ensure that minorities and women are fully represented on research teams, in postdoc and fellowship awards, and at meetings and conferences" (p. xxi).

Other foundations have made similar commitments. HHMI noted a core commitment to diversity, equity, and inclusion in its 2017 strategic plan, highlighting that the foundation plans to "actively use our resources—funding, community, and influence—to increase diversity, equity, and inclusion in our scientific community and beyond" (Howard Hughes Medical Institute, 2017, p. 4). HHMI has backed this plan with support for various individual fellowship programs. In addition, it also has established an Inclusive Excellence initiative to link together support from a number of institutions dedicated to increasing the number of under-represented minority students involved in science and engineering, thereby committing to funding both individual, institutional, and network level interventions on this important issue. The Wellcome Trust has also taken the lead on diversity and inclusion. It has made these concerns part of their core strategic "priority areas," provided funding to institutions and networks committed to advancing diversity in the biomedical and health sciences, and has reflexively looked at their own practices and grantmaking procedures (Wellcome Trust, n.d.a). Wellcome commissioned a

2017 reflexive study that investigated how well they had done in integrating diversity within their grantmaking and staff recruitment. One goal of the study was to ensure that "any policies and practices associated with awarding grants, and with appointing people to work for Wellcome, do not inadvertently disadvantage particular groups of people, thereby potentially limiting the flow of the best ideas" (Bridge Group, 2017, p. 2). The study made a set of recommendations to increase the use of best practices as part of its grantmaking, including interventions such as "ensuring that, at a minimum, individual selectors are aware about implicit bias," "setting of explicit and valid selection criteria…and clarity about the criteria being assessed at which stage," "introduce a specific expectation that all grant applicants will detail how their organization's research culture and standards promote diversity and inclusion," and "publish a summary of the diversity characteristics of Wellcome peer reviewers and Peer Review College members" (Bridge Group, 2017, pp. 18–19).

More recently, Wellcome launched a new effort to spur a conversation to rethink how to achieve a more positive and inclusive research culture. In a post on the organization's website, the organization's director, Jeremy Farrar, wrote that Wellcome has "an important role to play in changing and improving the prevailing research culture" and that "if we want science to be firing on all cylinders, we need everyone in the research system—individuals, institutions and funders—working in step to foster a positive working culture" (Farrar, 2019). Farrar continues by describing the changes that funder already has made to foster an improved research culture and, with this post, began a survey process to gather external perspectives about how additional progress could be made. He notes that, "we've already made improvements at Wellcome, including establishing and acting on our zero-tolerance stance to bullying and harassment, and making diversity and inclusion one of our first priority areas" and that "from now on we will be putting culture at the heart of everything we do, including the ongoing review of our science funding strategy" (Farrar, 2019). This last line is an indication of reflexivity and a recognition of the need to continually reflect these values within the decision-making approaches adopted by the philanthropy.

Establishing and sustaining institutions: creating long-standing organizational infrastructure for scientific research

Funding forward-looking research centers: producing the conditions for breakthrough science

The second column shifts attention to philanthropic support for institutions that look to conduct anticipatory, ground-breaking research. This modality is where some of the most prominent grantmaking undertaken by foundations funding science and technology takes place. The first category relates to philanthropic funding of institutions that aim to conduct ground-breaking, anticipatory research. As may be expected, philanthropies are particularly keen to fund work that is seen as being on the trailblazing, leading edge of a field. As discussed in Chapter 2, this kind of philanthropic support for research institutions has a long history, going back to support for what eventually became Rockefeller University. Therefore, while it is impossible to highlight the legions of examples that exist in this category, a few particular instances of philanthropic support for such institutional efforts stand out.

The Kavli Foundation is perhaps most well-known for its grantmaking in this manner, providing multi-million dollar grants to establish a number of high-profile research institutes in order "to advance fundamental research in the fields of astrophysics, nanoscience, neuroscience, and theoretical physics" (The Kavli Foundation, 2019a). As of 2019, twenty such Kavli-funded institutes have been supported across these four areas of science, mostly located in the United States with four based in other countries. Well-known universities receiving such funding include Stanford University, Massachusetts Institute of Technology, and the University of Chicago in astrophysics; Harvard University, Cornell University, and University of California Berkeley in nanoscience; Columbia University, Yale University, and Johns Hopkins University in neuroscience; and the University of California Santa Barbara in theoretical physics. Those located outside the United States are based at Peking University in China for astrophysics, Delft University of Technology in The Netherlands for nanoscience, the Norwegian University of Science and Technology for neuroscience, and the University of the Chinese Academy of Sciences in theoretical physics. Funding of these Kavli institutes generally is accompanied by the expectation that additional or matching funding can be secured, either internally from the host university or from other external sources.

Other science philanthropies provide similar kinds of institutional support for this kind of forward-looking research. For instance, the W. M. Keck Foundation established the Keck Institute for Space Studies at the California Institute of Technology and the Keck Graduate Institute of Applied Life Sciences within the Claremont College Consortium (W. M. Keck Foundation, 2019). Similarly, the Moore Foundation supports a number of pioneering research institutes at the California Institute of Technology, including the Institute for Quantum Information and Matter, the Center for Analysis of Higher Brain Function, and the Center for Ultrafast Science and Technology (Gordon and Betty Moore Foundation, 2019b). Many philanthropic efforts of this kind exist outside the United States as well. To take just one example, the Sainsbury Wellcome Centre for Neural Circuits and Behaviour is an innovative research effort housed at University College London and supported by the Wellcome Trust and the Gatsby Charitable Foundation. The aim of this center is to help advance research on the theoretical and empirical neurological underpinnings of decision-making, behavior, and learning by combining research and insights from multiple fields of investigation (Sainsbury Wellcome Centre, 2019).

Relatedly, there are also many examples that exist today of science phi-lanthropies supporting the development and construction of large-scale sci-ence instrumentation, often undertaken in the context of providing support for research institutions. Again, many examples abound, particularly in the field of astronomy. The W. M. Keck Observatory is a major optical and infrared observatory located in Hawaii, where the Keck Foundation and others have provided support for two, ten-meter diameter telescopes. The Simons Observatory, supported by the Simons Foundation and the Heising-Simons Foundation, is a new telescope facility being built in Chile's Atacama Desert to study cosmology and the origins of the universe. The Heising-Simons Foundation provides substantial funding for a host of instrumentation development purposes located at a variety of ground-based telescopes. The Moore Foundation is one of the founding funders of the planned Thirty Meter Telescope, also slated to be built in Hawaii. And, as will be discussed in the next chapter, the Sloan Foundation provided support to build what became the Sloan Telescope located at Apache Point Observatory in New Mexico. Outside of the United States, there are also instances of science philanthropies providing this kind of institutional support for critical research instruments. For example, the United Kingdom's national synchrotron, a high energy light research facility, is a jointly funded operation called Diamond Light Source that combines funds from the government's Science and Tech-nology Facilities Council and the Wellcome Trust to support this instru-mentation (Diamond Light Source, 2018).

Embedding inclusion and deliberation: institutional infrastructure to advance diversity and engagement

The second category in this column is a mode of grantmaking in which philanthropies support institutions to advance deliberation, inclusion, and broader deliberation of societal implications. As can be seen with the Meyerhoff Scholars Program model, many of the elements that contribute to the success of philanthropic funding programs oriented toward indivi-duals are deeply intertwined with programs focused on institutions and even networks. One article written by Freeman Hrabowski III and Peter Hen-derson observes that successful interventions addressing diversity and inclu-sion in science and technology need to utilize "multifaceted" approaches that are "based on what we call a 'social transformation theory of change' in which we create empowering settings for minority student achievement within a broader institutional change process focusing on transforming campus culture to emphasize inclusion and excellence" (Hrabowski III & Henderson, 2019, p. 71).

One good example of this attempt to help science and technology institu-tions move forward on this front is showcased in an analysis undertaken by the Wellcome Trust to assess the state of doctoral research training in the United Kingdom and determine what institutional changes are needed to make improvements. This analysis found that there is a "need for changes to PhD training that support a more positive research culture" and asserts that "Wellcome will set expectations regarding the appropriate structure of PhD training and the culture of research by fostering best practice among supervisors, directors, institutions and other funders, which will deliver changes in practice" (Wellcome Trust, 2018, p. 17). Additionally, Wellcome has focused on creating "a more positive culture for PhD training" by supporting "changes to improve the structure of PhD training" at institutions that the foundation funds (Coriat, 2018). This includes allowing grant-receiving institutions a fair amount of leeway and flexibility in the design and structure of their training programs, requiring improvements in mentoring and supervision, assisting in career transitions, focusing on promoting student mental health, and promoting a range of other diversity and inclusion practices. It is also one of the core institutional sponsors, along with government and industry supporters, of the Equality, Diversity, and Inclusion in Science and Health (EDIS) effort that aims to connect "organizations across the science and health field to develop a coalition with power to influence and drive evidence-based change" (EDIS, n.d.).

Two of the programs mentioned in the 2011 report from the National Academies discussed earlier, *Expanding Underrepresented Minority Participation*, fall into this category. These programs provide fellowships to under-represented minority and indigenous doctoral students at selected university partners, thereby bringing together both individual level and institutional level interventions. Like many of the programs mentioned above, these programs also focus on ensuring that significant attention is paid to student mentorship, which research shows is perhaps the key contributor to the ultimate success of under-represented minority students in science (National Academies of Sciences, Engineering, and Medicine, 2019b). The Sloan Minority PhD Program has worked with nine University Centers of Exemplary Mentoring across the country that have been selected based upon their willingness to provide internal institutional matching financial resources to expand the program's impact (Alfred P. Sloan Foundation, 2019b). Selected universities span a wide range of geographies, scales, and both public and private institutional types, including The Pennsylvania State University, Georgia Institute of Technology, University of South Florida, and the Massachusetts Institute of Technology, just to name a few. Under-represented minority students participating in this program are drawn from a wide array of scientific and engineering fields, including chemistry, mathematics, computer science, physics, agricultural sciences, and civil and environmental engineering, among others. Following a similar model, indigenous students who are American Indian or Alaska Native are supported across four participating university systems in the Sloan Indigenous Graduate Partnership program, with participating institutions including the University of Montana system, the University of Alaska system, the University of Arizona, and Purdue University.

Related to fostering policy and public engagement, in addition to supporting various individual fellowship programs as a way to bring scientists into the policymaking process, science philanthropies have also been supporting the establishment of new institutional centers that can serve as organizational hubs for these kinds of activities. One of the most high-profile efforts of this type is the provision of funds by eight philanthropies—including the Moore Foundation, Sloan Foundation, Rita Allen Foundation, and the Chan Zuckerberg Initiative, just to name a few—to create a new entity within the AAAS, called the Center for Scientific Evidence in Public Issues, with the purpose "to share scientific and technical evidence with policymakers working at all levels of government in the United States" (Ham, 2018, p. 1327). The Center for Scientific Evidence in Public Issues looks "to create timely, well-communicated evidence narratives—what scientists know about a topic, how they know it, what the evidence means, and how it relates to other public policy issues" (Ham, 2018, p. 1327). The purpose is to marshal the expertise available within the AAAS membership of scientists to bring scientific and technical knowledge to bear on societally relevant questions and challenges, with its first selected topic area relating to science associated with ensuring the security of electronic voting during elections (Korte, 2019).

Science philanthropies are also increasingly focused on supporting efforts and institutions that directly engage members of the public on science and technology topics. As an example, the Sloan Foundation has a long-standing program on Public Understanding of Science, Technology & Economics that looks to "give people a keener appreciation for the increasingly scientific and technological world in which we live and to convey some of the challenges and rewards of the scientific and technological enterprise" (Alfred P. Sloan Foundation, 2019d). The program draws on the language of C.P. Snow (1959) and the notion of "the two cultures" as a way of framing the need to better link together science with arts and the humanities. The goal of the program is described as aiming "to build bridges between the two cultures of science and the humanities and to develop a common language so that they can better understand and speak to one another—and ultimately to grasp that they belong to a single common culture" (Alfred P. Sloan Foundation, 2019d). This program supports the presentation of scientific research results, the lives of scientists, and scientific ways of thinking in multiple formats, including film, radio, television, theater, books, and various other new media modalities. Both the Simons Foundation (Simons Foundation, 2018) and the Wellcome Trust (Wellcome Trust, n.d.b) have also provided support to filmmakers to improve the depiction of science and scientists on screen in both fiction and non-fiction representations. Similarly, multiple funders—including the Sloan Foundation, HHMI, Moore Foundation, and Simons Foundation—have funded the Science & Entertainment Exchange at the National Academies to improve the connection between working scientists and the representation of science throughout the entertainment industry (Weber, 2019). Other philanthropies like the Rita Allen Foundation, Albert and Mary Lasker Foundation, and John Templeton Foundation have also worked together to identify best practices to communicate science to the public (Christopherson, Dill, & Pomeroy, 2019). The resulting report on this topic supported by these three foundations found that while sometimes an afterthought, effective communications by science philanthropies is increasingly important to amplifying the visibility and public appreciation of scientific research that is undertaken. It finds that, "as science philanthropies communicate with key stakeholders to empower scientific innovation, they require a range of talented strategic communicators in order to navigate changes in the environment and advance their essential work" (Dudo & Besley, 2019).

Constructing institutional reflexivity and responsiveness from the inside out: creating in-house research centers

The final type of giving in this category is the establishment of new institutions by a science philanthropy in ways that reflect the institution's interests, values, and ideals. One of the ways in which this kind of support is differentiated from the type of institution-oriented grantmaking discussed above is that in this mode of philanthropy, the research institution is mostly or perhaps wholly embedded in the philanthropy itself. This is a relatively newer kind of philanthropic intervention in science, one where the distinction between the foundation itself and the research being conducted becomes rather blurry. One prominent example of this kind of philanthropy is embodied in the Allen Institute. Founded in 2003 as the Allen Institute for Brain Science, the Allen Institute is a stand-alone research center named after its benefactor, Microsoft co-founder Paul Allen. Having broadened from its initial focus on brain science, the Allen Institute now comprises a series of collaborating research teams looking to make advancements across various areas within the biosciences, including cell science, immunology, and a focus on extending bioscience research globally. The Allen Institute places an emphasis on undertaking large-scale, collaborative team science and has "a commitment to share all we learn openly with the world," making its research publicly available for others to use (Allen Institute, 2019).

Another example is the creation of an in-house institutional research capacity within the Simons Foundation. The Flatiron Institute, established by the Simons Foundation in 2017 as part of the philanthropy itself, is embedded within the foundation and therefore is directly connected to pursuing the research interests of the Simons Foundation. The Flatiron Institute has adopted as its stated mission "to advance scientific research through computational methods, including data analysis, theory, modeling and simulation," explicitly tying it to the goals and objectives of the foundation overall (Simons Foundation, n.d.a). The Flatiron Institute is divided into four research centers focused on accelerating the computational aspects of astrophysics, biology, mathematics, and quantum physics, and it has a roster of top-notch scientific staff who conduct research in these areas. The Simons Foundation's 2017 annual report, which announced the opening of the Flatiron Institute, highlighted the very rationale for establishing this kind of organization as part of the philanthropy. "Flatiron Institute researchers don't have to apply for grants, freeing them to pursue long-term projects that might not be possible if continued funding were uncertain," it states (Simons Foundation, 2017). Underpinning this rather unique research capability within a foundation, the Flatiron Institute has a powerful in-house "computation infrastructure" that provides researchers access to high-performance computing resources, a level of research resources more commonly available at a university rather than at a philanthropic organization (Simons Foundation, n.d.b). Again, the Simons Foundation's annual report points to the ways in which the Flatiron Institute's organizational structure facilitates conducting research by leveraging high quality data science resources. "The financial model also means that software developed at the Flatiron Institute is freely available to all scientists and is built to last, receiving long-term support and continued development" (Simons Foundation, 2017). Both the Allen Institute and the Flatiron Institute are housed in dedicated buildings in their respective urban locales, Seattle in the former and New York City in the latter, specifically designed and built for the purpose of conducting scientific research. These extensive physical resources further enhance the ability of both institutions to not only have scientific impact but to ensure that they also are well-positioned to serve as central sites for research collaboration.

Another novel and interesting example of this type of philanthropic support for science is embodied in the Schmidt Ocean Institute. Not a grantmaking philanthropy in the traditional sense, the Schmidt Ocean Institute is self-described as a "private non-profit operating foundation" that is separate from the Schmidt Futures philanthropy (Schmidt Ocean Institute, 2019a). Established in 2009, its stated mission is to "advance oceanographic research, discovery, and knowledge, and catalyze sharing of information about the oceans" (Schmidt Ocean Institute, 2019a). The organization does not employ any scientists or research staff, nor does it give grants to researchers in a traditional sense. Instead, it maintains a state-of-the-art oceangoing research vessel and allows researchers to utilize this resource by providing instrumentation testing and support, technical assistance, and helping to standardize the reporting of results through a data management and data sharing platform. Collaborating researchers are able to utilize these technologies in exchange for making the science undertaken on the research vessel openly available. "All the scientists and researchers…have applied for ship time and are members of collaborating universities and institutions," notes the website of the Schmidt Ocean Institute (Schmidt Ocean Institute, 2019b). In many ways, then, this organizational form intriguingly combines elements of individual, institutional, and network backing by providing the research community access to a shared, cutting-edge scientific resource.

Weaving together individuals and institutions: advancing network-building for scientific research

Generating anticipatory, collaborative cohorts: forming linkages among early career scholars and connections across institutions

The third dimension in this framework focuses on the various ways in which science philanthropies provide funding for networks and network-building activities. In many ways, these kinds of network-level interventions are the most complex. They not only involve attempts to link together individuals and institutions, but they often include many varied and different tactics to strengthen relationships, build linkages, and create a sense of community among the various network participants. Science research networks supported by foundations can also come in many sizes, from smaller-scale endeavors that might involve just a handful or roughly a dozen researchers or institutions, to mid-sized networks that might include less than a hundred individuals, to larger networks that could include thousands of scientists and nearly fifty participating institutions. Beyond the potential to engage large numbers of individuals and multiple institutions, such networks often may involve collaborations across sectors, with foundations partnering with government and industry to advance research to grow the network over time, add in or match financial resources to grow the pool of available money, or provide in-kind assistance in the form of instrumentation, data access, or other necessary research infrastructure.

The first category in this dimension relates to philanthropic interventions that create a cohort of scholars or bring together institutions to undertake collaborative research projects. There are a number of such initiatives, many of which involve collaboration with funders from other sectors and an array of institutional stakeholders. One of the most well-known scientific efforts of this kind is the Brain Research through Advancing Innovative Neurotechnologies Initiative, commonly known as the BRAIN Initiative, in the United States. First announced in 2013 by former President Barack Obama, the BRAIN Initiative aims to achieve the transformative goal of "revolutionizing our understanding of the human brain" and "produce a revolutionary new dynamic picture of the brain that, for the first time, shows how individual cells and complex neural circuits interact in both time and space" (National Institutes of Health, n.d.). Based at the National Institutes of Health, this collaborative effort first received funds in 2014 and is designed as a twelve-year, $4.5 billion-dollar research program to achieve the research goals outlined in a strategic planning report titled *BRAIN 2025: A Scientific Vision*. Among other things, this document situated the BRAIN Initiative in the context of advancing and building on earlier, smaller-scale investments made by philanthropies, including the Sloan Foundation and the Swartz Foundation, in the areas of theoretical and computational neuroscience. The report highlighted that the best way to achieve transformational progress in the area of neuroscience research was through the establishment of "collaborative consortia" that would take place "through partnerships with foundations and private institutes that have broad in-house expertise" (National Institutes of Health, 2014, pp. 109–110). A more recent article from 2018 points out the importance of this move toward working in a more collaborative, network-oriented fashion, including the ability to bring together expertise from multiple disciplines such as biology, neuroscience, physics, chemistry, and mathematics to combining funding from multiple sources in government, industry, and philanthropy. "The BRAIN

Initiative signals a paradigm shift for neuroscience, as it requires the scientific community to work together toward a neural network understanding of the brain," write the authors (Mott, Gordon, & Koroshetz, 2018, p. 2).

The Kavli Foundation was among the science philanthropies that played a particularly key role in establishing and continuing the collaborative BRAIN effort (Pena, Stokes, & Behrens, 2019). They and three other philanthropies—the Simons Foundation, the Gatsby Foundation, and the Allen Institute for Brain Science—were instrumental in funding the first meeting that identified opportunities to conduct ground-breaking research at the intersection of neuroscience and other fields (Yuste, 2017). The Kavli Foundation continued to fund a series of planning meetings in conjunction with the Office of Science and Technology Policy that ultimately led to the development of the idea for the BRAIN Initiative (The Kavli Foundation, 2019b). In 2015, the Kavli Foundation announced a contribution of $100 million toward funding the BRAIN Initiative—half of which came from its own funds and the other half from university partners—that added to the initial financial commitments it made when the BRAIN Initiative network was initially established (Maldarelli, 2015).

Furthermore, as the collaboration has evolved, a central component of this network has been the establishment of the BRAIN Initiative Alliance (BIA), a centralized information portal that was established to "inform and engage the public and the scientific community about scientific successes emerging from the BRAIN Initiative, and opportunities for further discovery" (BRAIN Initiative, n.d.). The BIA includes the nearly 35 formal members and affiliate organizations that include government agency funders, university research centers, industrial partners, professional and technical societies, independent research organizations like the Allen Institute for Brain Science and the Salk Institute for Biological Studies, and science philanthropies. The two key science philanthropy funders are The Kavli Foundation and the Simons Foundation, along with involvement from the Pediatric Brain Foundation and the Brain & Behavior Research Foundation. At its five-year mark, the BRAIN Initiative is looking ahead to pose and answer new questions, not only investigating questions in neuroscience but also continuing to integrate social science research by interrogating issues in neuroethics. As one article describing the progress that has been made and the potential that remains to marshal this collaboration network in understanding how the mind and brain work, "with diverse scientists jointly working in novel team structures, often in partnership with industry, and sharing unprecedented types and quantities of data, the BRAIN Initiative offers a unique opportunity to open the door to a golden age in brain science and improved brain health for all" (Koroshetz, et al., 2018, p. 6434).

There are other multi-sectoral research collaboration networks that combine public, philanthropic, and private resources, yet in some cases it can be difficult to determine how much progress has been made. For instance, the National Microbiome Initiative was announced in 2016 as a more than $120 million effort of combined federal and philanthropic funding that would take place over four years to address key questions related to microbiology research that cut across areas such as the environment, human health, and food production. In addition to financial resources provided by various federal agencies, philanthropies like the Gates Foundation committed to supporting research that would study the relationship between microbiomes in agriculture and their relationship to human health, with non-profit organizations and universities also committed funding to extending research in this area (The White House, 2016). However, with little additional public information available, it is challenging to determine the impact of such a multi-sectoral and multi-partner funding initiative, let alone determine whether the announced funds to be provided were new resources directed at these questions or whether they mainly involved repackaging previously allocated or planned funding for this purpose.

Efforts like the BRAIN Initiative and the National Microbiome Initiative are good examples of the increased attention being paid to partnership and network building activities between philanthropic and government funders. One report on this topic found that, "as both philanthropy and government seek to expand their impact, new models of working together are beginning to emerge" (Ferris & Williams, 2012, p. 4). In the sciences, this can mean informal collaboration by way of foundations and governments collectively deciding to give grants to establish and sustain research networks. There are alternative, more formal modes of collaboration as well. For instance, some of these networking partnerships are being facilitated through the establishment of institutions known as federal foundations. These are linked to existing government agencies but, as separate non-profit institutions, allow philanthropic or private sector funding to be more formally aligned with government spending. One recent report describing the emergence of these partnership opportunities articulated the value of these institutions, stating that, "in the absence of clear contracting authorities, 501(c)(3) foundations have emerged to support missions of specific Federal agencies while remaining independent of the Federal entities…Through foundations, Federal agencies may be able to more freely accept gifts from non-Federal organizations to support their goals or agency missions" (Pena, Stokes, & Behrens, 2019, p. 21). There are numerous such philanthropic institutions, including the Foundation for the NIH, which supports research collaborations across academia, industry, and non-profit organizations; and the Foundation for Food and Agricultural Research and the Agricultural Technology Innovation Partnership Foundation, both at the United States Department of Agriculture, which link private and public resources to accelerate the commercialization of agriculture-related technology; and the Reagan-Udall Foundation for the Food and Drug Administration that works with that agency to advance regulatory science needed to ensure safety (Pena, Stokes, & Behrens, 2019). Scholars Steven Ezell and David Hart have also encouraged the idea of creating a Department of Energy (DOE) Foundation that would bring in private and philanthropic money to help scale up novel energy technologies developed at national laboratories (Ezell & Hart, 2017). These researchers go on to describe the multiple societal and public benefits that these kinds of institutions provide in terms of promoting multi-sectoral network building and the pooling of resources across philanthropic, government, and private donors.

> Such foundations benefit government researchers, donors, and the nation as a whole. For government researchers, foundation grants serve as a force multiplier, providing them with additional funding to focus on problems they are passionate about. Donors are able to mobilize outstanding researchers to tackle problems they care about…The nation gets more from the money it has already spent to build top-notch intramural research teams to focus on public problems. Foundations can help agencies like NIH and DOE speed the fruits of research into practice by supporting collaboration between their own laboratories and those affiliated with corporate and charitable foundation donors.
>
> (Ezell & Hart, 2017)

Beyond support for network building activities that take place across sectors, there are a number of instances of science philanthropies collaborating closely with one another to establish research networks in domains of shared interest. One of the best examples of this kind of intervention, whereby a science philanthropy provides support for research networks across topics and disciplines, is a program known as Scialog—a mashup of the phrase Science Dialogue—that has been organized and undertaken by the Research Corporation for Science Advancement (RCSA). Began in 2010, Scialogs are a series of annual meetings devoted to a particularly novel or emerging topic or set of research questions in a field that aim to link together and promote collaboration among early-career scholars conducting cutting-edge research. An article describing the purpose and details of the Scialog process notes that this network-building activity "rapidly generates novel, high-risk basic science ideas, catalyzes new multi-disciplinary collaborations among researchers previously unfamiliar with one another, develops networks of early career scientists, and empowers private foundations to work together effectively to enable convergence" (Wiener & Ronco, 2019, p. 1020). Each Scialog series typically consists of two or three meetings that take place over successive years, with roughly the same cohort of 50–60 selected early-career scholars participating as a way to build connections and form scientific research partnerships. Five Scialog series have taken place in areas across the physical and biological sciences that bring together scholars in astronomy, physics, chemistry, biology, materials science, and other disciplines to investigate topics from multiple disciplinary perspectives under headings such as Solar Energy Conversion, Advanced Energy Storage, Molecules Come to Life, Chemical Machinery of the Cell, and Time Domain Astrophysics.

A key innovation of the Scialog convenings is that instead of just having participants discuss the future of these research areas and identify hypothetical research projects that could be pursued, the focal point of these gatherings is to have early-career researchers, who have not worked with one another previously, prepare short proposals that outline highly innovative and risky research ideas. These proposals are then considered for funding by RCSA and other science philanthropies that have been brought in as funding partners on specific Scialog series, with the top ideas being provided with small amounts of seed funding to initiate pursuit of this idea, typically between $100,000 and $150,000 per project over one year of research. "Scialog Fellows are incentivized to form new collaborative teams, with diverse characteristics, and pitch on-the-spot ideas for seed funding of novel, cutting-edge projects," write the program leads of this effort (Wiener & Ronco, 2019, p. 1020). They note later in this piece that restricting proposal length to two pages and requiring collaboration among those who have not worked with one another in the past is deliberately designed to generate new ideas. "The rapid-fire environment sparks creative thinking that is not overedited, as often occurs in other grant proposal processes. Scialog seeks to remove caution which might otherwise consign highly original ideas to the trash bin" (Wiener & Ronco, 2019, p. 1022). Beyond the teams receiving funding at this smaller scale, there are other indicators of success, including larger-scale follow-on support from government agencies, continued pursuit of projects that did not receive funding during the initial review phase, and, over the longer-term, the formation of ongoing research relationships among leading faculty that are just beginning their careers.

Moreover, in addition to serving as network-forming infrastructure for the researchers themselves, the Scialog program has fostered networking and collaboration opportunities among science philanthropies as well. Most of the Scialog series have included other science philanthropy funders as partners, either as full co-sponsors at the outset, as co-funders that emerge over time, or even as one-off co-funders for particular projects that emerge from Scialog meetings. For instance, the Moore Foundation co-sponsored the two Scialogs that had more of a focus on biology, Molecules Come to Life and Chemical Machinery of the Cell, with the latter also involving the Paul G. Allen Frontiers Group; the Heising-Simons Foundation co-funded the Time Domain Astrophysics Scialog; and the Sloan Foundation collaborated on the Advanced Energy Storage Scialog. Other foundations, such as the Lyda Hill Foundation, have provided funding to individual research projects emerging from some of the Scialog meetings. Wiener and Ronco point out the value of these network interactions among science philanthropies provided by Scialog:

> Program officers from cosponsoring and other private foundations and federal agencies often attend Scialog meetings. Their involvement not only provides additional resources to support Scialog projects but just as importantly creates bidirectional access between Fellows and program officers, which allows for connections and projects beyond Scialog. Networking is both horizontal and vertical with Fellows forming connections not only among themselves but also with facilitators and program officers.
>
> (Wiener & Ronco, 2019, p. 1022)

Since 2010, over \$12 million has been awarded to collaborative research projects developed at Scialog meetings, with more to come as the Scialog series plans to expand in the years ahead.

In this way, the Scialog network-building activities are similar to other collaborative idea-generating endeavors undertaken by government funders. These are often known as sandpit exercises that bring together a group of scholars from a range of fields to work intensely over a short period of time to generate actionable and fundable research projects that involve multiple scientists from multiple fields and multiple institutions. In the United Kingdom, the Engineering and Physical Sciences Research Council (EPSRC) has pioneered the use of this network-building funding approach since 2004. As part of its "IDEAS Factory," these sandpit workshops have brought together a "dynamic range of individuals and skills needed to attack real world problems from every angle" and then "groups and ideas are formed, reviewed and potentially funded within five days" (EPSRC, 2018, p. 3). The National Science Foundation has also experimented with this mode of giving to support collaborative and potentially transformative research in the area of synthetic biology (Mervis, 2009).

A third foundation-funded network building activity that falls in this category is the National Academies Keck Futures Initiative (NAKFI), an effort funded by the Keck Foundation as a 15-year effort with \$40 million of support to The National Academies to spur interdisciplinary research networks and collaborations. Began in 2003, the goal was to create a network of researchers from across fields who could "advance the capacity of the research enterprise to address society's greatest challenges" (National Academies of Sciences, Engineering, and Medicine, 2018a, p. 1). The program had three related components. The first and primary element was organizing an annual Futures conference focused on a particularly challenging area of science, technology, or medicine that could be addressed by a network of collaborators from different fields and disciplines. These conferences spanned a wide range of topics, from genomics and synthetic biology to smart prosthetics and imaging science to ecosystem services and ocean science. As a report from the National Academies notes, "the initiative was intended to be a broad, national stimulus of creative inquiry that would enhance the spirit of collaboration and problem solving among accomplished and emerging research talent and their institutions," so that "as future leaders in universities and industrial laboratories they would organize and guide the research of the future and potentially encourage institutions to invent structures and strategies to advance joint science, engineering, and medical research in the service of improving the human condition" (p.1).

Building on these annual gatherings, the second component of these network-building activities included the provision of grants, awarded competitively, to pursue innovative research projects identified at the Futures conferences. "Seed grants awarded to conference participants enabled further pursuit of bold, new ideas generated at the conference that were not yet ready to compete for other funding," writes the summary report (p. 2). Nearly \$15 million in these seed awards was provided over the course of the program, approximately $1 million a year with each grant being on the order of $25,000 to $100,000 over two years. The resulting projects eventually raised over $150 million of additional funding secured from other sources to advance these collaborative research ideas further. Collaborators on each project would meet in person midway through the project to further promote networking and make adjustments as needed. The desire was to provide funding that would serve as "a critical missing link between bold new ideas and major federal funding programs" (p. 20). A third component of the program involved making an annual award to recognize effective efforts to communicate science and technology to the broader public. Collectively, these foundation-funded interventions helped create "broad, diverse, and better prepared networks of interdisciplinary and cross-professional researchers, scholars, and practitioners" that not only were accelerated by the provision of seed grants but were able to grow by leveraging funding from other sources (p. 14).

In many ways, these kinds of philanthropic interventions and public-private partnerships—the BRAIN Initiative, RCSA's Scialog program, and the NAKFI—relate back to roles that foundations played in the research enterprise earlier in the 20th Century, as discussed in Chapter 2. In his analysis on the history of science philanthropy, Kohler notes that,

> the partnership between philanthropic or government patrons and scientific researchers might well be more reciprocal, with program officers exercising a more active role in identifying priorities, not as bureaucrats and accountants, but as partners. Patrons might encourage communication and cooperation on problems of large significance by making more use of grants for group projects, or by developing centers in which research is integrated with innovative training or social services.
>
> (Kohler, 1985, p. 13)

In her study of science philanthropies, Murray also makes this point that the inter-relationship of public and philanthropic support for science is complementary and provides positive feedback loops. She writes, "while the interaction among funding sources is crucial, perhaps the most important role of philanthropy could be to serve as a locus of learning for federal agencies; philanthropists who experiment with new modes of selecting, organizing, and structuring research provide important insights for the management of research" (Murray, 2013, pp. 54–55).

Promoting networks for stakeholder deliberation: spanning the boundaries of research and practice

Moving to the second category in this group, these kinds of interventions involve efforts to extend deliberation and inclusion practices among multiple individuals and institutions. Many of these networking activities are relatively new. On the whole, the kinds of science philanthropy examples evident here tend to be in much more nascent phases than many of the other kinds of interventions discussed previously. For instance, science philanthropies have been among the set of funders supporting projects undertaken by the Expert and Citizen Assessment of Science and Technology (ECAST) network: a group of academic institutions, informal science centers, and non-governmental organizations working to develop and implement informed public deliberation approaches capable of facilitating dialogue on the governance of emerging technologies (ECAST Network, n.d.). This approach, called participatory technology assessment, aims to enable "laypeople, who are otherwise minimally represented in the politics of science and technology, to develop and express informed judgments concerning complex topics" (Sclove, 2010, p. vii). Science philanthropies, such as the Sloan Foundation, have provided support to ECAST member institutions to undertake public deliberation exercises focused on addressing governance options associated with research on solar geoengineering research (Kaplan, et al., 2019) and the advent of autonomous vehicles (Consortium for Science, Policy & Outcomes, 2019). The latter project grew out of earlier research supported by the Kettering Foundation, an operating foundation looking to further cooperative, community-oriented research practices.

Beyond these kinds of novel public deliberation activities, much of the recent focus in this area of network-building has involved philanthropic support for networks of scholars and universities that look to investigate and address the role of digital technologies throughout all aspects of contemporary life. As an example, five foundations came together in 2015 to establish the NetGain Partnership, aimed at cultivating a field known as public interest technology. Originally funded by the Ford Foundation, Knight Foundation, MacArthur Foundation, Mozilla Foundation, and Open Society Foundations, the NetGain Partnership focused on advocating for the free and open use of Internet content. In establishing this network, there was a recognition that more research was needed to more thoroughly investigate the impact of these new digital innovations on society and create a more robust evidence base for understanding the impact of implemented and proposed public policy (Freedman Consulting, LLC, 2016). This kind of undertaking laid the groundwork for the formation of the Public Interest Technology University Network (PIT-UN) that was launched in early 2019 with support from the Ford Foundation and Hewlett Foundation, along with backing from the New America think tank. PIT-UN consists of twenty-one participating universities and looks to establish "a new partnership dedicated to defining and building the nascent field of public interest technology, as well as growing a new generation of civic-minded technologists and digitally fluent policy leaders" (Ford Foundation, 2019). By examining the intersection of digital technologies with public policy, law, ethics, and the social sciences more broadly, PIT-UN aims to train students to integrate consideration of ethics, governance, and societal dimensions with the development of new digital technologies (Parthasarathy & Guston, 2019). Philanthropic support for PIT-UN is expected to lead to the development of new training curricula, faculty hiring, graduate student support, and novel data sharing and analysis initiatives. As just one example of this collaboration's early impact, Arizona State University announced the creation of a new Public Interest Technology Community Innovation Fellowship that will train staff based at science museums and other informal science learning centers about how to design and implement new public engagement, deliberation, and outreach processes related to emerging areas of science and technology (Consortium for Science, Policy & Outcomes, 2020)

There are other philanthropy-funded networking initiatives designed to scale the application and utilization of data science tools to address a wide range of societal challenges. The Social Science Research Council (SSRC)—one of the key organizations involved in galvanizing social science research and, as discussed in Chapter 2, itself established with philanthropic funding—noted in a 2018 landscape analysis report the need for more of this kind of network-building support from the donor community. It recommended that funders consider how to "design and implement new models for public-private research funding partnerships that include government, the private sector, the academy, and philanthropy" (Social Science Research Council, 2018, p. 11). Additionally, science philanthropies have a role to play in setting the expectation with their funding that best practices are followed as these novel data-intensive approaches to research take hold across many scientific disciplines. In particular, foundations can encourage that appropriate steps are taken to ensure that research findings resulting from the utilization of these data science methods are reproducible and replicable (National Academies of Sciences, Engineering, and Medicine, 2019c).

A number of philanthropic supported research efforts related to establishing data science research networks have begun to appear. In particular, The Rockefeller Foundation has announced a series of research and implementation initiatives over the course of 2019 designed to connect scholars and practitioners developing and applying data science approaches to address global challenges. In June 2019, it announced the launch of a partnership among four universities—University of Massachusetts Amherst, Columbia University, Carnegie Mellon University, and Colorado School of Mines—to apply predictive analytics and other data science tools for the purpose of predicting energy use patterns in emerging economies. Known as the Electricity Growth and Use In Developing Economies Initiative, this "consortium" of academic partners will apply advancements in data science to develop a tool that will provide "insights on electricity consumption growth to flow across borders and throughout the sector...by applying new machine learning techniques to geospatial data from satellites in conjunction with real electricity billing and consumption data from hundreds of thousands of emerging market commercial and residential customers" (The Rockefeller Foundation, 2019a). Similarly, in January 2019, The Rockefeller Foundation partnered with the Mastercard

Center for Inclusive Growth to establish a new collaborative effort, called Data Science for Social Impact, to bring data science tools and expertise into greater use within non-profit entities and government organizations (The Rockefeller Foundation, 2019b). In September 2019, it shared the details of a new Precision Public Health Initiative partnership involving various global development organizations and industry partners to apply the tools of machine learning, data science, and artificial intelligence to improve the delivery of public health interventions (The Rockefeller Foundation, 2019c).

Other foundations are involved establishing these kinds of partnerships as well. For example, the Knight Foundation announced a more research-oriented activity in this space, announcing awards to eleven universities and research centers for the purpose of creating "cross-disciplinary research centers and projects [that] will fill knowledge gaps on how society is informed in the digital age" (Knight Foundation, 2019). The selected research projects were broadly sourced and selected "through an open request for proposals process" and "are intended to catalyze additional resources to support this critical area of inquiry and enable universities and research institutions to match Knight's contribution" (Knight Foundation, 2019). Similarly, three funders—Wellcome Trust, Cloudera Foundation, and Omidyar Network—are partnering with Nesta, a non-profit research center in the United Kingdom, to initiate a series of small-scale pilot experiments aimed at using data science to gain a deeper understanding of how to address global challenges, a practice known as collective intelligence (Nesta, 2019).

Of course, it should be noted that there are potential operational risks that can hinder the effectiveness of collaborative funding partnerships, especially those that involve stakeholders from multiple sectors. For instance, eight funders came together in 2018 to partner with the SSRC to help provide an interface between Facebook and the social science research community to facilitate access to privacy-protected social media data from that company. While the goal of this Social Data Initiative was to "examine social media's impact on society, explore questions about the responsible use of social network data, and generate insights to inform solutions," the ability to successfully secure appropriately privacy-protected data from Facebook proved more problematic to implement than initially expected, making the effort unviable to continue (Social Science Research Council, n.d.). This led the philanthropic funding consortium to terminate the project and wind down the provision of small grants that were being made, while also supporting "an outside evaluation…that they hope will shed light on what went awry and how to proceed" (Mervis, 2019b, p. 1361).

Encompassing responsiveness in network-building: partnerships reflecting fundamental values and interests

Lastly, the final category in the table includes philanthropic support for and creation of multi-institutional collaborative networks and partnerships that reflect the demonstration and extension of a foundation's values, interests, and perspectives related to the RRI dimensions of anticipation, deliberation and inclusion, and reflexivity. This is an extensive area to explore, with the following chapter presenting two in-depth case studies in this domain: the first involving an internally oriented network of forward-looking grantees assembled by The Rockefeller Foundation, known as the Searchlight network, and the second an external network of scientists collaborating on a large-scale astronomical research project, the Sloan Digital Sky Survey (SDSS). Both of these foundation-supported networks reflect the various dimensions of RRI to a great extent, warranting closer attention and scrutiny.

There are other examples of these kinds of interventions, particularly those associated with the integration of an anticipatory mindset within a philanthropic context. For example, the Omidyar Network, an entity which provides both philanthropic resources and investment capital, formed an internal Exploration and Future Sensing team that looks to leverage the insights from the team's network and bring in-house an anticipatory perspective on the issues the organization deems in need of attention. This team continually "scans for emergent signals and trends, imagines futures very different from the present, and catalyzes dialogue and experimentation to test new avenues of change," leveraging a variety of expertise to anticipate a wide array of potential impacts from various technological developments, such as distributed manufacturing and quantum computing (Omidyar Network, n.d.). Moreover, the Omidyar Network was particularly catalytic in collaborating with the forward-looking research organization Institute for the Future to produce a toolkit called Ethical OS that can be used by researchers, entrepreneurs, and businesses interested in better anticipating the potential risks and associated societal implications of advanced digital innovations (Omidyar Network, 2018).

Another example of this kind of intervention is interest among science philanthropies in advancing the study of how research is practiced, often known as the field of science of science (Fortunato, et al., 2018) or research on research (Ioannidis, 2018). Fortunato, et al. (2018) summarize the field of science of science as "the practice of science itself under the microscope, leading to a quantitative understanding of the genesis of scientific discovery, creativity, and practice" (p. 1). Science philanthropies have supported the launch of at least two such networks of scholars and practitioners to advance these areas of inquiry. One is the Science of Science Funding Initiative at the National Bureau of Economic Research (NBER), which "seeks to improve understanding of effective methods of supporting scientific research" and "promote analysis of the links between research funding models, management strategies, and scientific outcomes that can inform decision-making by both private and public funders" (National Bureau of Economic Research, 2018). The second effort is the Research on Research Institute (RoRI) that has been supported by, and housed within, the Wellcome Trust. Formed as a collaborative consortium involving multiple science philanthropies, government funders, academic institutions, and other research partners, RoRI looks to serve as a collaborating body that can help accelerate analysis about how scientific research is financed, structured, and assessed in terms of its overall contribution to societal well-being. The effort is described as "an open and independent new initiative providing data, analysis and intelligence on how to make research systems more strategic, open, diverse and inclusive" (Research on Research Institute, 2019). An editorial in *Nature* published soon after the launch of RoRI calls on other funders to engage with this new institute. It also highlights key areas in need of attention, such as developing more holistic definitions and metrics of research excellence and outlining best practices toward how to establish a more welcome and inclusive culture of research. "The task of achieving a kinder, more welcoming research environment—one that rewards diverse approaches and embraces failure—is not something that Wellcome can achieve on its own," says the article (Nature, 2019). RoRI has already released two landscape analyses that examine key issues associated with the conduct of research, one on improving priority setting in science through the use of funding analyses (Waltman, Rafols, Jan van Eck, & Yegros, 2019) and another focused on improving methods for tracking the career trajectories of doctoral students (Hancock, Wakeling, & Chubb, 2019). The plan is for RoRI to act as a hub that will link together other research funders in the philanthropic and public spheres to share data and information about best practices and policies associated with the provision of support for and conduct of research (Holmes, 2019).

Collectively, the nine types of interventions explored in depth in this chapter reflect many, though not all, of the ways in which science philanthropies can further the research enterprise. The core mode of interaction by funders involves the provision of financial resources, first and foremost. Yet, this typology demonstrates that there are many other ways in which foundations can shape the direction of scientific research by influencing who does science, how it is conducted, and what values and principles are instilled in what is expected from grantees and the foundations themselves. These are just the kinds of tenets that science philanthropies increasingly need to place at the center of their decision-making processes to better enhance how they go about fortifying the societal relevance of research they support. In particular, the establishment and advancement of networks is a particularly critical component of contemporary science philanthropy, a type of intervention in which various characteristics discussed throughout this chapter are interwoven. The next chapter will explore two such case studies in great detail to illuminate how these various facets of science philanthropy operate together.

Bibliography

Alfred P. Sloan Foundation. (2016). 2015 Annual Report. Retrieved August 2019, from Alfred P. Sloan Foundation: https://sloan.org/storage/app/media/files/annual_reports/2015_annual_report.pdf.

Alfred P. Sloan Foundation. (2019a). Sloan Research Fellowships. Retrieved June 2019, from Alfred P. Sloan Foundation: https://sloan.org/fellowships/.

Alfred P. Sloan Foundation. (2019b). Diversity, Equity & Inclusion in STEM Higher Education. Retrieved July 2019, from Alfred P. Sloan Foundation: https://sloan.org/programs/higher-education/diversity-equity-inclusion.

Alfred P. Sloan Foundation. (2019c, April 10). Grant Application Guidelines – Research Projects. Retrieved August 2019, from Alfred P. Sloan Foundation: https://sloan.org/storage/app/media/files/application_documents/Sloan-Grant-Proposal-Guidelines-Research-Projects.pdf.

Alfred P. Sloan Foundation. (2019d). Public Understanding of Science, Technology & Economics. Retrieved September 2019, from Alfred P. Sloan Foundation: https://sloan.org/programs/public-understanding.

Alisic, E., & Hilgenkamp, H. (2018, September 7). New Voices, At Last. *Science*, 361 (6406), 953.

Allen Institute. (2019). What We Do. Retrieved July 2019, from Allen Institute: www.alleninstitute.org/what-we-do/.

American Association for the Advancement of Science. (2017). *Connecting Scientists to Policy Around the World*. Washington, DC: American Association for the Advancement of Science.

Atherton, C. (2019, March 27). Intentionally Improving Processes for the 51 Pegasi b Fellowship. Retrieved June 2019, from Heising-Simons Foundation: www.hsfoundation.org/intentionally-improving-processes-for-the-51-pegasi-b-fellowship/.

Ayoubi, C., Pezzoni, M., & Visentin, F. (2019, February). The Important Thing is Not to Win, It is to Take Part: What if Scientists Benefit from Participating in Research Grant Competitions? *Research Policy*, 48(1), 84–97.

BRAIN Initiative. (n.d.). The Alliance. Retrieved August 2019, from BRAIN Initiative: www.braininitiative.org/alliance/.

Bridge Group. (2017). Diversity in Grant Awarding and Recruitment at Wellcome: Summary Report. London, United Kingdom: Bridge Group.

California Council on Science & Technology. (2017, February 16). CCST Awards Grants to Create Science Policy Fellowships in Nine States. Retrieved July 2019, from California Council on Science & Technology: https://ccst.us/reports/science-and-policy-beyond-california/planning-grants/.

California Council on Science and Technology. (2018). State Fellowships Planning Grant. Retrieved June 2019, from Science & Policy Beyond California: https://ccst.us/reports/science-and-policy-beyond-california/planning-grants/.

Chambers, D., Preston, L., Topakas, A., de Saille, S., Salway, S., Booth, A., et al. (2017, May). Review of Diversity and Inclusion Literature and an Evaluation of Methodologies and Metrics Relating to Health Research. Retrieved August 2019, from University of Sheffield: https://wellcome.ac.uk/sites/default/files/review-of-diversity-and-inclusion-literature.pdf.

Chan Zuckerberg Initiative. (2019, October 24). Making Science Journalism More Diverse and Inclusive. Retrieved November 2019, from the Chan Zuckerberg Initiative: https://chanzuckerberg.com/newsroom/making-science-journalism-more-diverse-inclusive/.

Chang, W.-Y., Cheng, W., Lane, J., & Weinberg, B. (2019, July). Federal Funding of Doctoral Recipients: What Can be Learned from Linked Data. *Research Policy*, 48(6), 1487–1492.

Christopherson, E. G., Scheufele, D. A., & Smith, B. (2018, Spring). The Civic Science Imperative. *Stanford Social Innovation Review*, 16(2), 46–52.

Christopherson, E., Dill, H. T., & Pomeroy, C. (2019, August 6). Research Shows How to Advance Public Understanding of Science. Retrieved September 2019, from *The Chronicle of Philanthropy*: www.philanthropy.com/article/Explaining-Science-Isn-t/246848.

Consortium for Science, Policy & Outcomes. (2019). Our Driverless Futures: Community Forums on Automated Mobility. Retrieved November 2019, from Consortium for Science, Policy & Outcomes: https://cspo.org/research/driverless-vehicles/.

Consortium for Science, Policy & Outcomes. (2020, January 17). Announcing the Public Interest Technology Community Innovation Fellowship! Retrieved January 2020, from Consortium for Science, Policy & Outcomes: https://cspo.org/news/announcing-the-public-interest-technology-community-innovation-fellowship/.

Coriat, A.-M. (2018, June 18). A More Positive Culture for PhD Training. Retrieved July 2019, from Wellcome Trust: https://wellcome.ac.uk/news/more-positive-culture-phd-training.

Diamond Light Source. (2018). Governance. Retrieved August 2019, from Diamond Light Source: www.diamond.ac.uk/Home/Company.html.

Domingo, M. R. S., Sharp, S., Freeman, A., Freeman Jr., T., Harmon, K., Wiggs, M., et al. (2019, April 26). Replicating Meyerhoff for Inclusive Excellence in STEM. *Science*, 364(6438), 335–337.

Dudo, A., & Besley, J. (2019). *Identifying Best Practices for Communications Workforce at Science Philanthropies*. Princeton, NJ: Rita Allen Foundation.

ECAST Network. (n.d.). About. Retrieved August 2019, from ECAST Network: https://ecastnetwork.org/about/.

EDIS. (n.d.). Home Page. Retrieved August 2019, from EDIS: https://edisgroup.org/.

Else, H. (2019, May 1). Male Researchers' 'Vague' Language More Likely to Win Grants. Retrieved August 2019, from *Nature*: www.nature.com/articles/d41586-019-01402-4.

EPSRC. (2018). Welcome to the IDEAS Factory…Home of Innovation Since 2004. Retrieved August 2019, from EPSRC: https://epsrc.ukri.org/newsevents/pubs/welcome-to-the-ideas-factory-home-of-innovation-since-2004/.

Ezell, S., & Hart, D. (2017, December 20). A Department of Energy Foundation: An Idea Whose Time has Come. Retrieved September 2019, from *The Hill*: https://thehill.com/opinion/energy-environment/365850-a-department-of-energy-foundation-an-idea-whose-time-has-come.

Farrar, J. (2019, September 10). Why We Need to Reimagine How We Do Research. Retrieved September 2019, from Wellcome Trust: https://wellcome.ac.uk/news/why-we-need-reimagine-how-we-do-research.

Ferris, J. M., & Williams, N. P. (2012). Philanthropy and Government Working Together: The Role of Offices of Strategic Partnerships in Public Problem Solving. Los Angeles, CA: The Center on Philanthropy & Public Policy, University of Southern California.

Fineberg, H. V. (2016, October 27). Perspective: Infusing Science into Policy Decisions. Retrieved June 2019, from Gordon and Betty Moore Foundation: www.moore.org/article-detail?newsUrlName=perspective-infusing-science-into-policy-decisions&tagToFilterBy=ab660061-a10f-68a5-8452-ff00002785c8.

Ford Foundation. (2019, March 11). Higher Education, Philanthropy and Public Policy Sectors Unite in New Push to Develop Public Interest Technology. Retrieved August 2019, from Ford Foundation: www.fordfoundation.org/the-latest/news/higher-education-philanthropy-and-public-policy-sectors-unite-in-new-push-to-develop-public-interest-technology/.

Fortunato, S., Bergstrom, C. T., Borner, K., Evans, J. A., Helbing, D., Milojevic, S., et al. (2018). Science of Science. *Science*, 359(1007), eaao0185, 1–7

Freedman Consulting, LLC. (2016). *A Pivotal Moment: Developing a New Generation of Technologies for the Public Interest*. Washington, DC: Freedman Consulting, LLC.

Gordon and Betty Moore Foundation. (2014, October 2). The Gordon and Betty Moore Foundation Selects Awardees for $21 Million in Grants to Stimulate Data-Driven Discovery. Retrieved July 2019, from Gordon and Betty Moore Foundation: www.moore.org/article-detail?newsUrlName=the-gordon-and-betty-moore-founda tion-selects-awardees-for-$21-million-in-grants-to-stimulate-data-driven-discovery.

Gordon and Betty Moore Foundation. (2019a). Emergent Phenomena in Quantum Systems Initiative. Retrieved July 2019, from Gordon and Betty Moore Foundation: www.moore. org/initiative-additional-info?initiativeId=emergent-phenomena-in-quantum-systems.

Gordon and Betty Moore Foundation. (2019b). California Institute of Technology. Retrieved July 2019, from Gordon and Betty Moore Foundation: www.moore.org/ initiative-strategy-detail?initiativeId=california-institute-of-technology.

Gordon and Betty Moore Foundation. (2019c). Moore Inventor Fellows. Retrieved June 2019, from Gordon and Betty Moore Foundation: www.moore.org/initiative-s trategy-detail?initiativeId=moore-inventor-fellows.

Greider, C. W., Sheltzer, J. M., Cantalupo, N. C., Copeland, W. B., Dasgupta, N., Hopkins, N., et al. (2019, November 8). Increasing Gender Diversity in the STEM Research Workforce. *Science*, 366(6466), 692–695.

Ham, B. (2018, September 28). AAAS EPI Center Launch Brings Evidence to Policy-Makers. *Science*, 361(6409), 1327–1328.

Hancock, S., Wakeling, P., & Chubb, J. (2019). *21st Century PhDs: Why We Need Better Methods of Tracking Doctoral Access, Experiences and Outcomes.* London, United Kingdom: Research on Research Institute.

Hansen, S. (2019, April 9). UMBC's Meyerhoff Scholars Model Heads to UC Berkeley and UCSD through a $6.9M Investment from the Chan Zuckerberg Initiative. Retrieved June 2019, from *UMBC News*: https://news.umbc.edu/meyerhoff-czi/.

Heising-Simons Foundation. (2019). Women in Physics and Astronomy. Retrieved August 2019, from Heising-Simons Foundation: www.hsfoundation.org/programs/ science/women-physics-astronomy/.

Holmes, B. (2019, November 25). Joining Forces for Responsive and Responsible Research Funding. Retrieved December 2019, from Michael Smith Foundation for Health Research: www.msfhr.org/news/blog-posts/joining-forces-responsive-and-resp onsible-research-funding.

Howard Hughes Medical Institute. (2017, November). HHMI: Catalyst for Discovery. Retrieved July 2019, from Howard Hughes Medical Institute: www.hhmi.org/sites/ default/files/about/hhmi-vision-2017.pdf.

Howard Hughes Medical Institute. (2019). Hanna H. Gray Fellows Program. Retrieved August 2019, from Howard Hughes Medical Institute: www.hhmi.org/programs/ha nna-h-gray-fellows-program#Award.

Howard Hughes Medical Institute. (n.d.). Investigator Program. Retrieved June 2019, from Howard Hughes Medical Institute: https://www.hhmi.org/programs/biom edical-research/investigator-program#Overview.

Hoy, A. Q. (2019, December 20). AAAS Local Science Engagement Network Gets Under Way. *Science*, 366(6472), 1464–1465.

Hrabowski III, F. A., & Henderson, P. H. (2017, Spring). Toward a More Diverse Research Community: Models of Success. Retrieved July 2019, from *Issues in Science and Technology*: https://issues.org/toward-a-more-diverse-research-community-models-of-success/.

Hrabowski III, F. A., & Henderson, P. H. (2019, Winter). Challenging US Research Universities and Funders to Increase Diversity in the Research Community. *Issues in Science and Technology, 35*(2), 67–72.

Ioannidis, J. P. (2018, March). Meta-Research: Why Research on Research Matters. *PLOS Biology*, 16(3), e2005468, 1–6.

Jones, R., & Wilsdon, J. (2018). *The Biomedical Bubble*. London, UK: NESTA.

Kaplan, L., Nelson, J., Tomblin, D., Farooque, M., Lloyd, J., Neff, M., et al. (2019). *Cooling a Warming Planet? Public Forums on Climate Intervention Research*. Washington, DC: Consortium for Science, Policy & Outcomes, Arizona State University.

Kirshner, R. (2016, November 2). To Nurture Invention, Ditch the Shark Tank Model. Retrieved June 2019, from *Scientific American*: https://blogs.scientificamerican.com/guest-blog/to-nurture-invention-ditch-the-shark-tank-model/.

Knight Foundation. (2019, July 22). Knight Invests $50 Million to Develop New Field of Research around Technology's Impact on Democracy. Retrieved August 2019, from Knight Foundation: https://knightfoundation.org/press/releases/knight-fifty-million-develop-new-research-technology-impact-democracy.

Kohler, R. E. (1985, March). Philanthropy and Science. *Proceedings of the American Philosophical Society*, 129(1), 9–13.

Kolev, J., Fuentes-Medel, Y., & Murray, F. (2019). *Is Blinded Review Enough? How Gendered Outcomes Arise Even Under Anonymous Evaluation*. Cambridge, MA: National Bureau of Economic Research.

Koroshetz, W., Gordon, J., Adams, A., Beckel-Mitchener, A., Churchill, J., Farber, G., et al. (2018, July 18). The State of the NIH BRAIN Initiative. *The Journal of Neuroscience*, 38(29), 6427–6438.

Korte, A. (2019, June 28). AAAS' EPI Center Shares the Science of Election Security. *Science*, 364(6447), 1245–1246.

Lavery, J. V. (2018, August 10). Building an Evidence Base for Stakeholder Engagement. *Science*, 361(6402), 554–556.

Maldarelli, C. (2015, October 1). Kavli Foundation Invests $100 Million In Brain Research. Retrieved August 2019, from *Popular Science*: www.popsci.com/kavli-foundation-commits-100-million-for-brain-research/.

Mervis, J. (2009, May 29). Digging for Fresh Ideas in the Sandpit. *Science*, 324(5931), 1128–1129.

Mervis, J. (2019a, July 26). Vaunted Diversity Program Catches On. *Science*, 365(6451), 308–309.

Mervis, J. (2019b, September 27). Privacy Concerns Could Derail Facebook Data-Sharing Plan. *Science*, 365(6460), 1360–1361.

Mott, M. C., Gordon, J. A., & Koroshetz, W. J. (2018, November 26). The NIH BRAIN Initiative: Advancing Neurotechnologies, Integrating Disciplines. *PLOS Biology*, 1–5.

Murray, F. (2013). Evaluating the Role of Science Philanthropy in American Research Universities. In J. Lerner & S. Stern, eds., *Innovation Policy and the Economy, Volume 13* (pp. 23–60). Chicago, IL: University of Chicago Press.

National Academies of Sciences, Engineering, and Medicine. (2018a). *Collaborations of Consequence: NAKFI's 15 Years Igniting Innovation at the Intersections of Disciplines*. Washington, DC: The National Academies Press.

National Academies of Sciences, Engineering, and Medicine. (2018b). *Sexual Harassment of Women: Climate, Culture, and Consequences in Academic Sciences, Engineering, and Medicine*. Washington, DC: The National Academies Press.

National Academies of Sciences, Engineering, and Medicine. (2019a). New Voices in Sciences, Engineering and Medicine. Retrieved August 2019, from The National Academies of Sciences, Engineering, and Medicine: www.nationalacademies.org/newvoices/.

National Academies of Sciences, Engineering, and Medicine. (2019b). *The Science of Effective Mentorship in STEMM*. Washington, DC: The National Academies Press.

National Academies of Sciences, Engineering, and Medicine. (2019c). *Reproducibility and Replicability in Science*. Washington, DC: The National Academies Press.

National Academy of Sciences, National Academy of Engineering, and Institute of Medicine. (2011). *Expanding Underrepresented Minority Participation: America's Science and Technology Talent at the Crossroads*. Washington, DC: The National Academies Press.

National Bureau of Economic Research. (2018). The Science of Science Funding Initiative. Retrieved November 2019, from National Bureau of Economic Research: https://projects.nber.org/drupal/SOSF/home.

National Institutes of Health. (2014, June 5). BRAIN 2025: A Scientific Vision. Retrieved August 2019, from BRAIN 2025: A Scientific Vision: https://braininitia tive.nih.gov/sites/default/files/pdfs/brain2025_508c.pdf.

National Institutes of Health. (n.d.). What is the BRAIN Initiative? Retrieved August 2019, from *The BRAIN Initiative*: https://braininitiative.nih.gov/.

Nature. (2018, June 7). Science Benefits from Diversity. *Nature*, 558, 5.

Nature. (2019, October 3). Excellent Problem. *Nature*, 574(7776), 5–6.

Nesta. (2019, September 25). Wellcome Trust, Cloudera Foundation and Omidyar Network Join Forces with Nesta to Fund Grants. Retrieved October 2019, from Nesta: www.nesta.org.uk/news/wellcome-trust-cloudera-foundation-and-omidyar-network-join-forces-nesta-fund-grants-supporting-human-and-ai-collaboration/.

Omidyar Network. (2018, August 7). Omidyar Network Partners with Institute for the Future to Launch the Ethical Operating System: A Guide to Anticipating the Future Impact of Today's Technology. Retrieved August 2019, from Omidyar Network: www.omidyar.com/news/omidyar-network-partners-institute-future-launch-ethical-operating-system-guide-anticipating.

Omidyar Network. (n.d.). Exploration & Future Sensing. Retrieved August 2019, from Omidyar Network: www.omidyar.com/our-work/exploration-future-sensing.

Parthasarathy, S., & Guston, D. H. (2019, October 13). Colleges Must Play a Role in Bridging Ethics and Technology. Retrieved November 2019, from *The Chronicle of Higher Education*: https://www.chronicle.com/article/Colleges-Must-Play-a-Role-in/247308

Pena, V., Stokes, C. A., & Behrens, J. R. (2019). *Partnership Development in the Federal Government*. Washington: IDA Science and Technology Policy Institute. Retrieved October 2019, from Institute for Defense Analysis: www.ida.org/-/media/feature/publications/p/pa/partnership-development-in-the-federal-government/d10702final.ashx.

Research on Research Institute. (2019, September). Research on Research Institute. Retrieved October 2019, from http://researchonresearch.org/.

Rita Allen Foundation. (2019a). Rita Allen Scholars. Retrieved August 2019, from Rita Allen Foundation: http://ritaallen.org/scholars/

Rita Allen Foundation. (2019b). Civic Science. Retrieved August 2019, from Rita Allen Foundation: http://ritaallen.org/civic-science/.

Sainsbury Wellcome Centre. (2019). Funders & Governance. Retrieved July 2019, from Sainsbury Wellcome Centre: www.sainsburywellcome.org/web/content/funders-governance.

Schmidt Futures. (2019a). Schmidt Science Fellows. Retrieved July 2019, from Schmidt Futures: https://schmidtfutures.com/our-work/schmidt-science-fellows/.

Schmidt Futures. (2019b). Advancing Society Through Technology. Retrieved July 2019, from Schmidt Futures: https://schmidtfutures.com/our-work/technology-society/# investments.

Schmidt Ocean Institute. (2019a). About. Retrieved July 2019, from Schmidt Ocean Institute: https://schmidtocean.org/about/.

Schmidt Ocean Institute. (2019b). Frequently Asked Questions. Retrieved July 2019, from Schmidt Ocean Institute: https://schmidtocean.org/about/faq-2/#data_and_information_ sharing.

Schmidt Science Fellows. (2019). Overview. Retrieved July 2019, from Schmidt Science Fellows: https://schmidtsciencefellows.org/overview/.

Sclove, R. (2010). *Reinventing Technology Assessment: A 21st Century Model.* Washington, DC: Science, Technology and Innovation Program, Woodrow Wilson International Center for Scholars.

Simons Foundation. (2017). Flatiron Institute Inaugural Celebration. Retrieved July 2019, from Annual Report 2017 Edition: www.simonsfoundation.org/report2017/ stories/flatiron-institute-inaugural-celebration/.

Simons Foundation. (2018, August 24). "The Most Unknown" Available on Netflix, Youtube [Updated]. Retrieved September 2019, from Simons Foundation: www.sim onsfoundation.org/2018/08/24/the-most-unknown-selected-to-open-major-film-festival/.

Simons Foundation. (n.d.a). Flatiron Institute. Retrieved July 2019, from Simons Foundation: www.simonsfoundation.org/flatiron/.

Simons Foundation. (n.d.b). Scientific Computing Core. Retrieved July 2019, from Simons Foundation: www.simonsfoundation.org/flatiron/scientific-computing-core/.

Snow, C. P. (1959). *The Two Cultures.* Cambridge, UK: Cambridge University Press.

Social Science Research Council. (2018). *To Secure Knowledge: Social Science Partnerships for the Common Good.* Brooklyn, NY: Social Science Research Council.

Social Science Research Council. (n.d.). Social Data Initiative. Retrieved September 2019, from Social Science Research Council: www.ssrc.org/programs/view/social-da ta-initiative/.

The Kavli Foundation. (2019a). Institutes. Retrieved July 2019, from The Kavli Foundation: www.kavlifoundation.org/institutes.

The Kavli Foundation. (2019b). About the BRAIN Initiative. Retrieved August 2019, from The Kavli Foundation: www.kavlifoundation.org/about-brain-initiative.

The Pew Charitable Trusts. (n.d.). Pew Biomedical Scholars. Retrieved August 2019, from The Pew Charitable Trusts: www.pewtrusts.org/en/projects/pew-biomedical-scholars/ program-details.

The Rockefeller Foundation. (2019a, June 18). Four Leading Universities and The Rockefeller Foundation Launch Initiative Using Cutting-Edge Data to End Energy Poverty. Retrieved August 2019, from The Rockefeller Foundation: www.rock efellerfoundation.org/about-us/news-media/four-leading-universities-rock efeller-foundation-launch-initiative-using-cutting-edge-data-end-energy-poverty/.

The Rockefeller Foundation. (2019b, January 22). Mastercard and The Rockefeller Foundation Announce 'Data Science for Social Impact' with Initial $50 Million Commitment. Retrieved August 2019, from The Rockefeller Foundation: www.rockefellerfoundation. org/about-us/news-media/mastercard-rockefeller-foundation-announce-data-science-social-impact-initial-50-million-commitment/.

The Rockefeller Foundation. (2019c, September 25). Using Data to Save Lives: The Rockefeller Foundation and Partners Launch $100 Million Precision Public Health Initiative. Retrieved October 2019, from The Rockefeller Foundation: www.rockefellerfoundation.org/about-us/news-media/using-data-save-lives-rockefeller-foundation-partners-launch-100-million-precision-public-health-initiative/.

The White House. (2016, May 13). FACT SHEET: Announcing the National Microbiome Initiative. Retrieved August 2019, from The White House: https://obamawhitehouse.archives.gov/the-press-office/2016/05/12/fact-sheet-announcing-national-microbiome-initiative.

University of Maryland, Baltimore County. (n.d.a). About. Retrieved June 2019, from Meyerhoff Scholars Program: https://meyerhoff.umbc.edu/about/.

University of Maryland, Baltimore County. (n.d.b). 13 Key Components. Retrieved June 2019, from Meyerhoff Scholars Program: https://meyerhoff.umbc.edu/13-key-components/.

W. M. Keck Foundation. (2019). Special Projects. Retrieved July 2019, from W. M. Keck Foundation: http://staging.wmkeck.org/grant-programs/special-projects.

Waltman, L., Rafols, I., van Eck, N. J., & Yegros, A. (2019). *Supporting Priority Setting in Science Using Research Funding Landscapes*. London, United Kingdom: Research on Research Institute.

Weber, D. (2019, March 22). The Future of Science in Film. *Science*, 363(6433), 1253.

Wellcome Trust. (2018). *Wellcome Review of PhD Training in Biomedical Research*. London, UK: Wellcome Trust.

Wellcome Trust. (n.d.a). Diversity and Inclusion: Helping More Ideas Thrive. Retrieved August 2019, from Wellcome Trust: https://wellcome.ac.uk/what-we-do/our-work/diversity-and-inclusion.

Wellcome Trust. (n.d.b). Wellcome Screenwriting Fellowship in Partnership with BFI and Film4. Retrieved September 2019, from Wellcome Trust: https://wellcome.ac.uk/what-we-do/our-work/wellcome-screenwriting-fellowship-partnership-bfi-and-film4.

Wiener, R. J., & Ronco, S. (2019). Scialog: The Catalysis of Convergence. *ACS Energy Letters*, 4(5), 1020–1024.

Williams, T. (2017, April 3). A Foundation Aims to Strengthens Connections Between Scientists and Policymakers. Retrieved June 2019, from *Inside Philanthropy*: www.insidephilanthropy.com/home/2017/4/3/moore-hopes-to-strengthen-connections-between-scientists-and-policymakers.

Yen, J. W. (2019, December). De-Biasing the Evaluation Process of In-Person Review Panels for a Postdoctoral Fellowship. *Nature Astronomy*, 3(12), 1041–1042.

Yuste, R. (2017, November 2). The Origins of the BRAIN Initiative: A Personal Journey. *Cell*, 171(4), 726–735.

5 Case studies in science philanthropy network-building

The Rockefeller Foundation Searchlight network and the Sloan Digital Sky Survey

A deeper look at the implementation of RRI principles

Foundation support for the creation and sustainment of research networks is among the most interesting, yet understudied, areas of science philanthropy. Network-building often involves the combination of elements that underpin philanthropic programs geared toward individuals and institutions, plus the addition of other centralized coordination mechanisms that not only link together actors within a research network, but that also work to integrate findings, synthesize results, and extend the network's impact by sharing the network's outputs externally. In particular, the hub-and-spoke model of most research networks supported by science philanthropies nicely situate these collaborations as sources of ideas for other funders, both public and private, to pursue.

This chapter dives into the question of how research networks funded by science philanthropies reflect the RRI principles described in previous chapters. Two case studies will be examined, both of which I have had the privilege to be involved in supporting, engaging, and learning from as a funder representative. I have had the opportunity to write about each of these previously (Science Philanthropy Alliance, 2017; Juech & Michelson, 2012), and I have drawn on these earlier materials, with permission, in the following discussion. Reporting on these network-building engagements where I have experience is another way of drawing on the insights of the RRI framework that point to the importance of reflexivity when considering the societal implications of science, technology, and innovation. Of course, as Chapter 4 demonstrated, there are a number of other network-building activities undertaken by science philanthropies that could warrant further in-depth attention from this perspective. These include the Scialog program developed by the Research Corporation for Science Advancement (RCSA) (Wiener & Ronco, 2019) and the BRAIN Initiative that was partly initiated with support from The Kavli Foundation in partnership with the federal government (Pena, Stokes, & Behrens, 2019). These and other research networks facilitated by philanthropic funding warrant further analysis to not only tease out their RRI components, but to also identify commonalities and differences across collaborative efforts advanced by science philanthropies.

The first case study presented here focuses on The Rockefeller Foundation Searchlight network, a group of forward-looking, topically focused, and regionally oriented horizon scanning and trend monitoring organizations that conduct regular, ongoing scanning for novel ideas, research results, and signals as to where the world is evolving. The second case study is the Sloan Digital Sky Survey (SDSS), perhaps the most well-known and cost-effective astronomical survey in the history of the field. Both case studies highlight ways in which philanthropies, at least implicitly, can apply different notions of the RRI framework to their network-building funding activities. In doing so, they represent strong examples of reflexivity and responsiveness called out in the final category identified earlier in Table 3.1, providing support for the creation of multi-institutional collaborative partnerships that reflect a foundation's values and interests.

Examining these case studies in tandem highlights their complementary, yet distinctive, characteristics. The Rockefeller Foundation Searchlight network is an example of a philanthropy looking to build its own in-house capability in foresight, anticipation, and being systematic in examining its contextual environment. SDSS has adopted a process of regular review and assessment to ensure that it stays at the forefront of research in the field and that the collaboration is continually exploring cutting-edge research questions using state-of-the-art technologies. Both networks have, among their bedrock principles, the notion that bringing in a diversity of views and perspectives is critical to gaining long-lasting impact and provide insight to the questions that sit at the core of each network's purpose. For the Searchlight network, this meant including researchers from different cultures and communities from the staff based at the foundation. For SDSS, this means deliberately ensuring that the values of diversity, equity, and inclusion are explicitly interwoven throughout the collaboration's policies and procedures.

The Searchlight network was mainly an internally oriented entity, established to assist foundation staff in strategic decision-making and resource allocation based upon regularly updated knowledge about changing global conditions. SDSS is external to the funder, established by pioneering and enterprising scientists and engineers. In terms of duration, the Searchlight network was relatively short lived, taking place over a roughly five-year period as part of The Rockefeller Foundation's revamped idea generation processes. SDSS has been in operation for over twenty-five years and is still ongoing, with resources to continue into the middle of the 2020s decade. In terms of scale and budget, the Searchlight network was a relatively small-scale network consisting of twelve participating organizations, with approximately sixty researchers in total involved in its horizon-scanning and landscape analysis research processes. This led the Searchlight network to cost roughly one million dollars annually to sustain. SDSS is a multi-million-dollar project and has consisted of many partner institutions, nearly fifty-five in its latest phase, with approximately one thousand participating astronomers within the network alone and many others utilizing SDSS data from outside the formal collaboration. In terms of disciplinary scope, the Searchlight network was designed to cover a broad range of topics related to human development, with an emphasis on the developing world. Science and technology was one of the Searchlight network's core thematic components, joined by other social and cultural issues that were regularly investigated by the network researchers and participants. SDSS is, obviously, an astronomy and astrophysics research enterprise, yet it is facilitated and underpinned by groundbreaking developments in data science. In terms of geographic footprint, both networks are global in nature, with the Searchlight network deliberately designed to involve organizations based in different countries and regions. Due to its sheer size and relevance to the field, SDSS not only has participating members and collaborators in many countries, but it has grown to include scientific instrumentation located in two countries across two continents.

Finally, in terms of their network structure, both collaborations made use of similar coordination mechanisms to ensure that the project operates smoothly. Each involved a central management team, with the Searchlight network overseen by only a handful of staff internal to The Rockefeller Foundation and SDSS establishing an extensive collaboration management infrastructure drawing from scientists at various institutions. Both utilize annual gatherings—and in the case of SDSS, multiple sub-team annual meetings—to bring together researchers in the network to facilitate closer engagement and to identify potential research synergies. Both have also emphasized external dissemination of results. The Searchlight network added a component of synthesizing and visualizing its research findings using a variety of overlapping integrative approaches. SDSS not only shares its findings through the more traditional pathway of academic publications, but one of its distinctive outputs was being perhaps the first astronomical survey to regularly and systematically make all the collaboration's data publicly available, free to use by any astronomer or member of the public. In sum, both The Rockefeller Foundation Searchlight network and SDSS are useful instances to explore how the RRI dimensions of anticipation, deliberation and inclusion, and reflexivity and responsiveness are experienced in practice.

The Rockefeller Foundation Searchlight network: building funder capacity for anticipation, deliberation, and reflexivity

Bringing anticipation to philanthropy

Organizations across a range of sectors face a common challenge: how to track the current context in which they operate, how to identify future risks and opportunities, and how to create and implement a forward-looking strategy that guides decision making. This has led to a growing interest from researcher organizations, philanthropies, non-profits, and government entities to look for novel ways of generating, processing, and acting on timely information that has long-term relevance and significance (Miller, 2018; Fulton, Kasper, & Kibbe, 2010; Fulton & Blau, 2005). There is a long history of corporations utilizing scenario planning and other forward-looking strategy tools to better anticipate alternative futures for their companies (Schwartz, 1996; van der Heijden, 2005; Wilkinson & Kupers, 2014; Wack, 1985a; Wack, 1985b). More recently, there are also a growing number of examples of other kinds of organizations experimenting with various horizon scanning modalities in order to better track and respond to changes in their contextual environment. These include trend monitoring activities, such as those undertaken by the Global Environment Facility to better anticipate developments related to climate change and the environment (Rejeski, Leonard, & Libre, 2018). Internationally oriented nonprofit organizations, such as those working with the United Nations, have used scenario planning exercises to envision different futures that could be substantially different from the status quo (Pauwels, 2019). Scholars have begun to use prediction markets to crowdsource opinions about how a particular research topic might evolve, such as assessing the likely reproducibility of various scientific studies (Dreber, et al., 2015; Munafo, et al., 2015). Researchers and practitioners in the United States are also thinking about how to re-introduce some of these future-oriented technology assessment capabilities into government (Fretwell, Rejeski, Hendler, Peroff, & McCord, 2019). Along these lines, the Government Accountability Office underwent an organizational reform in early 2019 that established a new unit—called the Science, Technology Assessment, and Analytics Team—that has become responsible for carrying out forward-looking analysis on the societal implications of emerging technologies (Government Accountability Office, 2019). There are even efforts being explored by Congress about reviving the defunct Office of Technology Assessment (Malakoff, 2019).

However, the philanthropic sector has generally been slow to adopt these foresight practices to date, and they remain relatively rare in science philanthropies. This is particularly problematic since the practice of anticipating and tracking trends and envisioning different alternatives for how issues might evolve is a critical practice that could be harnessed to shape how philanthropies allocate their resources in support of science and how their grantmaking could have greater societal impact. As one blog post from leading foresight practitioners Catarina Tully and Louise Pulford has stated, "philanthropic foundations have traditionally given relatively little emphasis to foresight, but philanthropy is more exposed to future risk than the private or public sectors, in taking on untested or 'frontier' areas. The sector urgently needs a stronger focus on becoming 'future-fit': understanding how the trends of the next 10, 20 and even 50 years will impact its focus, operations and legitimacy" (Tully & Pulford, 2019). Similarly, a 2012 report titled *Scanning the Landscape 2.0* that described the value of horizon scanning in the context of philanthropy, notes the many benefits that come from institutionalizing this practice within a grantmaking organization, from providing "a way to see more broadly" to offering "a way to listen and respond" to exploring new opportunities as "a way to 'find the white spaces'" (Mackinnon, 2012, pp. 2–3). The report also notes that such efforts are effective in bringing different viewpoints to the attention of a philanthropic funder, including those from different constituencies, disciplines, and with more out-of-the-box ideas or solutions. Moreover, horizon scanning by science philanthropies can serve as one tool for having impact on, as the report notes, "the knowledge and effectiveness of an entire foundation, other organizations, and the field as a whole" (p. 18).

First conceptualized in 2009 and running for about five years, The Rockefeller Foundation began to address this gap by developing one of the first-of-its-kind trend monitoring and horizon scanning efforts in the philanthropic sector, conceptualizing and operationalizing an approach that surfaced cutting-edge intelligence about how various topic areas were changing with a distinctly on-the-ground perspective from individuals and institutions living and working globally. This undertaking was known as The Rockefeller Foundation Searchlight network. The Searchlight network was one early stage component of an eventual multi-pronged approach undertaken by The Rockefeller Foundation to restructure its internal research function and early idea generation processes. Having moved away from a program-based model during this period, The Rockefeller Foundation transitioned to an initiative model focused on achieving impact through problem-oriented, time-bound activities.

As detailed in a *Stanford Social Innovation Review* article reporting on these efforts, the first step in the initiative model was a "scan and search" phase, which was designed to evaluate "not only what might be the biggest opportunities for impact but also whether the foundation is well positioned to develop solutions" (Murray, 2018, p. 13). This "lengthy and rigorous process" involved examining the pressing nature of the problem, the potential availability of scalable solutions and systems level change, and the foundation's ability to have an impact through its grantmaking resources. To identify the most pressing problems that would be addressed as part of this initiative model, there became an evident need to create a regular, high-quality input stream of information to the foundation that would provide a broad evidence base for decision-making, elucidate risks and opportunities in the contextual environment in which the foundation operates, and point to innovative ideas that could spur new areas of investigation. The Searchlight network served as one of these important input streams, in addition to other sources of information gathered through expert convenings or from more technologically driven methods such as crowdsourcing or electronic information mining. It also offered a more local, granular perspective about how to interpret, contextualize, and better understand this incoming information, an added value that many of the other input streams do not provide as readily or as easily.

Specifically, The Rockefeller Foundation Searchlight network was designed to achieve the following three goals. First, illuminate important signals in the current contextual environment in which philanthropies and global development organizations operate. Second, learn from a diversity of opinions, methodological approaches, and points of view. Third, identify potential solutions or intervention opportunities for the foundation to pursue. The Searchlight network consisted of twelve organizations based in a diverse array of geographies and bringing to bear a wide array of perspectives, with each organization preparing a monthly trend monitoring newsletter that would be submitted to the foundation and that they were free to make available publicly and to other interested partners as well. Identifying new opportunities in global science and technology was one of the core goals of the assembled network members, in addition to a number of other topics related to global development that were relevant to The Rockefeller Foundation's grantmaking, a wide range of areas that included politics, health, economics, and culture. Determining which organizations would comprise the Searchlight function was strongly guided by the desire to establish a set of partners that would complement one another as a portfolio. With this approach in mind, an extensive selection process to identify potential participating organizations for the network took place in 2009 and 2010. A request for concept papers was sent to over thirty-five organizations globally that had already demonstrated experience in conducting this kind of work. Potential partners were asked to submit responses describing their organizational structure, trend monitoring experience, methodological approach, potential linkages with their ongoing work, references, previous writing samples, and researcher biographies. This solicitation returned eighteen submitted concept papers, which were then reviewed in detail. A selected number of organizations were contacted and asked to respond to an additional set of questions in writing and to prepare a sample newsletter.

Learning from diverse perspectives

Following the selection of an initial core group of organizations during the first phase, additional members of the network were added over time to achieve the final set of twelve. Participating member organizations came from universities, non-governmental organizations, small consulting companies, and even entities aligned with government research centers. Two institutions were located in the Americas, with research teams located at the RAND Corporation in the United States and a non-profit called Foro Nacional Internacional in Peru. Four participating think tanks were located in Africa, including the African Center for Economic Transformation in Ghana, the Center for Democracy and Development in Nigeria, chapters of the Society for International Development located in Tanzania and Kenya, and the South Africa Node of the Millennium Project in South Africa. Two network members were based in India, research and consulting organizations Intellecap and the Strategic Foresight Group. In Southeast Asia, four organizations participated in the Searchlight network, including research consultancies Noviscape in Thailand and Indochina Research in Cambodia, a government research unit called the National Institute for Science and Technology Policy and Strategy Studies in Vietnam, and a multidisciplinary academic research team based at the Lee Kuan Yew School of Public Policy in Singapore.

From the outset, the Searchlight partners were asked to take a non-directed approach to scanning, in order to provide their fresh point of view on the topics they covered. In doing so, the aim was to generate awareness that combined the provision of information with commentary and interpretation that reflected each organization's perspective. It was expected that the primary outputs of this content, trend monitoring newsletters produced on a roughly monthly basis, would reflect each organization's point of view, topical area of expertise, and knowledge of local conditions. Participating organizations created these newsletters by monitoring secondary sources in their regions, including academic journals, think tank reports, conference proceedings, newspapers, magazines, grey literature, websites and blogs, local language sources, and activities occurring in their own networks. The newsletters contained both secondary-sourced quantitative data and qualitative insights, such as findings from interviews, case studies, and narrative description. Each newsletter pulled together this trend analysis information for distribution to The Rockefeller Foundation as well as to the wider research, non-profit, and policymaking communities. Some of the newsletter material was eventually disseminated through academic publications (Lyakura, 2009; Damrongchai & Michelson, 2009; Eyakuze & Muliro, 2014) and consolidated for ease of sharing via a single website platform called FutureChallenges.org, which was at that point funded by the Bertelsmann Foundation in Germany (FutureChallenges, n.d.). Collectively, these newsletters outlined a rich mosaic of themes, patterns, and concepts that provided early indications of how various forces related to science, technology, economics, and other topic areas might intersect with one another over time and suggested a wide range of concrete intervention opportunities.

The initial set of monthly Searchlight newsletters began to be produced in late 2009 and early 2010. This early period was conceived as a learning opportunity, with each organization receiving substantive feedback from The Rockefeller Foundation staff on each newsletter. The newsletters continued to evolve over the course of 2010 and into 2011, demonstrating the value of continued iteration and close back-and-forth between the producers of horizon scanning information and the primary recipients of the analysis. By the middle of 2012, over 300 Searchlight newsletters were produced. The network continued operation through 2013 and was eventually closed in 2014. The Searchlight network's written output was complemented by regular communications with each network organization member. There were also a series of annual in-person meetings that brought together the main representatives of each participating institution. The focus of these meetings was to help ensure continual improvement of the scanning process and to help solidify interpersonal connections within the group. These annual network convenings were deliberately held in different locations around the world and led by different members of the network, in part to further reflect the importance of gaining diverse perspectives from local contexts. The initial planning and implementation conferences were held at The Rockefeller Foundation Bellagio Center in Italy in 2009 (Institute for Alternative Futures, 2009) and 2010 (Society for International Development, 2010), in Mumbai, India in 2011

(Intellecap, 2011), in New York City in 2012 (Institute for Alternative Futures, 2012), and in Nairobi, Kenya in 2013 (Muliro & Eyakuze, 2014), with summary reports produced after almost all of the meetings to share findings of the discussions and to serve as informational resources for the field.

Emphasizing integration, visualization, and dissemination

It quickly became apparent that the strategic value of the information produced by the Searchlight network horizon scanners could be amplified if the findings from the entire body of work were synthesized and visualized together in a user-friendly way. The importance of this integrative component of the material arising from the Searchlight network emerged as a consensus view and as an explicit next step from discussions that took place during the network's annual meeting held in 2010. The goal for developing this integrative component was not only to add value to the network as a whole, but also to contribute to the wider field of horizon scanning and to use the body of Searchlight information as a test case for applying different synthesis and visualization methodologies. Given the variety of relevant approaches that could be deployed for these synthesis and visualization purposes, there was substantive value in experimenting with multiple methodologies. Doing so offered complementary and divergent points of view that generated a wide-ranging set of results for multiple audiences. Similar to the tactic that was taken in identifying and selecting the primary Searchlight network partners, the synthesis and visualization partners were identified through a competitive selection process. Approximately fifteen relevant organizations in the academic, non-profit, private, and public sectors were contacted to judge their interest in participating and then asked to prepare a concept paper to outline their approach to this synthesis and visualization work. Seven organizations responded with initial concept notes, and due to the consistently high level of these submissions, follow-up conversations were held with all seven finalist organizations. In the end, four organizations were selected to take the information created by the Searchlight network partners and produce independent synthesis and visualization outputs designed to highlight cross-cutting themes emerging from the corpus of newsletters that had been produced by the network members. Drafts of all the resulting synthesis and visualization outputs were reviewed by representatives of the Searchlight network throughout the process and, particularly, at two important junctures. The first formal review occurred at an early stage check-in meeting, held in Bangkok in 2010, with a select number of Searchlight organizations based in Asia. The second formal review occurred at the in-person meeting of all Searchlight member organizations held in Mumbai in 2011. All the resulting synthesis and visualization analyses were published and shared in multiple venues to further extend the reach of the network's outputs, including papers compiled in a special issue of the journal *Foresight*.

The lead synthesis and visualization partner was the Institute for the Future (IFTF), a non-profit research organization based in Palo Alto, California that conducts a variety of forward-looking analyses in conjunction with a wide range of organizations. IFTF used a qualitative process of reading through the Searchlight newsletters and breaking down the information contained in each newsletter into individual signals. A signal can be defined as a specific innovation or disruption that has the potential to grow in scale and geographic distribution, such as a new product, a new practice, a new market strategy, a new policy, or new technology. Following this review process, IFTF then created a database of about 600 signals emerging from the Searchlight newsletters, tagging each signal in the database to develop an initial and more rudimentary visualization of the key trends and innovations identified in the Searchlight newsletters. This analysis was then iteratively revised and resulted in the primary output of hard-copy and digital versions of an interactive map called *Catalysts for Change* that utilized insights from the systems thinking literature (Meadows, 2008) to identify a set of "action zones" indicating relevant problems and opportunities warranting philanthropic intervention, all based on individual signals arising from the Searchlight newsletters (Institute for the Future, 2012a; Vian, Chwierutt, Finlev, Harris, & Kirchner, 2012). Second, IFTF created a workshop toolkit and a related set of templates designed to help organizations, communities, and individuals put the information contained in the map into practice. Finally, IFTF conducted a time-bound, web-based serious game that aimed to engage a broad community of interested participants in a unique conversation about the ideas and innovations emerging from catalysts for change, action zones, and signals described in the map. This public and interactive game, which took place over 48 hours in early April 2012, succeeded in engaging over 1,600 participants from around the world, who played over 18,000 idea "cards" online, while also leveraging the Searchlight network members to serve as game guide moderators (Institute for the Future, 2012b).

The second synthesis and visualization partner involved scholars affiliated with The Frederick S. Pardee Center for the Study of the Longer-Range Future at Boston University, which developed a methodology that took the qualitative information from the Searchlight newsletters and turned it into quantitative data. This team created a database of selected Searchlight articles produced through December 2010 and undertook a standardized coding and scoring format for each article. Each article was then coded across four primary concepts and eleven secondary concepts. Using statistical and data-mining algorithms, a set of patterns and trends were extracted from the articles at the global and regional levels, with the synthesis presented by using a number of visualization modalities (Gopal, 2012; Gopal & Najam, 2012). A third synthesis and visualization partner was a team based at the Manchester Institute of Innovation Research at the University of Manchester, which reviewed the Searchlight newsletters using semantic text analysis and network mapping tools to identify particular trends, issues, and uncertainties. They also studied a set of external sources of information to provide a comparative approach and a top-down framework to structure the analysis. Further analyses were conducted at the continent level (Asia, Africa, and Latin America), at the country level, and at the thematic level, with the resulting visualizations including various sophisticated network maps that identify linkages between different actors and between different concepts that emerged in close association with one another within the Searchlight newsletters (Saritas & Miles, 2012).

Finally, the fourth synthesis and visualization partner was the Risk Assessment and Horizon Scanning Programme Office, located in the National Security Coordination Secretariat in the Prime Minister's Office in Singapore, which undertook their synthesis research project on a pro bono basis. This team applied two different synthesis and visualization processes to the Searchlight newsletters. The first, called SKAN-to-Trend, consisted of an eight-step process of classifying data that involved selecting a subset of newsletters for deeper investigation, using text extraction tools to identify relevant keywords and emerging themes. Using concepts from systems thinking, this team created a series of systems analysis maps to highlight important relationships between drivers and to generate alternative policy options for consideration. The second approach, called the Issue-to-Indicator Process, was developed to identify potential policy response options generated from the analysis (Chan & Chng, 2012). The adoption of and philanthropic support for multiple, complementary synthesis and visualization methods helped to pull together findings from this diverse range of horizon scanning activities, combining qualitative and quantitative, automated and non-automated, and top-down and bottom-up methods. They also helped to show how different audiences can be reached effectively, from engaging the members of the lay public to producing materials for experts in the field.

A key takeaway for science philanthropies drawn from the experience of establishing the Searchlight network is that creating such a global endeavor on this scale requires an iterative process linking together talented and committed individuals and institutions dedicated to a common goal. It reveals the value of applying anticipatory horizon scanning and trend monitoring for the philanthropic sector, where many of the topics and problems addressed are rather complex, challenging, and hard to disentangle from one another. Overseeing such work requires diligence, open-mindedness, and a willingness to pursue new directions of thought, action, and grantmaking as they emerge. Interacting closely with the Searchlight partners provided a multi-layered view of the world that was constantly evolving and shifting over time. Receiving such a high volume of information from different perspectives helped to avoid groupthink and offered a more holistic and nuanced perspective. It shows that horizon scanning methodologies can be applied to address a range of organizational needs, from illuminating the contextual environment to stimulating idea generation. In sum, the establishment of this type of internal–external trend monitoring network is one way that science philanthropies can start to take steps and act with the long-term future more explicitly in mind.

Sloan Digital Sky Survey (SDSS): leading the way in cutting-edge science, diversity, and the adoption of responsive practices

Regularly looking ahead to achieve groundbreaking scientific discoveries

Since 1992, the Alfred P. Sloan Foundation has supported the establishment and continued operations of the Sloan Digital Sky Survey (SDSS), a pioneering collaboration of astronomers, cosmologists, and astrophysicists that now makes use of two telescopes located in both hemispheres to study some of the most pressing research questions in astrophysics and cosmology. In the 25 years since the Sloan Foundation's first grant to the project, SDSS has become one of the most important, most productive, and most highly cited telescopic surveys in the history of astronomy (Madrid & Maccetto, 2009; Zhang & Yongheng, 2015). As its website states, the result of this research is that SDSS "has created the most detailed three-dimensional maps of the Universe ever made, with deep multi-color images of one third of the sky, and spectra for more than three million astronomical objects" (Sloan Digital Sky Survey, 2018b).

Moreover, through its collaborative institutional management system and diverse funding model, SDSS has become one of the most influential forces shaping not just the practice and culture of astronomy today, but it has influenced the way many large-scale collaborations across scientific fields share data and organize their management practices.

SDSS has a long, rich, and complex history that involves some of the leading astronomers and data scientists working in the field (Finkbeiner, 2010). Prior to SDSS, astronomical survey research was conducted by exposing and developing photographic plates, a long and tedious process, and the collected data was owned by the scientists who gathered them and difficult for others to access. The underlying idea for a digitally enabled astronomical survey was led by astrophysicist Jim Gunn of Princeton University, who pioneered the use in astronomy of new digital camera technologies called a charge-coupled device that records images and spectra by converting light into digital information. The new device would lead to the creation of digital cameras and detectors that would allow for the establishment of the first electronic, searchable and computable map of the universe. Representatives from government funding agencies and the Sloan Foundation were intrigued by the potential of this new technology to transform the practice of astronomy by moving to the analysis of digital information recorded of millions of stars, galaxies, and other astronomical objects such as quasars. Access to this data would facilitate the study of many new and important questions in astronomy that scientists were starting to explore, such as the chemical composition of stars, how galaxies are formed and interact with one another, how quickly the universe is expanding, and the nature of physics surrounding black holes.

A new telescope designed for the purpose of housing this digital astronomical survey was needed and was subsequently built at Apache Point

Observatory in southeastern New Mexico. Following completion of what is now called the Sloan Telescope in 2000, SDSS began operations and has been structured in a series of phases, each about five years long and focused around a set of targeted research questions. The first phase—SDSS-I, which ran from 2000 to 2005—concentrated on producing an initial image map of a portion of the night sky. The second phase, SDSS-II (2005–2008), included an investigation of the stars in the Milky Way galaxy's halo and contributed to the study of the universe's acceleration and dark energy. By the third phase, SDSS-III (2008–2014), SDSS fully transitioned away from taking digital images of objects to utilizing spectrographs designed to record the constituent spectra of astronomical objects in visible and infrared wavelengths. This allowed astronomers to better probe the structure of the Milky Way and create what remains one of the largest three-dimensional maps of galaxies. Phase four, SDSS-IV (2014–2020) not only saw the survey extend research from previous phases, but it began expanding to a second observing site located in the Southern Hemisphere, which allows scientists to study the core of the Milky Way galaxy in ways not possible in the Northern Hemisphere. This involved starting to make partial use of the Irénée du Pont Telescope located at the Las Campanas Observatory in Chile. In 2017, the Sloan Foundation approved support for a fifth phase of SDSS, SDSS-V, that will run from 2020 to 2025, which will involve almost the complete dedication of time on the du Pont Telescope to the SDSS observing program.

Due to this regular interval review and survey re-assembly process, SDSS is constantly looking ahead to identify and address some of the most pressing questions in the fields of astronomy and astrophysics. For this reason, it has been the source of some of the most groundbreaking and influential discoveries that shed light on the nature and origins of the cosmos. Consider just a few of its major discoveries. SDSS research has led to the production of highly precise maps detailing "the large-scale structure of the Universe…which have become a central pillar of the standard cosmological model that describes our understanding of the history and future of the Universe" (Sloan Digital Sky Survey, 2018d). SDSS research has made headlines with findings that include precise measures of the expansion rate of the universe (Sloan Digital Sky Survey, 2014), identifying the impacts of dark energy and dark matter on the expansion rate of the universe (Sloan Digital Sky Survey, 2016a), the nature of activity associated with supermassive black holes that sit at the centers of galaxies (Sloan Digital Sky Survey, 2016b; Sloan Digital Sky Survey, 2018e), studying the habitability of planets (Sloan Digital Sky Survey, 2017a), and identifying the origin and distribution of chemical elements beyond our solar system (Sloan Digital Sky Survey, 2017b).

Since the beginning of its funding for SDSS, the Sloan Foundation has provided over $72 million (in 2016 dollars) across 18 grants, which have been awarded following a rigorous review process involving evaluation by numerous external subject matter experts. The Sloan Foundation has historically provided 20–25% of funding for the collaboration, with the remainder having to be raised by the leads of each phase. This innovative university subscription model has made SDSS less reliant on government funds as its phases have progressed. SDSS-IV currently has nearly fifty-five collaborating member institutions, and SDSS-V already has nearly thirty participating member organizations. The process of periodic grant renewals and the adoption of this subscription model has helped ensure that the collaboration stays relevant as the field evolves, responding to changing research priorities and regularly adopting new technologies. Other fields, such as biology and chemistry, have also begun to experiment with ensuring the sustainability of their data repositories using this kind of consortium funding or membership fee model, to good success (Bourne, Lorsch, & Green, 2015; Kaiser, 2016; Oliver, Lock, Harris, Nurse, & Wood, 2016). In the SDSS institutional member consortium funding model, universities or other independent research centers pay to join the collaboration in exchange for having the opportunity to not only serve in collaboration governance roles and shape the scientific research agenda, but also to gain immediate access to SDSS data once it is produced and before it goes public.

Broadening engagement through data sharing

It is this public release of all SDSS data, undertaken with the encouragement of Sloan Foundation staff at the outset of the project, that has made SDSS such a touchstone in the sciences and is perhaps what the collaboration is most well-known for in other fields of research. Prior to SDSS, research projects in astronomy were mostly characterized by scientists keeping their data proprietary; scholars on a team had access to it, but extensive data sets were not shared with others in the field or with the public at large. SDSS took an additional step in making its data freely available after an embargo period of one year, not only to collaboration members but to the greater astronomy community and to the public worldwide. One indicator of the impact of this open data sharing approach is that out of the over 9,000 papers that have been published using SDSS data, 80% of these papers have been written by scholars from outside the collaboration. Collectively, these scientific articles have received over 400,000 citations (The SOA/NASA Astrophysics Data System, n.d.). The integration of these open data sharing principles early on in SDSS's history had a profound impact on establishing a wider culture of data sharing in astronomy. One recent document describing the characteristics that make SDSS an archetype of a mid-scale program in astronomy noted that, "the large impact of the data releases is impressive to foundations and agencies and helps to get non-member institutions familiar enough with SDSS data to consider joining, both of which help ultimately to fund the project long-term" (Blanton, 2019, p. 8).

Because of its open availability, many subsequent astronomical surveys have relied on SDSS data, and the SDSS data platform has served as a model for other large-scale astronomical surveys. One analysis of SDSS's impact on the field noted that it "has proven beneficial to nearly every subfield of astronomy" (Pasquetto, Sands, Darch, & Borgman, 2016, p. 1587). The software originally developed for broadly sharing SDSS data, known as the SkyServer, has been generalized for use and subsequently renamed SciServer to indicate its application in many different scientific domains beyond astronomy, including soil ecology, oceanography, genomics, materials science, fluid dynamics, and other areas of cosmology (SciServer, n.d.). These open data sharing practices also led SDSS to become one of the first large scale research projects to facilitate and promote citizen science, allowing members of the public to meaningfully contribute to the research effort by helping to categorize the shapes of different galaxies (Borgman, Sands, Darch, & Golshan, 2016). This project, known as Galaxy Zoo, began in 2007 and has continued for over a decade with multiple rounds of citizen science research activities. It now has "the largest number of publications based on citizen scientists input," and it too spawned a more generalized follow-on effort in other areas of science, a project called Zooniverse, that include targeted citizen science efforts in areas as diverse as biology, ecology, animal science, atmospheric science, social science, and other areas of physics as well (Zooniverse, n.d.).

Furthermore, the adoption of open data release practices as a model for SDSS has led other projects to refer to SDSS as a metaphor for the broad-based utilization of large-scale data analysis in other fields. To take just one example, The Kavli Foundation launched a project in 2014 called the Kavli HUMAN Project at New York University, with the goal of collecting biological and behavior data from 10,000 participating individuals over a twenty-year time period to analyze how biological and social factors relate to one another. SDSS was used as a core analogy by the lead researchers to describe this impetus to bring big data collection and analytics to the social sciences. Describing how SDSS marshalled data science to transform the field of astronomy, the leads of the Kavli HUMAN Project articulated how they plan to bring the same perspectives to bear on the study of the human condition. "Over the course of the last decade, however, advances in computers, smartphones, the Internet, and large-scale biological measurement have made it possible to construct automated counterparts to the Sloan Apache Point Telescope for the study of humanity," they write (Azmak, et al., 2015, p. 174). They go on to argue that, "just as the Sloan Digital Sky Survey and the Human Genome Project revolutionized the disciplines of astronomy and genetics, a large-scale synoptic study of a population could revolutionize our understanding of human behavior, health, and well-being" (Azmak, et al., 2015, p. 187). While it remains unclear whether SDSS is a well-founded analogy and metaphor for the Kavli HUMAN Project, the very fact that other scholars refer to this distinctive elements of the SDSS collaboration more than twenty-five years after they were established is one indicator of how forward-looking these data sharing practices were when instituted at the outset and how influential they remain today.

Taking the lead on diversity, equity, and inclusion

Beyond helping to support the establishment of open data principles in SDSS, the collaboration—again with the encouragement and support of the Sloan Foundation—has also been instrumental in supporting the integration of diversity, equity, and inclusion principles and practices throughout the collaboration. One article reporting on diversity measures within the SDSS collaboration emphasized the role that the Sloan Foundation played in animating more attention to diversity issues, noting that, "with the approval of additional funding for the SDSS-IV in 2012, the Sloan Foundation requested that the SDSS management report on efforts to recruit women into the project leadership" (Lundgren, et al., 2015, p. 777). More recently, a report from the leads of SDSS-IV further reflected on the role that the Sloan Foundation played in emphasizing the need for more diversity within the collaboration. This report states, "SDSS did not take steps to address and mitigate the issue [diversity] until the Sloan Foundation identified it during its review of SDSS-IV in 2012. This history illustrates the important role that funding agencies can play in establishing priorities" (Blanton, 2019, p. 3). It continues by noting, "the Sloan Foundation made the gender balance and overall inclusiveness of the project and collaboration a truly existential issue that we had to address" (Blanton, 2019, p. 3).

SDSS took up these challenges, establishing two committees—one focused on the participation of women in the survey, the other focused on engaging a larger number of historically under-represented minorities—which eventually merged together to address these diversity and inclusion issues holistically under a single umbrella entity called the Committee on Inclusion in SDSS (COINS). Over time, SDSS has undertaken a series of steps to make significant advancements on this front, including the adoption of best practices throughout the collaboration, establishing expectations about diversity among leadership and senior management teams, and ensuring the participation of women and under-represented minorities throughout the collaboration. For instance, COINS put together a series of guiding resources to establish a more "inclusive environment" within the survey, including a Code of Conduct to set expectations about participant behavior, a best practices document to give more detailed content on this front, plus additional resources to help inspire more open participation throughout the various in-person and virtual meeting formats that take place as part of the scientific research process (Sloan Digital Sky Survey, 2018a). SDSS members undertook a demographic and diversity survey, coupled with qualitative interviews, to better understand the contours of these issues within the collaboration. The study found that while progress still needs to be made, SDSS has a higher percentage of women in the collaboration when compared to the broader field of astronomy and that the percentage of under-represented minorities in the collaboration was on par with the field of astronomy, but which still falls well below the demographic composition of these groups in the United States (Lundgren, et al., 2015).

To address the particularly challenging issue of involving a larger number of under-represented minorities in the collaboration, the Sloan Foundation provided support to SDSS in 2015 and then again in 2018 to initiate a new dual-level mentoring effort called the Faculty and Student Team (FAST) program. The FAST program is designed to bring university research teams with larger fractions of under-represented minorities into the SDSS fold. In this model, existing SDSS researchers help mentor faculty from these teams new to the collaboration, and then the new faculty members mentor their students, most of whom are under-represented undergraduate minorities. The SDSS website description highlights the expected long-term impacts and goals of the program. By providing "teams with specialized training, data rights, and financial support to help them begin working with SDSS data," the expectation is "ultimately…FAST teams will build long-term research relationships with SDSS collaborators and be a lasting and productive part of the collaboration," it states (Sloan Digital Sky Survey, 2018c). Five diverse teams have been selected for participation from universities located across the country, including two at the City University of New York and one each at DePaul University in Chicago, New Mexico State University, and the University of California, San Diego, with additional teams to be added to the network over time. The program is already having success in addressing the "structural inequalities that often hinder students in underrepresented groups from entering astronomy and other sciences" (Sloan Digital Sky Survey, 2017c). Over its first two years, two-thirds of the teams consisted of under-represented minority undergraduate students and a handful have already successfully applied to graduate programs in astronomy or physics, with more planning to do so going forward. Participants in this program made fifteen science presentations at the 2017 American Astronomical Society meeting, one of the largest professional gatherings of astronomers in the world (Sloan Digital Sky Survey, 2017c).

Lastly on this diversity front, with the two most recent SDSS phases, SDSS-IV and SDSS-V, having observation footprints both in the Northern Hemisphere (United States) and now in the Southern Hemisphere (Chile) for the first time, the collaboration paid close attention to ensuring the integration of researchers and scholars from the Chilean astronomical community. Scientists, engineers, technicians, and decision-makers from Chile were engaged early in the planning efforts. A press release from 2017, with versions in both English and Spanish, announcing the launch of the SDSS-IV partnership with the Las Campanas Observatory based in Chile featured the many ways in which Chilean astronomers were engaged as central, core members of the collaboration (Sloan Digital Sky Survey, 2017d). Many subsequent SDSS blog posts and press releases have been written in both languages, and a number of cross-national training opportunities and exercises have taken place that have linked astronomers from both countries, including holding a joint workshop devoted to finding collaborative ways of presenting and communicating SDSS findings to the public. Additionally, in 2017, the collaboration's annual meeting was held in Chile as one way of honoring the participation of their astronomy community in SDSS.

Lessons learned: how to infuse research network design with an RRI perspective

There are a number of cross-cutting, generalizable lessons emerging from both of these case studies. These findings can be relevant to a wide range of collaborations supported by other philanthropies and donors in the public and private sphere.

First, the Searchlight network, in particular, demonstrated the value of developing an internal process that can *enhance current strategic awareness*. It provided a high frequency input stream of information related to The Rockefeller Foundation's contextual environment, with selected partners having identified a diverse array of valuable information sources that the foundation would not have been able to access otherwise, either because they are not easily accessible electronically or because they involve resources or events that are highly local in nature. Each partner organization has developed different methodologies for identifying information of interest as well as providing distinct and unique viewpoints on the subjects they covered. This helped contribute to the foundation's risk management strategy and allowed the foundation to extend its information gathering reach in a way that would not have been possible otherwise.

Second, the Searchlight network also helped *ease the identification of intervention opportunities*. The trends identified by the Searchlight network partners were collectively used to inform The Rockefeller Foundation's overall strategic framework and planning efforts, as well as highlighting potential solutions or intervention opportunities that the organization could consider as part of its early stage initiative work. Ideas about potential intervention opportunities were excerpted from the Searchlight newsletters and stored in an internal idea generation platform. These ideas could be used as building blocks for other staff as they develop strategic approaches to structuring new grantmaking initiatives at the foundation. Information from the Searchlight newsletters was also regularly and actively shared with staff across the organization and used as a base of information for strategic analyses and trend papers prepared for senior management.

Third, SDSS raises a number of intertwined lessons for science philanthropies looking to fund large-scale science networks. Of clear importance is having *grantee institutions and networks identify pressing scientific questions at the outset*, which should drive and determine the type of data collected and not the other way around. Engaging the scientific community during this process is critical and necessary. Similarly, establishing open data access and sharing policies early on in a collaboration can facilitate broader use of datasets and accelerate discoveries within the scientific community. While basic science projects can take longer to realize, and even end up being more expensive than expected, there can be potentially transformative returns on this investment. Research networks that span multiple years and decades should not only expect evolution in scientific fields, but they should plan for and anticipate technology obsolescence that will inevitably shape the research collaboration as it progresses. Moreover, perhaps the most important role for funders to play is in paying attention to governance issues and ensuring that there is high-quality and dedicated scientific leadership in place that has developed and implemented an effective management structure to keep the network on track. Philanthropies must also make explicit at the beginning of the collaboration the importance of diversity, equity, and inclusion considerations. Finally, funders must encourage the development and implementation of an innovative and collaborative funding model that engages scientific research institutions in order to ensure project sustainability as well as ensure that the project stays relevant as it proceeds over time.

Taken together, these lessons point to a key takeaway for science philanthropies interested in establishing a forward-looking capacity: there is *no one-size-fits-all approach* to advancing research networks. Such networks are unique and highly dependent on the characteristics of the participating individuals and institutions. Therefore, a customized approach is required to work with each organization in the network to develop the parameters for their respective activities and to ensure there is agreement about roles and responsibilities. Recognizing that each participating organization has their own strengths, challenges, and institutional interests indicates that there is not a standard template that can be followed in establishing such a network. The aim should be to assemble a set of organizations that complement one another in terms of the topics they cover, the methodologies they adopt, and the perspectives they offer.

Moreover, both the Searchlight network and SDSS demonstrate the benefit of engaging with a *broad diversity of opinions perspectives*. Searchlight partners contributed to a reframed understanding of local, regional, and global issues by providing their unique interpretation from a regional perspective. This on-the-ground presence was particularly valuable in places where The Rockefeller Foundation worked but did not have a permanent presence or an office. Similarly, close collaboration between American and Chilean astronomers allowed SDSS to rather seamlessly expand its observing program across the entire night sky and access regions of viewing that were wholly unavailable to SDSS for the first two decades of its existence. Both show how global research networks—whether internal to an organization or situated externally in a field—can operate productively across spatial and temporal distance.

Both collaborations clearly have also made *global dissemination and outreach of knowledge* key elements of the networks, albeit at different scales and scopes. Though certainly smaller in its reach than SDSS, content from the Searchlight network could be brought together and synthesized to highlight trends and patterns. Many Searchlight organizations not only distributed their newsletters within their own local, national, and regional networks, but they also brought this information to life through events such as speaker series, workshops, and other discussions based on the Searchlight information they collected. A number of participating organizations created specific websites to feature their Searchlight content, and Searchlight material was often featured in other writing, blog posts, magazine articles, and opinion pieces. Much Searchlight content has also been picked up and re-posted on well-known blog sites. By almost any measure, SDSS is an accomplishment that revolutionized the field of astronomy, where a relatively modest series of investments has helped to establish one of the most productive astronomical facilities in history that has brought a greater understanding of our universe to a wide swath of the population. SDSS advanced a model of international scientific collaboration that provided a template for how institutions could share funding and work together. Its open data policies and its multi-institution subscription model helped ensure the involvement of a large fraction of the astronomy community. Yet it has done so by first identifying interesting scientific questions, which then drive the type of data that is collected and shared broadly.

Yet there are also some caveats to keep in mind in terms of the oversight and management of such research networks. One important point of learning is that both networks continued to benefit from *regular iteration and feedback* from their philanthropic funder to ensure their efforts remained closely aligned with the funder's interests over time. In the case of the Searchlight effort, it took considerable time to establish such a global network. With The Rockefeller Foundation being the primary recipient of the Searchlight newsletters, there was a need to provide regular feedback and to respond to multiple iterations of the outputs, especially at the outset of the organizational partnership, as a way to create sustained and lasting value. A small team of approximately five foundation staff were formed to read, review, and provide feedback on each Searchlight newsletter, identifying the points and ideas that were of interest and those that might have missed their mark. This iterative feedback process allowed the Searchlight organizations to ensure that their outputs could be adjusted as needed. In the case of SDSS, the provision of feedback took place in the context of the Sloan Foundation's proposal review process at the outset of each SDSS phase, with SDSS proposals following the same rigorous, external peer-review approach that the Sloan Foundation has established for all proposals it actively considers.

Establishing and maintaining such networks can take *considerable amounts of time*, often over a year of planning, budgeting, and strategic review at the outset and then again at critical junctures during the network's lifespan. The Searchlight network took over a year to get off the ground, including the open call for applications held by the foundation, followed by another year of learning and adjustment during the grantmaking phase. Preparations for the latest, fifth phase of SDSS started nearly four years before the collaboration began observations, with an initial year of planning activities to broadly scope the extent and interest in its future scientific program. Initial funding for SDSS-V was provided nearly three years before it began scheduled observations in 2020 because of the need to undertake infrastructure upgrades and hardware build-out.

A related strategic risk to point out is perhaps unexpected: the very naming of such networks and the adoption of the foundation's name in the collaboration heading. SDSS and the primary telescope took on the Sloan Foundation's name early in its history, an honor provided by the founders to recognize the foundation's critical contribution to initiate the project. The Searchlight network, though not formally adopting The Rockefeller Foundation name, was inevitably linked with the foundation given its strategic focus and the foundation's central role in establishing the idea, providing the necessary support, and serving as the sole benefactor. Naming a project or network after the foundation has its advantages and disadvantages. While it can give the foundation recognition for its support, it can also hinder fundraising with other sources. It is obviously a signal to the wider philanthropic community that the funder is invested in the network succeeding. However, it may also prove challenging to grantees to secure additional support if the adopting of a funder's name provides the impression to other potential donors that additional resources are not needed or that the founding donor will cover all the associated costs of the network.

Finally, both case studies point to the need to recognize the *ongoing evolution of such networks*, even when their goals and expected outcomes are clear. In the case of the Searchlight network, it became apparent that no matter how insightful or forward looking the Searchlight function proved to be on a regular basis, there remained an ongoing need to digest and consider the information it produced in light of The Rockefeller Foundation's strategy and interests. This strategic interpretation from trend information to strategic relevance is highly crucial to getting the most out of a philanthropy-oriented trend monitoring network. Having a team that knows the recipient organization well is critical in identifying the relevant points of intersection between the incoming information and its potential uses and applications. For instance, such a team can determine if a piece of information should be held and stored as background for a later date or whether such information is particularly timely as part of ongoing conversations and therefore requires more immediate attention. SDSS's success over a longer period of time across two and a half decades would not have been possible without its ongoing evolution and transformation as astronomical observing technologies advanced and as the collaboration's unique capabilities shifted over time. The process of periodic grant reviews and phased renewals ensured that the project had to evolve with the changing field, and the university subscription model helped ensure that SDSS was responding to the changing interests in the field as well as to changes in technology. For instance, as it became clear that the digital imaging technology used in earlier SDSS phases was soon to be surpassed by other facilities, the collaboration switched its focus exclusively to conducting wide-field spectroscopy across the visible and infrared spectrum, the latter of which has remained at the forefront of facilities in astronomy. Other developments that expanded the geographic footprint of the collaboration over successive phases led to new partnership opportunities that would not have been possible in previous iterations of the collaboration.

In conclusion, even with one project being foundation-driven and the other being more community- and field-driven, both The Rockefeller Foundation's Searchlight network and SDSS demonstrate many of the qualities that lead to effective research network formation, persistence and, in one case, closure. It is an effective combination of dedicated researchers asking important scientific questions, utilization of the right collaboration schemes, establishing effective management structures, and employing data sharing policies and expectations that facilitate broader use of the knowledge that is generated. In many ways, both are experiments. The establishment of the Searchlight network was an attempt to demonstrate the value of applying anticipatory horizon scanning and trend monitoring to the philanthropic sector, where many of the topics and problems addressed are rather complex, challenging, and hard to disentangle from one another. SDSS focused on answering important questions in astronomy and astrophysics using a collaborative model and adopting the tools and techniques from data analytics to elucidate these mysteries more accurately, more quickly, more efficiently, and more transparently that had been done previously. Its innovative funding model engaging multiple scientific research institutions has helped ensure the project's sustainability. In the end, both efforts showcase how science philanthropies can apply the spirit and perspective of the RRI principles to improve their own practices and to infuse such values and ideals within scientific research networks that they fund.

Bibliography

Azmak, O., Bayer, H., Caplin, A., Chun, M., Glimcher, P., & Koonin, S., et al. (2015). Using Big Data to Understand the Human Condition: The Kavli HUMAN Project. *Big Data*, 3(3), 173–188.

Blanton, M. R. (2019). The Sloan Digital Sky Survey as an Archetypal Mid-Scale Program. Retrieved July 2019, from Sloan Digital Sky Survey: www.sdss.org/wp-content/uploads/2019/07/BlantonMichaelR.pdf.

Borgman, C. L., Sands, A. E., Darch, P. T., & Golshan, M. S. (2016). The Durability and Fragility of Knowledge Infrastructures: Lessons Learned from Astronomy. *Proceedings of the Association for Information Science and Technology*, 53(1), 1–10.

Bourne, P. E., Lorsch, J. R., & Green, E. D. (2015, November 5). Sustaining the Big-Data Ecosystem. *Nature*, 527(7576), S16–S17.

Chan, J. C., & Chng, L. D. (2012). Understanding Pathways of Poor and Vulnerable Communities. *Foresight*, 14(6), 511–529.

Damrongchai, N., & Michelson, E. S. (2009). The Future of Science and Technology and Pro-Poor Applications. *Foresight*, 11(4), 51–65.

Dreber, A., Pfeiffer, T., Almenberg, J., Isaksson, S., Wilson, B., et al. (2015, December 15). Using Prediction Markets to Estimate the Reproducibility of Scientific Research. *PNAS*, 112(50), 15343–15347.

Eyakuze, A., & Muliro, A. (2014). Dispatches from the Frontline: Using Pro-Poor Foresight to Influence Decision-making. *Development*, 56(4), 456–463.

Finkbeiner, A. (2010). *A Grand and Bold Thing: An Extraordinary New Map of the Universe Ushering in a New Era of Discovery*. New York, NY: Free Press.

Fretwell, E., Rejeski, D., Hendler, J., Peroff, K., & McCord, M. (2019). Science and Technology Policy Assessment: A Congressionally Directed Review. Washington, DC: National Academy of Public Administration.

Fulton, K., & Blau, A. (2005). Looking Out for the Future: An Orientation for Twenty-First Century Philanthropists. San Francisco, CA: Global Business Network and Monitor Institute.

Fulton, K., Kasper, G., & Kibbe, B. (2010). What's Next for Philanthropy: Acting Bigger and Adapting Better in a Networked World. San Francisco, CA: Monitor Institute.

FutureChallenges. (n.d.). *Searchlight*. Retrieved July 2019, from FutureChallenges: https://futurechallenges.org/searchlight/.

Gopal, S. (2012). Global Synthesis of Searchlight Reports Using Knowledge Discovery and Visualization. *Foresight*, 14(6), 468–488.

Gopal, S., & Najam, A. (2012). Connecting the Dots: Information Visualization and Text Analysis of the Searchlight Project Newsletters. Boston, MA: The Frederick S. Pardee Center for the Study of the Longer-Range Future, Boston University.

Government Accountability Office. (2019, January 29). GAO Deepens Science and Technology Capabilities. Retrieved July 2019, from Government Accountability Office: www.gao.gov/about/press-center/press-releases/gao_deepens_science_tech.html.

Institute for Alternative Futures. (2009). Foresight for Smart Globalization: Accelerating & Enhancing Pro-Poor Development Opportunities. Alexandria, VA: Institute for Alternative Futures.

Institute for Alternative Futures. (2012). Scanning for a Brighter Future: Report from the 2012 Searchlight Workshop. Alexandria, VA: Institute for Alternative Futures.

Institute for the Future. (2012a). Catalysts for Change: Paths Out of Poverty. Retrieved July 2019, from Institute for the Future: www.iftf.org/our-work/global-landscape/catalysts-for-change/catalysts-for-change-project/.

Institute for the Future. (2012b). Summary of an Experiment in Global Engagement. Retrieved July 2019, from Institute for the Future: www.iftf.org/uploads/media/IFTF_SR-1535_CatalystsforChange_SummaryExperimentinGlobalEngagment-sm.pdf.

Intellecap. (2011). Searchlight Convening: The Future of the Urban Poor. Mumbai, India: Intellecap.

Juech, C., & Michelson, E. S. (2012). Innovation in Horizon Scanning for the Social Sector: An Introduction to the Searchlight Function. *Foresight*, 14(6), 439–449.

Kaiser, J. (2016, January 1). Funding for Key Data Resources in Jeopardy. *Science*, 351 (6268), 14.

Lundgren, B., Kinemuchi, K., Zasowski, G., Lucatello, S., Diamon-Stanic, A. M., Tremonti, C., et al. (2015, August). The SDSS-IV in 2014: A Demographic Snapshot. *Publications of the Astronomical Society of the Pacific*, 127(954), 776–788.

Lyakura, W. (2009). Prospects for Economic Governance: Resilient Pro-Poor Growth. *Foresight*, 11(4), 66–81.

Mackinnon, A. (2012). Scanning the Landscape 2.0: Finding out What's Going On in Your Field. New York, NY: GrantCraft.

Madrid, J. P., & Maccetto, F. D. (2009). High-Impact Astronomical Observatories. *Bulletin of the AAS*, 41(2), 913–914.

Malakoff, D. (2019, April 30). House Democrats Move to Resurrect Congress's Science Advisory Office. Retrieved July 2019, from *Science*: www.sciencemag.org/news/2019/04/house-democrats-move-resurrect-congress-s-science-advisory-office.

Meadows, D. H. (2008). *Thinking in Systems: A Primer*. Oxon, UK: Earthscan.

Miller, R. (2018). *Transforming the Future: Anticipation in the 21st Century*. Oxon, UK: Routledge.

Muliro, A., & Eyakuze. (2014). Editorial: Future of Foresight. *Development*, 56(4), 435–439.

Munafo, M. R., Pfeiffer, T., Altmejd, A., Heikensten, E., Almenberg, J., Bird, A., et al. (2015). Using Prediction Markets to Forecast Research Evaluations. *Royal Society Open Science*, 2(150287), 1–8.

Murray, S. (2018, Winter). Unconventional Wisdom. *Stanford Social Innovation Review*, 13–14.

Oliver, S. G., Lock, A., Harris, M. A., Nurse, P., & Wood, V. (2016). Model Organism Databases: Essential Resources that Need the Support of Both Funders and Users. *BMC Biology*, 14(49), 1–6.

Pasquetto, I. V., Sands, A. E., Darch, P. T., & Borgman, C. L. (2016). Open Data in Scientific Settings: From Policy to Practice. CHI 2016, 1585–1596.

Pauwels, E. (2019). The New Geopolitics of Converging Risks: The UN and Prevention in the Era of AI. New York, NY: United Nations University.

Pena, V., Stokes, C. A., & Behrens, J. R. (2019). Partnership Development in the Federal Government. Washington: IDA Science and Technology Policy Institute. Retrieved October 2019, from Institute for Defense Analysis: www.ida.org/-/media/feature/publica tions/p/pa/partnership-development-in-the-federal-government/d10702final.ashx.

Rejeski, D., Leonard, S., & Libre, C. (2018). Novel Entities and the GEF Background Paper. Washington, DC: Environmental Law Institute.

Saritas, O., & Miles, I. (2012). Scan-4-Light: A Searchlight Function Horizon Scanning and Trend Monitoring Project. *Foresight*, 14(6), 489–510.

Schwartz, P. (1996). *The Art of the Long View: Planning for the Future in an Uncertain World*. New York, NY: Doubleday.

Science Philanthropy Alliance. (2017, December). Taking to the Stars: The Alfred P. Sloan Foundation's 25-year Partnership with the Sloan Digital Sky Survey. Retrieved September 2019, from Science Philanthropy Alliance: www.sciencephilanthropyalliance.org/wp-con tent/uploads/2017/12/Sloan-SDSS-philanthropy-story-pdf-for-web.pdf.

SciServer. (n.d.). Science. Retrieved July 2019, from SciServer: www.sciserver.org/integra tion/.

Sloan Digital Sky Survey. (2014, April 7). Astronomers from the Sloan Digital Sky Survey Make the Most Precise Measurement Yet of the Expanding Universe. Retrieved July 2019, from Sloan Digital Sky Survey: www.sdss.org/press-relea ses/astronomers-from-the-sloan-digital-sky-survey-make-the-most-precise-measure ment-yet-of-the-expanding-universe-2/.

Sloan Digital Sky Survey. (2016a, July 14). Astronomers Map a Record-Breaking 1.2 Million Galaxies to Study the Properties of Dark Energy. Retrieved July 2019, from Sloan Digital Sky Survey: Astronomers map a record-breaking 1.2 million galaxies to study the properties of dark energy: www.sdss.org/press-releases/astronomers-map-a-record-breaking-1-2-million-galaxies-to-study-the-properties-of-dark-energy/.

Sloan Digital Sky Survey. (2016b, May 25). Supermassive Black Holes Cause Galactic Warming. Retrieved July 2019, from Sloan Digital Sky Survey: www.sdss.org/press-releases/supermassive-black-holes-cause-galactic-warming/.

Sloan Digital Sky Survey. (2017a, January 5). Between a Rock and a Hard Place: Can Garnet Planets Be Habitable? Retrieved July 2019, from Sloan Digital Sky Survey: www.sdss.org/press-releases/between-a-rock-and-a-hard-place-can-garnet-planets-be-habitable/.

Sloan Digital Sky Survey. (2017b, January 5). The Elements of Life Mapped Across the Milky Way by SDSS/APOGEE. Retrieved July 2019, from Sloan Digital Sky Survey: www.sdss.org/press-releases/the-elements-of-life-mapped-across-the-milky-way-by-sdssapogee/.

Sloan Digital Sky Survey. (2017c, January 5). The Sloan Digital Sky Survey: Working Hard to Improve Inclusion in Astronomy. Retrieved July 2019, from Sloan Digital Sky Survey: www.sdss.org/press-releases/the-sloan-digital-sky-survey-working-hard-to-improve-inclusion-in-astronomy/.

Sloan Digital Sky Survey. (2017d, March 29). Seeing the Whole Galaxy with a "Second Eye on the Sky". Retrieved July 2019, from Sloan Digital Sky Survey: www.sdss.org/press-releases/seeing-the-whole-galaxy-with-a-second-eye-on-the-sky/.

Sloan Digital Sky Survey. (2018a). COINS. Retrieved July 2019, from Sloan Digital Sky Survey: www.sdss.org/collaboration/coins/.

Sloan Digital Sky Survey. (2018b). The Sloan Digital Sky Survey: Mapping the Universe. Retrieved July 2019, from Sloan Digital Sky Survey: www.sdss.org/.

Sloan Digital Sky Survey. (2018c). Faculty and Student Team (FAST) Initiative. Retrieved July 2019, from Sloan Digital Sky Survey: www.sdss.org/education/faculty-and-student-team-fast-initiative/.

Sloan Digital Sky Survey. (2018d). Science Results. Retrieved July 2019, from Sloan Digital Sky Survey: www.sdss.org/science/.

Sloan Digital Sky Survey. (2018e, January 8). How Massive is Supermassive? Astronomers Measure More Black Holes, Farther Away. Retrieved July 2019, from Sloan Digital Sky Survey: www.sdss.org/press-releases/how-massive/.

Society for International Development. (2010). Building a Searchlight Function: Workshop Report and Participant Reflections. Washington, DC: Society for International Development.

The SOA/NASA Astrophysics Data System. (n.d.). Astrophysics Data System. Retrieved July 2019, from The SOA/NASA Astrophysics Data System: https://ui.adsabs.harvard.edu/.

Tully, C., & Pulford, L. (2019, April 5). Future-Fit Philanthropy: Why Philanthropic Organisations will Need Foresight to Leave Lasting Legacies of Change. Retrieved August 2019, from *Alliance Magazine*: www.alliancemagazine.org/blog/future-fit-philanthropy-why-philanthropic-organisations-will-need-foresight-to-leave-lasting-legacies-of-change/.

van der Heijden, K. (2005). *Scenarios: The Art of Strategic Conversation*. Chichester, UK: John Wiley & Sons.

Vian, K., Chwierutt, M., Finlev, T., Harris, D. E., & Kirchner, M. (2012). Catalysts for Change: Vizualizing the Horizon of Poverty. *Foresight*, 14(6), 450–467.

Wack, P. (1985a, September). Scenarios: Uncharted Waters Ahead. *Harvard Business Review*, 63(5), 72–79.

Wack, P. (1985b, November 63). Scenarios: Shooting the Rapids. *Harvard Business Review*, 6, 139–150.

Wiener, R. J., & Ronco, S. (2019). Scialog: The Catalysis of Convergence. *ACS Energy Letters*, 4(5), 1020–1024.

Wilkinson, A., & Kupers, R. (2014). *The Essence of Scenarios: Learning from the Shell Experience*. Amsterdam, The Netherlands: Amsterdam University Press.

Zhang, Y., & Yongheng, Z. (2015). Astronomy in the Big Data Era. *Data Science Journal*, 14(11), 1–9.

Zooniverse. (n.d.). Galaxy Zoo. Retrieved July 2019, from Zooniverse: www.zooniverse.org/projects/zookeeper/galaxy-zoo/about/results.

6   Reflections from the field

Perspectives on the societal responsibility of science philanthropy

Exploring the experience of giving for science

The previous chapters highlighted the various ways in which the societal responsibility of science philanthropy is becoming more evident in grantmaking programs and more reflexively embedded in foundation policies and practices. Science philanthropies are starting to weave together support for high-quality scientific research while simultaneously addressing a broader set of considerations that advance a forward-looking mindset, trying to engage members of the public, diversifying who is conducting science, and being more responsive to societal needs. Yet there is more to this story than is apparent just from analyzing examples and case studies that draw on journal articles, foundation strategy documents, website postings, blogs, or magazine profiles. Instead, much of the rationale that underpins these approaches only becomes apparent by talking to the people involved, especially the leaders and practitioners who are responsible for setting the direction of philanthropic institutions. Understanding these viewpoints is critical to gaining a fuller appreciation of the ways in which science philanthropy works today and how it might better address the themes of responsible innovation going forward.

For that reason, I undertook a year-long process of interviewing over 20 science philanthropy representatives, analysts, grantees, and partners to gain a deeper, more nuanced sense of their views associated with how these organizations are already working to reflect the principles of the RRI framework and how they can do so even more concretely in the years ahead. The majority of the interviewees currently work as leaders and staff members in science-funding foundations and span a range of positions, including presidents who guide the overall strategic direction of these institutions; program directors, program officers, and program managers who are responsible for developing and implementing the day-to-day matters of proposal review and grant awarding; and staff in a variety of other positions inside and outside science foundations. In addition to philanthropy, interviewees were based in academic, non-profit, and consulting positions, all of whom were actively involved in working with science philanthropies in some capacity. Many of the interviewees had earlier experience in government, industry, or other kinds of philanthropic institutions, ensuring that these interviews represented a wide range of perspectives, sectors, and institutional types. The majority of the respondents were based in the United States, along with some located in or originally from Europe, and many of the interviewees had extensive experience working on international projects and globally oriented grantmaking. These interviewees were broadly representative in their collective assessments of how science philanthropies can and should approach the tasks they are undertaking, as evidenced by the common themes and even the terminology brought up across the interviews. The interviews took place either in-person or by phone, and the resulting conversations were recorded and transcribed, with only light edits to the transcripts undertaken where necessary to ensure clarity and consistency.

Interviewees both in and outside of science philanthropies not only shared their thoughts on what they think these institutions are able to achieve when it comes to societal responsibility, but they also expressed concerns, revealed critiques, and provided suggestions and recommendations about where these institutions might improve as the field progresses and as new entrants become involved in supporting scientific research. Learning from their words, through the direct quotations presented here, is valuable and constructive. While in almost all instances the interviewees were willing to allow their names to be used here, out of respect for the privacy of their positions and opinions, I have decided not to identify them by name. As a science philanthropy professional, I was continually aware of, and regularly acknowledged, the reflexive nature of these interviews with each discussant. I indicated during every interview that I was conducting this analysis in my personal capacity and that their responses would have no bearing on any current or future professional engagement they may have with me or my employer. Additionally, I have included my assessment and interpretation of the perspectives shared in the analysis below, while clearly differentiating between what was said by a respondent and my perspective on the points being made.

Realizing responsibility: establishing a new culture of science philanthropy

It quickly became apparent that many interviewees had an interest in taking stock of the resurgence of science philanthropy that has taken place over the last decade or so. They recognized that even as these institutions have been built on the long, robust tradition of philanthropic funding for research that originated in the early decades of the 20th Century, as discussed in Chapter 2, the practices and interests of science philanthropy today are inevitably changing and differing from what has come before. Partly this is due to the emergence of a number of newer philanthropies focused on science. For example, one science philanthropy expert highlighted the explosive growth in wealth that has emerged on both coasts—on the West Coast, largely due to the technology sector, and on the East Coast, largely due to the financial sector—and how that infusion of interest and new money is impacting science philanthropy. "I think that the great wealth that has been accumulated in individuals in those two areas has led to new philanthropists at a rate which I don't think has been seen since the Gilded Age," said this interviewee. Another interviewee seconded this point, noting that the growing interest among wealthy individuals giving directly to science, or establishing philanthropic institutions to do so, has impacted the ways in which science philanthropy takes place. "The traditional foundations had to change, adapt, and respond to the new wave of science philanthropists. It just seems like a very different ecosystem for supporting science than the original," noted this individual. I think this is a prescient and accurate insight, and one that serves to underpin many of the RRI-related practices that are discussed throughout this book. Bringing RRI considerations to the forefront requires that science philanthropies operate differently, in particular in terms of paying attention to factors such as broader public engagement, deliberation, diversity, and inclusion.

One of the factors that has led to this resurgence of science philanthropy is an increased willingness by many of these new science funders, and for many existing science philanthropies as well, to try to diversify the range of institutions whose research they support. New donors are becoming more interested in moving beyond funding "their favorite university," as one interviewee said, to identify grantmaking opportunities where their resources might be most useful and valuable. In my view, this is a welcome development, one that has led to an increased recognition among scientists and research institutions about the potential to tap into this emerging next wave of the science philanthropy ecosystem. "I have certainly detected more awareness among the scientific community that foundations are funding actual research," mused one interviewee based at a non-governmental research organization. Of course, as was noted in Chapter 1, each of these funding institutions has adopted different policies and practices that can make this changing landscape difficult to navigate. One researcher reflected on the advice that they give junior scholars interested in engaging newly formed science philanthropies, saying that "the first thing I tell them is every foundation is different and they are different in a lot of ways. It is not just their mission, but things like their receptivity to doing new things to how hands on they are once you get a grant." Furthermore, this interviewee noted how important it is for scientists seeking funding to learn how individual foundations operate, from understanding their high-level missions and thematic areas of interest, all the way down to paying attention to the details of their review timelines, deadlines, and proposal expectations. "You really have to know when things happen with that particular foundation, because if you miss that window, then you are kind of out of the picture," concluded this scholar. The spirit of this advice closely matches the outlook that I usually share with researchers interested in approaching science philanthropies for funding. A fair amount of time is needed by prospective grantees to learn as much as possible about how different foundations operate, how they select projects for funding, and the ways in which they make decisions. Without that information, it can be a challenge for researchers to effectively identify the most promising potential donors to support their work.

Beyond paying attention to institutional philanthropies, or even the giving of high-net-worth individuals, another interviewee described the need to widen the lens of attention even further. For instance, this respondent emphasized that attention should be paid to how universities direct their endowment spending toward research purposes, noting that the corpus of most endowments often stem from philanthropic giving. This respondent lamented that, "when we talk about philanthropy for science, we usually focus on foundations, or individuals giving money for research," while the most substantial amount of philanthropic money for science comes from endowment spending at universities drawn from "legacy philanthropy." Even as this endowment spending on research has grown in recent years, this individual worried about potentially negative implications that have led to increased inequalities across institutions. "There are consequences to this, which are very important, and one is the most obvious, is that the playing field has become much less level for universities and nonprofit research institutes that want to perform basic research." I would argue that one of the reasons as to why there is insufficient attention on this aspect of the science philanthropy landscape is the difficulties inherent in parsing how different universities draw on their endowment and direct such spending for scientific research. Furthermore, this individual was troubled by what this uneven distribution of resources means for scholars, faculty, and researchers at institutions where endowment spending is lower. "It used to be in the 1960s that if you hired great people, they could get all the money they needed from the federal government. But now, the difference between being at a well-endowed institution and a poorly-endowed institution can mean the difference between success and failure." Overcoming these hurdles is a key challenge for science philanthropies. Insights drawn from the RRI framework could help indicate some of the ways in which science philanthropies could play a role in addressing these inequalities, such as by more deliberately looking to allocate resources to faculty and institutions that have less opportunity to draw on internal endowment spending. If these inequities are not addressed in a timely manner, this person warned that only scholars from a select few institutions will have sufficient access to financial resources to carry out their research.

As this institutional ecosystem of science philanthropy has evolved, respondents also noted that a tension has emerged about the ways in which science philanthropies determine how to proceed in terms of funding research, whether the decision criteria should focus solely on the quality of science under consideration or whether broader societal and social responsibility dimensions should be part of the decision-making process. In essence, interviewees were musing on questions related to changing the culture of the research enterprise that were discussed in detail throughout Chapter 4. As argued earlier in this book, one science philanthropy staff member echoed the idea that differentiation among foundations is welcome and that not all philanthropic supporters of science need to answer this question in a similar way. In short, this interviewee noted that the field of science philanthropy is not monolithic. Different institutions can and should decide how much they want to take into consideration societal implications to different degrees. "I think they should let a thousand flowers bloom…there isn't to me any particular reason to think that there's only one best way to do it or that the field as a whole should somehow come to an agreement that we should fund things this way or this is how we should do it," rejoined this foundation staff member. Yet, on the other hand, this individual also noted that because foundations enjoy favorable tax status provided by governments, allowing them to make grants in the first place, there is inevitably a role to play in thinking about the societal impacts of science philanthropy. "The public has an interest in what science philanthropy does, right? We are giving science philanthropists tax credits, so maybe we want to make sure that these philanthropists are deploying these sources to what we think of as the best, most pro-social [way]," remarked this interviewee.

Clearly there is a tension here, one that arises in some of the examples discussed in previous chapters. There is a simultaneous interest in science philanthropies remaining differentiated along many different lines, yet there is also an overarching desire for these institutions to continually find better ways of operating more with societal interests in mind. I think there is an opportunity to harmonize these perspectives. Not only can science philanthropies address societal responsibility in many different ways, but even those funders that choose to remain squarely focused on supporting basic research can still integrate RRI themes in the work they undertake. For instance, examples discussed in previous chapters have shown that there are relatively easily implementable steps that science philanthropies can take to deliberately expand their pool of grantees or to integrate reflexive practices that allows them to better consider the societal implications of what they do. In fact, one researcher who has worked in academic, non-profit, and industry settings made this very point during their interview, commenting on the need for government funders and science philanthropies to think more in terms of a portfolio management strategy. "I personally think if you are trying to assemble a government research portfolio, you have to have components of each. You should have basic use, un-inspired science, and applied, use-inspired science and technology development, and that is how a balanced national innovation portfolio should go."

Moreover, one researcher who regularly seeks funding from foundations commented that they and their colleagues welcome this breadth of interests among institutions. It allows them to pursue support for both basic and more applied purposes simultaneously. They asserted that it is imperative for science philanthropies to sponsor both kinds of activities, "as there are certain scientific endeavors that are solely based on fundamental, basic science where there is no immediate societal payoff, and then there is the exact opposite." Another scholar also asserted a need for science funders to support a continuum of projects, from basic research to research designed to be more oriented toward addressing societal challenges. "I think there is a reason to have both the kind of use inspired research, specifically aimed at solving that problem, but also more basic research." A different individual stated that there are many ways, both large and small, for scientists and science philanthropies to increase the societal relevance of their research, with each researcher needing to be more self-reflective about how they are best positioned to achieve these goals. "Some people like talking to journalists, some want to go to DC, and some want to stay in their community," contemplated this individual, going on to say that what is important for both researchers and funders is that they begin to take whatever steps in these directions that they can.

Contributing to this challenge is that, even despite the rise of science philanthropy in recent years, both those based at philanthropic institutions and those in other sectors recognize that government and federal support for research continues to dwarf the resources available for giving by philanthropic institutions. One science philanthropy funder noted as much, stating that in their organization, "we have to understand where private money can make a difference, because our amount is so much smaller than the federal agencies can spend or that a corporation could spend on its own internal research." There was a sense among interviewees that despite their relatively lower levels of resources, science philanthropies continue to play key roles in the research ecosystem *exactly because* of their ability to adopt various different strategies that fit their unique characteristics. One foundation program lead described the need for each foundation to pinpoint their strengths in order to achieve impact. "What you have to do is identify what aspects your organization can bring...or do particularly well, that maybe others don't do, or don't do as well, that you have an opportunity to make a difference," articulated this interviewee. Yet even taking this valid point, I would contend that science philanthropies can go a step further and, even while operating to maximize their respective strengths, can infuse responsibility more thoroughly into their respective organizations. For instance, one kind of intervention that science philanthropies have typically adopted is provide funding for projects, or components of projects, that government agencies are unable, unwilling, or uninterested to support. In a sense, this kind of grantmaking already demonstrates an element of societal responsibility, as much of this research that falls between the cracks of government funding often includes components that may be more anticipatory, risky, or societally oriented. As one respondent put it, "what foundations can do...is they can sort of fill the gap, things that for one reason or another, the federal government is unwilling to do or is not ready to do." Another researcher noted, "I have definitely appreciated the flexibility the foundations have, the ability to explore new potential research directions." This individual claimed that, "I don't know if sampling is the right word, but you are able to be a little more speculative than say, a federal agency…They certainly do have programs that try to be more speculative, but I think foundations are particularly adept at that." Willingness to support speculative ideas that could have outsize societal impacts is a hallmark of the RRI framework and are another kind of intervention that science philanthropies could excel at supporting if they so choose.

Many interviewees imagined that there are a variety of reasons as to why foundations might be well-positioned to help initiate new lines of inquiry. A key factor is that many foundations have, as part of their stated organizational mission and goals, a desire to be more risk-taking. Therefore, pursuing novel research prospects fits squarely within such mandates. One practitioner conjectured that "foundations have the added value they quite often are closer to the application area and hear from the field in a more direct manner than government. I think just by being able to tap into the ecosystem of grantees or ecosystem of organizations that they partner with will give them, probably, a better sense of opportunities." Of course, for many researchers, receiving foundation funding also serves as an indicator of quality and provides a social marker of legitimization for a project, methodology, or individual that can then be communicated and utilized to secure additional government funding. One researcher who often seeks financial support from foundation and government sources noted as much. This interviewee supposed that, "the cost of getting funds…sometimes it can reach the value of the grant itself. Obviously, if it costs you ninety-nine cents to get a dollar, technically it is definitely worth it. Even if it costs you a buck fifty to get a dollar, it may still be worth it, because you send out signals" that a research project is of high quality. That expert concluded by expressing, "frankly, that just goes to show the importance and power of foundations, philanthropists, donors in general."

Another longtime observer of philanthropic and federal funding noted that foundations can actually use their smaller overall budgets, when compared with federal funders, to their advantage. "In general with foundations, a little bit of money can go a long way, and it can fund some of the most creative ideas that would have a hard time getting through any sort of peer review system" run by government funders, reflected this individual. One foundation program head also noted how their organization recognized the ability of foundations to provide small amounts of money early in a research project to help get it started. "Small amounts of money still can make a big difference when people are thinking about proofs of concept, when they are trying new ideas, when they are seeing if something might work, so seed funding small amounts in fundamental science makes sense." As Chapter 4 showed, one angle that science philanthropies often employ in the context of realizing societal responsibility is in focusing their support on early career researchers, who generally face difficult prospects of getting funding from the federal government and often confront an uphill climb for resources. For instance, one foundation program leader stated that their organization decided to focus on this cohort of early career scholars "because small amounts of money early in a career can have a big difference. Whereas, as a person advances in their career, if they are successful, they have more grant funding, larger grants, and so on. But at the beginning of the career, small amounts can be catalytic and can be very important."

However, as will be discussed more in depth later in this chapter, there were also concerns that science philanthropies can and should do more to live up to these ideals. One veteran observer of philanthropy opined that the extensive talk in the philanthropic community about addressing funding gaps is often masked by the fact that many funders ultimately have a clear sense in advance of what they want to do. "I think many of the philanthropic organizations say they want to identify the gaps where the government is not doing things, where other philanthropists are not doing things. But when they start out with a strong opinion about what they want to support, sometimes that is very difficult," said this interviewee. In my assessment, this is also a fair critique, albeit requiring a fair amount of nuance. On the one hand, funders may have spent a substantial amount of time designing their strategic plans to guide their grantmaking. On the other hand, as this respondent accurately notes, science philanthropies have a unique potential to respond to unanticipated submissions of good ideas and move in new directions in ways that more constrained funders, such as government agencies, are not able to do, at least as quickly. "I think there is a challenge in really identifying where philanthropy can make a difference," declared this respondent. This challenge is particularly difficult when trying to make grants or provide funding in areas that are under-explored in a particular field.

Foundations can conduct funding landscape analyses to gain a better sense about which topics might be receiving less funding from government and other donors, yet in the end, the decision about which areas to enter and which to avoid often comes down to internal strategic decision-making factors. That is why being guided by an overarching strategy is critical within the philanthropic sector. Without the identification of at least notional boundaries provided by an organization's mission, vision, and areas of interest, foundations working in all domains, including science and technology, run the risk of not being as effective or catalytic with their funding as they could be.

Anticipation in practice: broadly scanning for new ideas

Related to this point, I concur with the many respondents who described how important it is for science philanthropies to adopt a more open disposition and willingness to pursue novel ideas from a wide range of sources. Strategies for surfacing new ideas vary considerably among organizations. Many foundation staff who were interviewed noted that the broader their network of contacts and relationships are, the more extensive and comprehensive the incoming input stream of ideas seem to be. As one foundation program director expressed, "I like to describe it as advanced networking." This interviewee continued by characterizing their networking strategy thusly: "I talk to everybody who will talk to me…and I will ask these very open-ended questions. Sort of, 'What do you think is really cool that's going on right now, but that you are not working on yourself?'…Getting them to talk about other things, and other people, and other institutions other than themselves, and it is sort of like this game of connect the dots." Finally, this interviewee concluded this part of the conversation by relaying the details of their thought process when it comes to scanning for new ideas:

> If one person says, "Oh, there's person X. They're really cool." I think, "Oh that is good." File away in my little mental Rolodex. I talk to Person Two, and [they say], "Oh, there is this person X." It is like, "Oh, interesting. The same person X, or the same topic X, or the same institution X."…I'm looking for everything all the time. But when I start getting multiple people all commenting about the same topic, the same person, the same institution, [I think], "Oh wait, two years ago someone told me about topic X. So many people think that something is happening here. I need to go dig deeper into that whatever that is."…Being able to collect collective wisdom is really powerful.

The views of a representative from another foundation resonated on this point, describing how important it is to engage the research community when identifying new areas of investigation, especially by asking subject matter experts about who else they know who is working on a particular problem of interest. As they affirmed, "when you call experts, the thing to do is always say 'Who else should I be talking to? Who are the people that you would recommend we talk to?'"

Another science funder described how they rely on insights from the social sciences to underpin their approach of seeking out multiple points of view when determining which research areas to pursue. "There is all this social science work on wicked problems and complex problems. In the face of that complexity, institutions and approaches to addressing it are likely to be more robust if they are pluralistic. If you have a bunch of different buckshot approaches, instead of a silver bullet approach, it can feel messier and less efficient but…[this silver bullet approach] can backfire because you are losing diversity of thought." Other funders seek input from the research community in related ways as well. Said one science philanthropy program leader who oversees funding programs for academic research, "when we are thinking about funding researchers at universities, we often have ideas that come up from them…If we are looking at a big strategic priority area, then what we need to do is almost do the mapping before we begin to understand where we fit in the system and who else we would need to engage with if we were trying to make a change happen." Another funder got more specific, giving details on the various strategies they use to identify research opportunities. "For us, it is really important to find a niche and we use a variety of methods," noted this interviewee. "We stay up to date on *Science* and *Nature*. We try to have an ear to the ground from the National Academies. We have a science advisory board, and we take input from them about ideas."

While a number of science philanthropies draw on external subject matter experts to serve as science advisors, participate as review committee members, or conduct landscape analyses, at least one interviewee suggested that science foundations should do more to collaborate on their idea generating processes. "I wonder if there is some sort of analogy to the decadal review type process, where a group of foundations could actually go to a scientific discipline and say, 'Help us sort through a list of your priorities,' but in this case, it would actually be 'Give us the top ten things that aren't being funded by federal government.'" I think this is a particularly interesting idea in the sense that it would facilitate learning and systematize ways in which foundations identify and pursue new ideas. Moreover, this approach is likely to be efficient and cost effective, as funders could pool their resources to undertake such structured reviews and avoid having to duplicate the effort. Lastly, by pooling resources and linking networks, these processes could be helpful to regularize what can become a bespoke and sometimes narrow input process and serve to socialize new ideas among a broader range of funders. As one science philanthropy program leader noted, foundations need to pay attention to a more diverse set of perspectives from across different research communities and gain a deeper sense of the needs they face. In their view, listening to what a community requires to be successful is a critical skill. "You have to figure out what the community is thinking about, who the thought leaders are in that community, and also not have hubris," this individual mused. "Don't just assume because that you think you know that things are going to be better. You have to actually listen to people, and understand where they are coming from…It requires an awful lot of time and effort."

Conversely, some researchers in the field highlighted that, because of the high-level view that many foundation program leads have about the fields in which they work, those in the research community can benefit greatly from learning about the perspective of funders, thereby welcoming feedback that often comes from conversations with foundation staff. One researcher avowed as much, commenting that "in my opinion, and I am not just saying this to flatter you, there is nobody better to talk to than a foundation officer about a project you are wanting to do, because you have this great view of the landscape." This interviewee continued by expanding on this idea:

> You have worked with a lot of other grantees, you attend a lot of conferences, you really have this kind of 360 degree view of the research landscape and the policy landscape. That is just incredibly helpful, and you can give us pointers on projects, you can connect your grantees. That is actually a really useful function that is beneficial, both to the work, but also just for the design of a new research project. I think that kind of deep and broad knowledge that foundations can offer to a prospective grantee are sort of the two top functions that I think you have.

One foundation representative noted that the need to engage the scientific community is one of the reasons that donors new to science can find it difficult to identify effective entry points. If those donors do not yet have established networks within the scientific community, developing them can be challenging and time consuming. This interviewee remarked that for those who are entering an area of science for the first time, there is often "not a natural point of entry" into funding such research. These new donors "need people who understand the systems and speak the language" of science. As previous chapters have discussed, this is one of the core rationales behind the creation of the Science Philanthropy Alliance by established foundations, to help newer donors learn how to go about funding science effectively. In fact, one interviewee commented about the extent to which it is difficult for new donors to get started in funding science. "These folks who want to support science find it frightening," said one respondent, as these individuals or institutions do not have the long-standing history, review procedures, or readily available scientific expertise to assess the quality of competing research proposals. This interviewee rounded out this notion, saying "it is so easy to make mistakes, it is so easy to give all your money to some charismatic scientist and then have the scientific communities scoff at you and say you are wasting your money." Donors, both established and new to science, do not want to be misled or duped into funding research that cannot withstand scientific scrutiny. This respondent elucidated this point further:

> I think that may be true in all areas of philanthropy, but it is particularly true in science because the expertise in any field is spread over many institutions, and if you want to make a difference, there are many ways of doing it. But if you want to make a difference by creating a new program, then you have the problem with finding out who are the best people, where are they, and how do you support them, and you have to figure out what mechanism you are going to use.

Adding to this challenge is that science funders have become increasingly interested in finding ways of pinpointing truly breakthrough ideas. The head of one science philanthropy shared their organization's outlook on this topic, which is that new discoveries generally only come from getting researchers to work out of their comfort zone, either by conducting research in different institutional forms or by collaborating with scholars from other disciplines. In order to facilitate discovery, funders "almost have to remove people from the current institutional milieu" in order to "pursue work that is heterodox" and that "questions the status quo," said this respondent. These are certainly two strategies that can help lead scientists to conduct pathbreaking work, and as has been discussed, the formation of in-house research centers within science philanthropies serves as an example of how to implement this approach. One observer and practitioner in this field discussed the ways in which newer "philanthropists are trying new structures," with some testing out the establishment of in-house research centers and others setting up their organizations in different corporate forms to allow them to have influence in the scientific enterprise using a wider array of financial tools.

Yet I would also argue that there are other ways for scientists to advance new ideas within existing institutional settings, especially if science philanthropies provide incentives to researchers to follow these new directions. For instance, one researcher shared the viewpoint that another productive way for foundations to advance science is to focus on promoting interdisciplinary research. This individual noted that, "I think for things that are really, truly revolutionary, you have to kind of bring different fields together because people don't know each other in other fields." Another scholar commented on the rise of prize-oriented philanthropy to promote innovation. The use of prizes has gained more attention in recent years within the philanthropic community as donors look to invert the traditional model of grantmaking, with awards only made once a set of clear and demonstrable goals has been accomplished. This scholar characterized the situation by stating, "both the feds [federal government] and the philanthropies have perhaps over the past decade or so, been experimenting with prizes...I think the literature is pretty clear that they work...only if there is a very clear goal or aim to the competition."

Nevertheless, despite these generally positive takes on how science philanthropies source ideas from their respective networks, concerns also arose in the discussions—concerns that I also share—as respondents worried about whether science philanthropies seek to fund a sufficiently diverse set of researchers. Many researchers who were interviewed shared consternation about the invitation-only stance that many foundations have toward considering unsolicited proposals. Critiques were voiced that foundations can have their own set of preferential grantees and that they too often look to fund a relatively limited pool of individuals or institutions. One respondent shared that, "you will see a good number of foundations where things are invitation only, they are only going to invite certain people to submit a proposal to them. And that always irritates me, because...they are not necessarily willing to take, to even consider, somebody who had a new idea that might be new to the spectrum." One researcher stated bluntly, "there is an ability for me to make a personal relationship [with foundations]...Now there are advantages and disadvantages to this. The disadvantage is this can lead to corruption or nepotism, where if there is some kind of improper relationship between a grant giver and a grantee, the best project doesn't get funded." One interviewee acknowledged the power dynamics that exist between those giving and asking for funding. This individual pointed out that funders have a need to be mindful of this power differential, asserting that "the funders just have a lot more power than the research proposal writers."

In fact, a third interviewee raised the concern that this more interpersonal approach to grantmaking can influence how extensively proposed projects get reviewed. This individual said, "I think that in some quarters, there is a perception that foundation-funded research is not always vetted to the same extent as, for example, the National Science Foundation would vet a proposal." This interviewee commented on how the importance of these interpersonal dynamics arose more commonly in the philanthropic world than in the provision of government funding. A fourth interviewee reiterated this point, recounting how their interactions with science philanthropies over time had been "seemingly idiosyncratic" and "that perhaps the reputation for flexibility is well earned, but that flexibility comes at a cost of probably greater emphasis on social networks and personal relationships." This person continued by saying, "I think there is at least a significant external perception, possibly a reality, that there are...a set of relationships between known PIs [primary investigators] and known program officers." This is a fair point raised about an uneasiness with the concentration of support that may be given to a select number of researchers. "I think it is probably the case that, at this point, there is some chasing of prestige by funders, perhaps both public sector and philanthropic, where the reputations of funders are enhanced by the reputations of the people they fund. So, you end up with a much less well distributed funding system that you ought to have," said this interviewee.

In addition to raising questions about how science philanthropies source ideas, interviewees also raised questions about foundation capacity to assess and review proposals. One respondent noted that while many existing philanthropies have developed extensive grant selection processes, many newer donors have less explicit assessment processes and review criteria. This individual pronounced that while long-standing foundations have "a process that is pretty visible that has been kicked around, the tires have been kicked for decades," they expressed a concern that "there are fewer and fewer foundations that actually look or feel anything like NSF, or anything the government would fund. I just think they are more directive; they have almost become NGOs [non-governmental organizations]." This respondent broadened this appraisal by describing how new donors may even be bringing a different set of ethical considerations to the funding of science. This respondent hypothesized by saying, "the other thing that worries me is 'What kind of value and ethical system do these people bring into the funding space?'" They continued to conjecture that, "there was this kind of idea that these people were kind of visionaries and potentially could be trusted, it was like 'do no evil'. And then it became 'move fast and break things.' I am afraid that ethos goes into their funding." I contend that a balance needs to be struck between the speed and flexibility of a review process, on one hand, and its depth and thoroughness, on the other. As has been shown, each set of criteria speaks to a different set of values that those inside and outside of science philanthropy aim to have expressed, often simultaneously: on one side, nimbleness and agility and, on the other, rigor and analysis. In my experience, there is generally no hard-and-fast rule about how to balance these factors; situational awareness, recognition of context, and good judgement are what is needed in each instance to determine when speed or rigor should take precedence.

Furthermore, an additional criticism that arose in the interviews is the need to avoid following a herd mentality when it comes to deciding which programmatic paths to follow or which grants to make. One science philanthropy staff member mentioned that "my argument is we have more to fear from groupthink, as an industry, than we have to fear from the assumption that we should all be doing the same kind of thing." That individual pointed out that one of the results of this "groupthink" mentality is the preponderance of biomedical and disease-specific research funding within the philanthropic community. "Most science funding…is medical research. It gets a tremendous amount of attention. There are tons of foundations everywhere on it…They are giving money to doctors and they are trying to find new treatments, they are trying to find a cure." That is not surprising, given the critical importance and high stakes of those interventions, yet it often overshadows or crowds-out support for other forms of investigation.

Finally, respondents also noted that, even given the progress that has been made on these issues of late, science philanthropies can and should continue to do more to further address diversity, equity, and inclusion issues as they scan the landscape for funding opportunities. Chapter 4 highlighted some of the ways in which foundations are working to pay more attention to these considerations in terms of how grantees are chosen for funding and which researchers ultimately receive funding awards. One science philanthropy program leader noted that even just acknowledging the inevitable presence of implicit biases in decision-making, and then proactively working to address them, are critical steps that every grantmaking institution needs to adopt. This interviewee documented the many steps their organization took to better account for these diversity, equity, and inclusion dimensions within their grantmaking. "In one of our science fellowship programs, we have redone everything, from throwing out a nominations process and doing an applications process; now handling all the applications in-house to understand the demographics [of applicants]; redoing our application to include a Diversity, Equity, and Inclusion statement; and redoing how we do the panel review based on research that has shown best practices." This interviewee reflected further on their foundation's experiences in trying to hold themselves to a higher standard when it comes to these matters. "Everyone has biases, and what we have come to the conclusion at our foundation…is, we need to understand what those biases are. We need to understand how we intervene knowing that those biases are there and how to create a more diverse pool of grantees by confronting those biases, using known research of how to deal with those biases to as much as possible minimize them." This interviewee concluded by providing an encouraging and uplifting message regarding how other funders could follow in their footsteps. "We re-defined what success looked like. We have that capability, and we could serve as role models…Everybody can be doing better."

Diversifying perspectives: are science philanthropies sufficiently flexible and willing to take risks?

As mentioned initially above, in addition to the notion that science philanthropies should pursue a broader range of ideas by a wider array of potential grantees, interviewees also contemplated the extent to which science philanthropies demonstrate flexibility and nimbleness in what they do. This is a consideration reflected on by interviewees from both inside and outside philanthropic institutions and one that arose repeatedly during the interviews. For instance, one researcher shared their view that philanthropies can often fund interdisciplinary research more easily than government agencies. They noted, "I think a foundation can fund interdisciplinary, non-siloed research in a way that many government funding mechanisms fail to do." Moreover, this person expressed that, "government funding mechanisms are pretty siloed and often in today's scientific challenges, what we want to do is assemble the best team across disciplines and solve a problem, which may or may not fall within a disciplinary boundary." One foundation program officer posited that one indicator favorably demonstrating that philanthropies can operate rather flexibly is that "natural scientists, engineering researchers, and social scientists [are] increasingly turning to foundations for money for the stuff that the public sector, at least in the U.S., just seems unwilling to fund." Another foundation program leader echoed this point, a commonly held view among science philanthropy staff members. "What we like to think is that certainly, as foundations, we are able to be agile. We are able to make decisions in a way that enables us to capitalize on something that could ultimately lead to a system change in terms of the way that government funders work," noted this respondent. This interviewee continued by describing the broad leeway and freedom that foundations have in funding science as they see fit.

Interviewees identified different aspects of flexibility that science philanthropies have demonstrated. One researcher pointed to instances where some foundations have expressed an increased willingness to support research that might result in a range of different outputs that go beyond academic, peer-reviewed publications. "If I apply for some sort of government grant, my types of outputs would be much more narrowly defined. [Foundation funding] gives me so much flexibility to achieve the outcomes I want and...support a diversity of outputs that is helpful toward achieving overall outcomes." Another dimension of this flexibility is the ability of philanthropies to provide funding at the very early stage of a project, either to generate new ideas or to develop new relationships with individuals or institutions. One science philanthropy program officer expanded on this notion, describing how their organization determines where to allocate its resources. "We are looking for early seed, for cross disciplinary [ideas], for inputting an idea that works in a totally different field into a new field," stated that respondent. Another researcher reiterated this point, noting that many foundations can more easily provide small amounts of seed funding rather quickly, an underappreciated characteristic of their contribution to the research enterprise.

The issue then becomes whether this operational flexibility translates into an increased appetite for funding riskier research projects. As one interviewee contemplated, "I think it is an open question as to whether foundations are indeed funding riskier research." This respondent expounded on this point, describing their personal perspective "that foundations remain willing to experiment with new modes [of funding science]…which become models for how federal agencies can encourage more risky research." Even determining what exemplifies a riskier project was up for debate. "One of the challenges is we don't have any measures of riskiness. We don't know when a research project is high-risk, high-reward," pondered this interviewee. The lack of agreed-upon definitions or measures as to what would constitute risky research is a key barrier here. Philanthropic support for scientific research that, say, utilizes methodologies which are untried or untested is a different kind of risk-taking than, say, funding early career scholars who may not yet have an extensive history of accomplishments on their resume. Another practitioner noted that even as science philanthropies are pushed to be more risk-taking that an increased penchant for funding risky projects might have its own downsides and drawbacks. Referring to the ability of foundations to pursue ideas as they see fit, this interviewee pronounced, "I think there is a big risk there that if they do too many crazy things, the public will say they are not using their money well." Again, a tension exists here between science philanthropies looking to advance cutting-edge science with trying to do more to address concerns of societal responsibility. Being willing to devote more money to high-risk projects could lead the work that funders support to be less centered on having immediate societal impact.

While many shared the view that science philanthropies are more flexible and are able take more risks than government or industry funders, there were also dissenting voices among the group of interviewees that are important to note. One respondent called this assessment of foundations being more flexible and risk-taking to be mostly theoretical rather than experienced in practice. One scholar stated as much, commenting that, "I guess that the inherited wisdom has been that foundations are more flexible, more agile, are able to move into new areas of research in a leading way. Faster than the federal government, take a little more risk, and then move out of areas as the feds [federal government] move in, if and when they move in." Unfortunately, in this person's view, "I have really no great sense of whether that ever really was or, whether that if it was, whether that is still in fact the case. Because in broad brush strokes, it seems to me that the same kinds of overall profiles occur with private philanthropy as with federal spending." In other words, this interviewee has the view that all the talk about philanthropies being flexible and risk-taking is mainly rhetoric. This expert further detailed their views by referring to the ways in which philanthropic and government funding for science has tended to converge in terms of style and approach. This interviewee expressed the perspective that, over the years, both of these types of science funding organizations have moved toward funding larger-scale research projects in the biomedical and physical sciences, more so than in other areas of the natural sciences or in the social sciences. "At least in broad brushstrokes, there is seemingly a great similarity between the overall areas of funding" undertaken by government and philanthropic support for science, concluded this interviewee, raising doubts about the extent to which a commitment to move in new directions is really a hallmark of activity within science philanthropy.

Extending science philanthropy to new domains: finding new intervention opportunities in data science and climate change

Related to this question of whether or not science philanthropies are more or less willing to take risks and to support more speculative efforts in certain fields, respondents tended to mention a handful of topic areas where they thought that science philanthropies are starting to become more interested in advancing cutting-edge research. Perhaps not surprisingly, many interviewees thought that more foundations should be funding more research to accelerate novel discoveries in the physical sciences. "There are opportunities being missed in the physical sciences because there is not as much attention," declared one individual, a point recited by many others with whom I spoke. One program director noted the relative lack of funding by philanthropies in the physical sciences was a key reason for their foundation working in these domains. This person recounted that, "there is really a need to make sure that people don't lose sight of the importance of fundamental science...I think people have a difficulty of understanding why fundamental science is so important." That respondent continued by suggesting their institution's emphasis on supporting research in the physical sciences is a deliberate effort to carve out a unique niche in the science philanthropy landscape, again referencing the predominance of funding for biomedical research. For instance, this program officer announced that, "we have chosen to operate in the space primarily of the physical sciences because a whole lot of money has come in to play that can support biomedical development." Along these lines, another interviewee relayed that, "of course, there is a huge disparity between physical sciences and life sciences. There is a disparity in federal funding as well, but I think it is even more extreme than philanthropy."

A second topic area that received substantial attention during the discussions as being a key area for funding among science philanthropies is data science. In particular, interviewees referred to many of the themes that arise from the RRI framework, stating that foundations should pay more attention to funding research that centers on how data analytics tools and techniques can be applied to address societal challenges. One expert highlighted the contribution that science philanthropies are already making in this domain, all the while cautioning that when it comes to sifting through the breathless claims often associated with the rise of data science that "the big challenge, as always, is to understand what is hype and what is real." This data science expert continued by presenting the view that "big data and data science can make an impact in a variety of ways that are of importance to philanthropy... improving the way they go about solving public problems or the way big data can be applied to solving the problems that philanthropists care about." In particular, interviewees pointed out that a particularly impactful role that science philanthropies could play is by supporting the training and education of scholars to develop skills in multiple domains. Foundation funding can help foster the advancement of individuals who have developed expertise in specific scientific disciplines along with the practices of cutting-edge data science. This aforementioned expert put this point as follows: "It is important to develop those [research] questions by teaching what I call 'bilinguals,' by which I mean people that have familiarity or are experts in one domain but are also data scientists or have familiarity with data science."

Yet, despite the vast promise, foundations still face many challenges when entering the domain of data science. For one, this individual observed that some foundations may not have the requisite technical knowledge to extensively engage the data science research community. "Quite often, they don't have data scientists on staff. They don't really have a sense of what is required," said this respondent. Interviewees also shared the perspective that established philanthropic organizations may need to adjust how they approach and work with grantees in the field of data science. For instance, given how quickly the state of research in data science can change, I would concur with the interviewees I spoke with, who suggested that foundations should begin to adopt practices that better align with the rapid pace at which these fields evolve. As an example, some of the experts challenged the notion of having fixed grant metrics and firm deliverable expectations at the outset of a project. Data science research can be highly unpredictable and iterative, they said, so that measuring progress toward a particular fixed end goal as part of an innovative data science research effort can be highly challenging. Relatedly, they also noted that research using the tools of data science tends to advance in short bursts of activity. It is less plausible for these projects to have to follow a two- or five-year research plan established at the outset of a project, remarked one interviewee, even though typical foundation funding might expect such linear developments. "You have to have a more agile approach," said this individual, one that better conforms to the particular norms of different fields of research.

Another key challenge a respondent identified is the tendency of funders to focus mainly on utilizing methodological approaches that data science provides without paying sufficient attention to the importance of the research question that these methods are geared toward addressing. "In order for data science to matter, you need to focus on the questions that matter that data science can help address," said one interviewee. In more than one instance, interviewees lamented missed opportunities where philanthropic funding went more toward advancing exciting data science interventions as opposed to working more deliberately to answer a particular research question that was of interest to a broad range of stakeholders, including citizens and members of local communities. To address this problem, interviewees identified opportunities for foundations to use data analytics more reflexively, to better understand their own operations, to identify under-explored or missed opportunities, and to illuminate trends within their own grantmaking about which these institutions might be unaware. Some suggested that science philanthropies build out additional expertise in data science within their professional staff. Others suggested changes to how foundations set their strategic direction and choose program areas for further exploration. As one interviewee questioned hypothetically, "'To what extent can data science also be a tool for actual decision-making within foundations?' is an aspect that has not been sufficiently focused on."

Interviewees noted that data science presents an opportunity for foundations to support multidisciplinary research that not only combines the natural sciences and the social sciences, but also that intersects with humanities and the arts. One funder pointed out that bridging the gap between research and ethics when it comes to data science is a space that is ripe for foundation intervention. "If you can influence the outcome of the product and what actually hits the market and infuse it with more ethics, then that is really what we would classify as norm shifting," said this respondent. "There's going to be a whole learning curve for everyone in this space, I think, to understand what ethics mean in tech." In this person's view, foundations have a central role to play in nurturing those conversations and helping to create the conditions that would allow stakeholders from different fields and disciplines to come together. "At the end of the day," they summarized, "it is just an exercise of asking the right questions at the right time in the product cycle in order to make it better."

In addition to helping realize advancements in the application of data science techniques in different domains of science and technology, another area of investigation that interviewees discussed in depth, and that they thought of as being poised for philanthropic intervention, is helping to address climate change and environmental challenges. There was general consensus that foundations have a critical role to play in developing new approaches to help society develop mitigation and adaptation strategies in response to the impacts of climate change. However, there was also a sense that the philanthropic community needs to adjust how it currently approaches these issues. One interviewee involved in funding climate change related activities reflected on this point by posing the following question to their fellow philanthropic community: "If you wanted to spend money effectively around climate change mitigation, how would you think about doing the work differently?" This respondent continued by noting that philanthropies need to support more diverse approaches and a range of different interventions. "There is a large debate to be had about what the proper role of government should be in responding to this threat, but the point is foundations have done a lot of work to limit our options, to limit the conversation," stipulated that individual. In particular, this expert took the view that philanthropies engaged in addressing climate change needed to redirect funds toward supporting high-risk, and potentially high-reward, basic science research. This interviewee did not foresee other funders or stakeholders in the field, whether government or industry, putting the necessary resources into backing this kind of research. "It should be obvious to anyone that there are going to be investments that need to be made in basic science and a whole range of things where private capital just can't go. There is no return on investment, or if there is a return on investment, it is five, or 10, or 20 years out, and it is completely unpredictable."

Moreover, a number of interviewees responded that in addition to supporting more basic science to address the challenges posed by climate change, there are another series of efforts in this area in substantial need of attention from the philanthropic community. These relate to better engaging members of the public, particularly in terms of supporting larger-scale dialogue and engagement efforts, along with efforts that apply scientific findings to inform policymaking. Doing so, in the views of many experts I spoke with, has the potential to improve how foundations are held accountable to society at large, not just in terms of addressing the climate challenge but even more broadly on a host of other issue areas. "The questions of accountability with philanthropy tend to be more about a handful of people, basically at institutional philanthropies, who can decide the terms of the debate for climate policy," said one foundation representative. In other words, this concern loops back to the critiques of philanthropy that were discussed in Chapter 1, with the apprehension being that a small number of grantmaking institutions can have a potentially outsized influence on the questions that are and are not being addressed by researchers. It is important to emphasize that this point is particularly salient for funders involved in climate science and policy: whenever philanthropies involved in this area choose to narrow or expand the focus of their funding, such decisions have larger-scale, widespread societal ramifications that must be kept top of mind.

Another interviewee meticulously summarized the pitfalls that some philanthropies have experienced when it comes to thinking about their role in ensuring the societal responsibility of grants made in the areas of climate and energy. This interviewee observed:

> Efforts to engage the public, I don't think they have been very effective for a whole variety of reasons, and we have not been very good at learning from our mistakes…There is kind of a basic assumption that the science is in some way the problem and that if we could just persuade people of the science that suddenly the public would kind of jump on board with the solution set, our preferred solution set. I think that became obviously wrong a long time ago, but it still seems to be kind of our default mode of thinking about this stuff.

A similar perspective that emerged from interviews with subject matter experts on this topic is that philanthropies have the potential to intervene in many different ways in terms of tackling climate change. In fact, many respondents noted that since philanthropies have less money to spend than government funders, a better way for these institutions to direct their dollars is to identify niche areas or under-explored topics that foundations can help advance. Following this initial infusion of philanthropic funding, these researchers might then be able to reach the point where they are competitive for larger amounts of government funding down the line. One foundation representative commented that, "I think it is hard to overstate the power philanthropy has in framing research priorities and action priorities on public policy. I think that might be where we have the most power." Moreover, this philanthropy representative noted that without a deliberate and explicit process for identifying research priorities, foundations may simply be "throwing more money" at the problem of climate change and are unlikely to achieve results that respond to societal needs. "There has been a lot of complaining about the size of the energy research budgets being so small relative to other sectors. I think that is fair, but I am also not of the view that just like throwing more money at it is going to solve the problem," said this individual. This interviewee continued by laying out their strategic considerations about how to best direct philanthropic dollars in this area. This individual stipulated, "the way that I think about our portfolio at a philanthropy around energy innovation is 'What can we do to impact, sort of reform, the way that money is spent, rather than just fund more of it?'"

Lastly, many interviewees stressed an idea that refers back to the final dimension of the RRI framework laid out in Chapter 3: the need for philanthropies to apply the principles of societal responsibility more reflexively, to themselves. For instance, one foundation representative suggested, "I will say that I have been sort of surprised...how little actually the evidentiary basis seems to matter at a lot of foundations." This interviewee stressed that foundations that focus on funding research need to consistently look for opportunities to draw on evidence when it comes to informing how they make decisions and in determining which projects to support. Another interviewee raised a related point, describing that there is a need for foundations to marry evidence-based decision-making with a deeper appreciation and understanding of the worldviews that are present in the public at large. This funder noted, "there is a need for value judgments or value observations that go along with agreeing to certain scientific outlooks." Moreover, this funder shared the view that scientific research, while necessary, cannot often adjudicate among the many complex issues that arise when it comes to addressing climate change. In their view, disagreements over values cannot be solved by science alone, nor by research undertaken in a single discipline. Instead, it requires research that is more integrated across the natural and social sciences, research that, to paraphrase their view, combines work in sociology and economics with work in fields like engineering or the health sciences. "In most cases, you are going to need to understand communities or their social values" along with the basic physical, chemical, or biological functions of a natural system, said this interviewee. In short, "there is no ready scientific answer...because it depends so much on community, different perspectives, and different needs" across various stakeholder groups, requiring that philanthropies continually reflect on whether they have a sufficiently diverse array of scholars, practitioners, and institutions represented in their grantmaking portfolio.

Advancing collective responsiveness by realizing partnerships and promoting learning

In addition to these specific disciplinary opportunities where philanthropies can have an impact in terms of fostering research that is societally relevant, another critical aspect associated with philanthropic involvement in the scientific enterprise that emerged throughout the interviews relates to the potential for learning across sectors and seeding new partnerships. In particular, a number of discussions centered on the importance of foundations working together more frequently and helping to expand collaborative research partnerships. In many instances, respondents commented on the ability of foundations to support research that could subsequently go on to receive federal funding. One science policy expert noted as much, stating that, "we have ideas for federal policies coming from the foundation sector…science policy inspiration is something that goes from the foundation sector to the federal sector." As an example of such "inspiration" flowing from the philanthropic sector to government, this expert portrayed how the qualities and characteristics of many fellowship programs started in foundations tend to inform and influence similar fellowship programs run by government funders.

In fact, when describing the potential of science philanthropies to promote learning across sectors and help advance funding partnerships, a number of interviewees happened to use the same word to describe the nature of these activities: matchmaker. I find this linguistic similarity particularly intriguing, as it reflects a shared view about the nature of collaboration among foundations. One science funder proclaimed that, "we really see ourselves as matchmakers, as network builders." This individual continued by fleshing out different dimensions of this idea relating how their institution approaches partnership building, recounting that they aspire "to identify something to work on together where both organizations feel that it can really advance areas that they are interested in, where they have a benefit from working together. They see that as mutually beneficial." This respondent gave further detail on their perspective about how to work collaboratively across organizations:

> I think there are a lot of obvious reasons why foundations should work together. If you are in a space where you want to advance a certain area of science, and more than one foundation is coordinating, it has an opportunity to be more effective. I think it also sends a message to the people that might be involved that might get funded that more than one foundation considers this area important. There is a shared view of why this is an area that we should try to advance.

As someone who has been involved in developing and participating in a handful of partnerships across philanthropies, I can attest that the rationale shared above very much matches the strategic reasoning that foundations typically use to justify the formation of funding partnerships. Going one step further, another foundation representative stressed the broader societal value of foundations working more closely together to realize synergies that strengthen grantmaking across institutions. "I think what would be lovely to see, in terms of how philanthropies work, is that there is greater partnership in areas where it suits and meets people's needs, so that you could get much more of an impact by collaborating." Societal responsibility is enhanced when foundations deliberately work to see their respective funding as part of a larger system and look to find ways of strengthening the ways that their own grantmaking links with others. Conversely, a program manager at a non-governmental research organization lamented what happens when this matchmaking function falls short and prospects for collaboration are not realized. "That is kind of this missed opportunity," highlighted this individual, "where you have funds available, and you have a set of proposals, and there is just no matchmaker to put them together."

One observer of the science philanthropy landscape noted an uptick in interest among science-oriented foundations to partner with one another, particularly interactions between existing and new institutions, in order to share learning and best practices. This interviewee described how "partnerships between emerging philanthropies and the established ones" have become increasingly common, in part, because many new "philanthropists don't even understand themselves exactly what they want to do." This individual accentuated how such partnerships between established and emerging philanthropic institutions have great potential in terms of sharing best practices across organizations and giving new donors a sense of what kinds of policies and procedures might work well and which ones might have drawbacks. Collaborations among existing and established philanthropic organizations also allow these institutions to take advantage of their complementary characteristics. For instance, partnerships can bring together funders focused on different disciplinary areas, scientific fields, career stages, and geographies to work together. One foundation representative described how there is "important fundamental science that could really benefit from bringing together early career folks, networking them, bringing them across disciplines" in ways that are only possible by multiple foundations collaborating with one another. "We have been willing to work, for example, in the spaces that bring physicists and biologists together, or chemists and biologists together, recognizing that things in fundamental science that they discover may end up having impact in biomedical [science] or could be very important, but also need cross-disciplinary connections," reported this interviewee. This person further affirmed that, "we recognize that we have an opportunity to do that. We have got a lot of emphasis on the cross-disciplinary connection of people as we choose problems."

However, both researchers and practitioners sounded notes of caution as well when it came to the details that accompany the implementation of funding partnerships. While there are many benefits to partnerships between multiple foundations and between philanthropy and government, I can also attest that realizing their full potential is not easy or straightforward. One philanthropy representative described this conundrum by suggesting that, "partnerships are actually really, really, really hard, and everybody wants them." This interviewee continued by stating that "partnerships are so much more subtle than that." For instance, one respondent mentioned that when embarking on multi-institutional funding partnerships, foundations have to be willing to share, or even give up, some of the credit and attention they might normally receive when supporting research on their own. "Where philanthropies have got a key role to play is in…contributing to systematic change or contributing through capitalizing something with recognition that you can't get sole attribution," avowed this interviewee. In other words, achieving successful collaborative partnerships among science philanthropies involves much more than merely combining funds or pledging additional dollars for research. Funders need to align on a whole host of different critical factors, from gaining agreement on the desired outcomes of the collaboration to determining how key decisions about resource allocation will be made.

This respondent expounded further on both the opportunities and challenges that arise from foundations looking to partner with one another more closely, making clear that the rationale for partnership needs to go beyond a mere desire to augment funding levels with each other's resources. "It is not just moving money around," said this interviewee. "It is the expertise, and the connections, and the motivations, and the interests, and all of those things are wrapped up and have to be understood and dealt with really carefully, so that it is more than just the sum of the parts." This respondent concluded by reaffirming that successful partnerships are characterized by bringing together the strengths of different philanthropies to realize greater societal impact. "If you really want a partnership to make a difference, it has got to take advantage of all of those different components, so it really does do something more and something special, and only then is it worth it."

Recommendations for the path ahead: embracing complexity, addressing global challenges, and recognizing the value of a long time horizon

This chapter has assessed the views from scholars, practitioners, and observers of the science philanthropy community about how to address a number of important considerations when it comes to advancing various dimensions of societal responsibility of research and innovation. To summarize, respondents discussed the need to establish a new culture of science philanthropy, emphasized the importance of broadly scanning for ideas, expressed the importance of operating in a more flexible and risk-taking manner, called for a willingness to examine new domains and fields of study, and signified the centrality of learning and devoting resources to collaborative funding partnerships. Furthermore, interviewees communicated their hopes, expectations, and recommendations about what science philanthropies can do as interest grows in paying more attention to matters of societal responsibility.

So, what has been learned from this critical assessment of these views? To start, there was a strong sense that philanthropic funders of science and innovation can do even more *to support efforts that take a more integrative, systems-level view of the fields in which they are involved.* One philanthropy representative called on these institutions to more fully embrace, and work to address, the complexity of the challenges they wish to solve. This individual offered, "I think the issue is, when we look at foundations and philanthropy much more generally, motivations are quite different in some areas. Whether or not we truly understand how the whole system works is an interesting question in its own right." This interviewee reflected on their own institution's continual push in this direction. "One of the things we try and do is we try and push broader issues in relation to how the system's structured," they said. When it comes to training doctoral students, for instance, this individual recommended looking beyond narrow indicators or metrics of success. "It is not just about the excellent science of the programs...we are trying to change the culture and the way in which training is delivered, structured, so that it is looking at the individual. It is looking at where that individual might end up in the system."

I argue that foundation leaders should continue to devote substantial energy to infusing their organizations with this societally oriented mindset, with many interviewees marking this idea as critically important as well. Foundation staff and leaders need to remain sensitized both to the needs of the research community and to the ongoing necessity of better connecting the results of basic scientific research to society at large. Asked how these linkages could be bolstered more intentionally, one researcher expressed that the more the societal relevance of science and technology is considered to be part of the core mission of science philanthropies, the better these institutions will be positioned to fund research, training, and other activities that makes these relationships more apparent and more central. Another researcher encouraged these decision-makers to set targets or benchmarks for how much of their grantmaking resources would go toward ensuring that their research has a greater impact on society. To underline the importance of this point, this scholar even alluded to a biblical reference about how much of one's resources should be donated for charitable purposes. This individual recommended to foundation leaders to "tithe your research portfolio to getting your research into society," encouraging funders to be more unambiguous in drawing the connections between basic science and its application toward tackling societal challenges.

A second suggestion that arose from these conversations was that science philanthropies can and should do more *to fund research that is deliberately aimed at answering pressing global questions.* One funder representative counseled that, "the hope is that fundamental science is going to then bear on these big challenges." This interviewee raised a set of such questions in need of more research, areas where science philanthropy help can contribute in providing suitable answers: "How do you prevent nuclear war? How do you get resources distributed? How do you deal with epidemics, pandemics, and so on?" This person recommended that even when funding basic research, more science philanthropies should operate

with the need for these end-result societal impacts in mind. "I guess my fundamental belief is that the foundations that support science should be thinking about
how what they are doing can have an impact on that biggest picture," advised this
interviewee.

A third recommendation that arose from these conversations was that science
philanthropies have a unique ability *to connect short- and long-term time horizons
when it comes to assessing the impact of their work.* There was a two-fold rationale
for this conclusion. As noted in the introductory chapter, foundations have a
rather distinct ability to support research that aims at multiple time horizons,
exactly because of the freedom they have to operate. This becomes doubly true
for philanthropies focused on supporting science and technology, because the
results of basic research also often take a long time to turn into new innovations
that are broadly diffused. One science philanthropy staff member endorsed this
idea by indicating that, "basic science has a time horizon that requires patience,
and it is really hard for many people to wait that long." They summarized this
notion by surmising that, "you get some really fantastic, big things from those
investments. They just can't tell you what they are. Nobody can. Not even
scientists can tell you what the outcomes are going to be, but they can be truly
game changing, and will radically change what happens everywhere else."

Other funders and researchers voiced similar observations about the importance of marrying the near-term with the long-term, especially given the
uncertainty associated with how scientific research progresses. This is partly
why a number of researchers postulated the importance of science philanthropies allowing for a high degree of flexibility when it comes to supporting
research, as there is the potential for unexpected, serendipitous discoveries to
become ever-more important in future years. One foundation representative
described the need for foresight and the importance of making early stage
investments in basic research given long payoff times. "There have to be some
things where investing now for a future, uncertain benefit is a thing that
happens. Surely there must be opportunities to do that," they said. Another
researcher expressed a similar sentiment, postulating that, "answers are going to
come from research that you never thought was applicable in the first place,
but 30 years down the road it turned out to be applicable." I would argue that
while there are tensions between funding research that aims to have a more
immediate societal impact and work where such societal relevance is farther out
in the future, science philanthropies are exactly the kinds of institutions that
are well placed to mediate among these dual goals. On this front, one interviewee hypothesized that, "we need…a little more tolerance for uncertainty,
that we don't know quite how it is going to benefit, but we have faith that the
general process of human discovery."

In conclusion, even though science philanthropies operate in diverse ways
across many dimensions, interviews with some of the leading thinkers and
practitioners on this subject indicate that there is a surprising amount of
agreement surrounding the common challenges that these institutions are
working to address and what steps are needed to help move the field of

science philanthropy forward. While consensus in thinking is never to be expected, the reverberation of similar sentiments from those operating in different roles and in different institutions is telling. These commonalities indicate that it is possible to achieve a shared understanding of the role of science philanthropy in society, even if each institution continues to operate in slightly different ways.

I would be remiss by not ending with my own take on the collective set of interviews. I was particularly heartened by the sheer number of individuals who feel compelled to make the world better as part of their daily job and who expressed their dedication and enthusiasm for improving how science philanthropy operates. Moreover, these discussions also indicate that individuals are facing the uncertainties ahead with introspection, an impressive degree of nuance in thinking, and a commitment to achieve both the goals of their particular institution and science philanthropy in general. Given that the field is not static, though, I anticipate that these views will continue to evolve as well, especially as the modalities of science philanthropy transform in the years ahead as new practices are adopted, as new institutions are formed, and as new ways of working are employed. One researcher was so galvanized by the prospects about the next stages of development for science philanthropy that they envisioned a promising "new horizon" ahead.

The next two chapters will examine elements of this "new horizon" in more detail and consider some of the ways that the field as a whole may change in the coming years. This will be done by examining alternative approaches to science philanthropy in Chapter 7 and then, in Chapter 8, conclude with a presentation of a series of imaginative, forward-looking scenarios about the future of science philanthropy.

7 Novel modes of responsibility
New approaches to science philanthropy

Emerging alternative approaches in science philanthropy

The previous chapters have demonstrated how combining the three main dimensions of the RRI framework (anticipation, deliberation and inclusion, and reflexivity and responsiveness) with three main types of philanthropic intervention in the research enterprise (at individual, institutional, and network levels) yields a robust framework for understanding the various kinds of foundation-funded activities in this domain. As shown in Chapter 6, many of the perspectives and viewpoints underlying this typology are apparent in present-day thinking that is taking place from a number of individuals working within the science philanthropy community. Many of the interventions discussed so far still have their earliest roots in the genres of philanthropic grantmaking for science that was practiced in the 20th Century, albeit updated and with adjustments made to reflect changing contemporary needs and practices. However, there are further disruptions to this ecosystem that are starting to emerge, disruptions that may move in different directions over time and could come to characterize a larger share of how science philanthropy is practiced in the years or decades ahead. Drawing on a range of examples, this chapter will explore such developments and highlight some of the new directions in which science philanthropy may be headed and how they connect with the RRI framework.

A key element of these novel modes of philanthropic support for science is that they are increasingly doing away with the traditional structures of philanthropy and, in some instances, are even modifying the very notion of the traditional grantor-grantee relationship. Nevertheless, as Table 7.1 depicts, the RRI framework largely continues to serve as a useful theoretical construct to better understand how each of these alternative approaches reflects different dimensions of societal responsibility. At the same time, reality rarely—if ever—exactly fits such heuristic models, and that is also the case here, where some of these novel approaches start to strain against, and sometimes even challenge, neat categorization. I would argue that this lack of perfect fit is welcome for a number of reasons. First, it is the very probing of boundary cases that helps understand the limits of theoretical frameworks and push forward thinking on that front. Second, our understanding of what constitutes societal responsibility will evolve as the framework is applied in different contexts and with respect to different stakeholder groups. Third, it is also indicative of a point made in earlier chapters, namely that the practice of science philanthropy will continually change as new institutions are formed, as donors try new intervention approaches, and as the practice of scientific research advances over time.

The first of these novel approaches, which has already been discussed to some extent in previous chapters, reflects the RRI dimension of anticipation, as science philanthropies look to experiment with *new organizational structures for scientific research*. As we have seen in many of the examples discussed so far, philanthropies are typically structured as non-profit entities separate from the grant-receiving individuals or organizations to which they are providing funds. In short, an independent philanthropy makes grants to an independent grantee institution. In this new mode of science philanthropy, however, the presence of a separate, stand-alone, grant-receiving institution disappears. Instead, science philanthropies are moving toward establishing research

Table 7.1 RRI and alternative approaches to science philanthropy

Typology Dimensions	*Alternative Approaches to Science Philanthropy*
Anticipation	**New Organizational Structures for Scientific Research** Research centers created within science philanthropies and instances where foundations maintain research instrumentation *Examples: Simons Foundation Flatiron Institute, Schmidt Oceans Institute*
Deliberation and Inclusion	**New Donors through Crowdfunding and More Equitable Award Allocation Mechanisms** Individual members of the public providing support for scientific research through crowdfunding platforms and experimenting with new ways of randomly distributing resources to achieve more equitable outcomes *Examples: Experiment, Kickstarter, use of randomization in grantmaking*
Reflexivity and Responsiveness	**New Selection Criteria and Indicators of Success** Funders look for different indicators of quality, success, and risk-taking to inform proposal and grantee selection, including the adoption of prized-based philanthropy *Examples: Open Philanthropy Project, The Audacious Project*
Challenging the RRI Framework	***Remaking and Dissolving the Philanthropic Form*** Emergence of different corporate structures to support scientific research and creation of pooled funds from multiple donors *Examples: Chan Zuckerberg Initiative, Emerson Collective, Founders Pledge*

entities and organizational structures within the foundation itself, with the philanthropy no longer making grants to an independent grantee institution. An example presented earlier was the establishment of the Simons Foundation's Flatiron Institute. Another way in which foundations are moving away from the notion of funding a separate, independent grantee organization is that some science philanthropy interventions are no longer in the form of giving grants to an organization at all. Instead, science philanthropies are starting to serve more as the providers and maintainers of research instrumentation, with the foundation responsible for the management, oversight, and control of these tools, as in the case of the Schmidt Ocean Institute discussed in Chapter 4. In other words, instead of giving a grant to a university or research center to buy or build scientific research instrumentation, this novel approach entails the science philanthropy building, procuring, or maintaining research instrumentation as part of their philanthropic efforts. The rationale provided here is that by structuring at least a part of their philanthropic efforts as providing instrumentation as in-kind support, these interventions will serve to address a pressing or forthcoming need that will help to directly unlock additional scientific research.

The second of these new approaches involves the emergence of *new donors through crowdfunding and more equitable award allocation mechanisms*. On the first component, support for science is increasingly being provided by a broader range of individuals beyond high-net-worth donors or philanthropic institutions. The rising prominence of crowdfunding platforms for scientific research, such as websites like Kickstarter and Experiment, has led to increased opportunities for scientists to go directly to members of the general public and receive funding for their research projects. These online platforms allow any scientist to present their research widely and allow any individual to select projects that interest them and direct their funds as they choose. While the amounts of money provided to or received by any one particular research project are often relatively small, especially when compared with the amount that might be received from philanthropic or government sources, these platforms are aimed at more fully democratizing giving to science. At the moment, these crowdfunding approaches are mostly supplementary to the core research funding that scientists receive from other sources. However, the prominence of these crowdfunding platform sites has grown in recent years, as funding from other sources has become squeezed or harder for scientists to secure. Even if the total amount of money a scientist may receive is rather small from these giving platforms, crowdfunding sites provide researchers with access to a much larger pool of donors. Moreover, scientists do not have to go through the many bureaucratic hurdles they face to secure grants from foundations or government. These platforms also help to improve public engagement with science, as members of the public directly allocate resources to their preferred areas of interest. Sometimes this crowdfunding comes in the form of charitable contributions. Yet, in other instances, some of these funds actually serve as investments, with members of the public potentially able to have their financial outlays paid back if the research leads to the commercialization of a new product. The rise of crowdfunding for science is, in many ways, a counterpart to the rise of citizen science that has influenced how research is conducted; members of the public not only can conduct science now, but they can fund it as well. On the second component, there is rising interest among both funders and researchers in trying different ways of awarding grants to achieve more equitable outcomes. In particular, this approach includes the adoption of randomization to allocate awards. Experimentation with this alternative is based on the view that given limited resources available, the unpredictability of the research enterprise, and the difficulty inherent in selecting among many worthy proposal applications, that the fairest and most just way of selecting grant recipients among qualified applicants involves selection by lottery-like mechanisms. While this tactic remains in its infancy and has a long way to go before any extent of mainstream adoption by science philanthropies, just the fact that it is starting to receive even a modest amount of attention is indicative of its potential appeal to help overcome bias and lead to a more diverse and inclusive set of funded researchers.

The third of these alternatives approaches involve science philanthropies adopting *new selection criteria and indicators of success* as part of their review processes. These changes have emerged from science philanthropies looking for ways to reflexively rethink how they assess and evaluate research quality and, in turn, determine how to select different kinds of research projects for funding. These changes have been mainly driven by science philanthropies looking to alter how they identify and eventually fund what may be viewed as high-risk research projects. In more traditional modes of science philanthropy, foundations typically make funding decisions by selecting proposals based on their presumed likelihood of success; the greater the likelihood of success, the greater the likelihood of funding. As previous chapters have shown, science philanthropies use various assessment protocols to determine potential research success, including holding open requests for proposals, organizing expert review panels to help adjudicate the quality of different proposed projects, or directly soliciting proposals that funders believe have a high degree of potential for impact. Increasingly though, as interest within the philanthropic community in funding research that is both high-risk and high-reward has grown, newer philanthropic funders of science have begun to adopt different proposal selection criteria and change what they view as indicators of proposal quality. In fact, some of these newer funders are going as far as seeking out projects and proposals that have been declined or rejected elsewhere because they were deemed too risky. In other words, these funders are moving toward deliberately selecting projects where the initial chances of success appear low, at least by conventional evaluation standards, yet where they think there may be the potential for a transformational payoff in the future in terms of realizing breakthrough discoveries.

Finally, the last of these novel approaches features the *remaking and dissolving of the philanthropic form* altogether, a development both that gets to the very heart of what foundations are supposed to do and also serves to push against the limits of the RRI framework itself. In this category, both the presence of a not-for-profit foundation and a not-for-profit grant-receiving entity are being replaced by various novel institutional forms that draw on for-profit business models. Specifically, this involves science funding entities establishing themselves not as foundations but as limited liability corporations (LLCs). This move presents various trade-offs, as it impacts the charitable nature of the funds provided. However, some donors are choosing this path as it provides the ability to utilize different kinds of financial support mechanisms when backing science. These corporate forms not only provide donors with the ability to make grants for basic scientific research, they also give the ability for donors to make private investments in, and even take ownership stakes in, firms that might result from funded basic research. Experimentation with this alternative approach is mostly taking place from science funding bodies located around the Bay Area on the West Coast, especially as Silicon Valley philanthropists have started to become more involved in supporting science. There are other related changes happening with giving by high-net-worth individuals as well. While these individuals may have previously opted to start their own foundations or give money directly to science projects of their own choosing, there is growing interest in turning over the responsibility of researching and selecting projects to pooled fund mechanisms, called donor advised funds (DAFs). Under this arrangement, resources from a number of different donors can be combined and deployed in a more collective manner, often through an institution that brings together subject matter experts and advisors who are better positioned to identify promising research projects than an individual donor alone. Each of these four transformations to the philanthropic system has substantial ramifications for the funding of science, to be discussed in more detail below.

Anticipating future research needs: establishing new organizational structures for scientific research

The first alternative approach noted in Figure 7.1 highlights changes in the notion of a grantee institution existing separate from the funder. Examples like the Allen Institute, the Flatiron Institute at the Simons Foundation, and the Schmidt Ocean Institute all point to this new model, one in which the philanthropy brings the research enterprise in-house, blurring the distinction between the grantee conducting research and the philanthropy funding this work. There are a number of reasons why a science philanthropy might move in this direction. One is a desire by the philanthropy to have more direct oversight and influence on what research is performed and how that research is managed. Bringing a grantee institution in-house obviously gives the funding organization more control over all facets of the research effort. A second potential reason is that this organizational structure helps to free the researchers from the requirement of continually seeking out funds for their science. Instead, those resources are made directly availably by being in a foundation, proving a level of financial security that might not otherwise exist and allowing scientists to focus squarely on undertaking their investigations without having to spend the time and effort needed to fundraise. Third, the funder may also be able to reduce transaction costs and realize economies of scale if the research is conducted in-house. Of course, doing so also requires that the host foundation be responsible for covering all the costs and expenses of that novel institutional entity, reserving this approach for only the most well-resourced philanthropic institutions. A fourth reason for moving in this direction is that the establishment of an in-house research organization has the potential to influence the operational culture of other areas of that philanthropic institution. Foundations that establish these in-house research centers also typically provide grants externally as well, so the expectation may be that having working scientists based at the foundation can help inform how that external grantmaking is provided. For instance, this is one of the reasons noted by the Simons Foundation for launching the Flatiron Institute. Their 2017 annual report describes the envisaged contribution that the formation of this in-house research center would have on the foundation's overall culture. The report notes that "the institute's rapid growth has already shifted the staff composition of the Simons Foundation as a whole, which, a short time ago, focused only on grant-making. The addition of an in-house research organization has influenced other divisions of the foundation" (Simons Foundation, 2017).

Beyond the establishment of in-house research entities within science philanthropies, these foundations have also started to move in a different direction by being the ones to maintain and oversee the management of unique research instrumentation and infrastructure. That is the case with Schmidt Ocean Institute, which has been pioneering this mode of support by taking on the responsibility of equipping and deploying an oceangoing research vessel, called the *Falkor*, with state-of-the-art robotic and data science instrumentation. Time on such research vessels is in high demand within the scientific community, and by focusing on crafting and sustaining such an instrument, Schmidt Ocean Institute is able to supply the oceanographic research community with an increased ability to explore the ocean using a variety of tools by air, on the surface, and underwater. Its 2017 annual report described the goals of taking this approach as helping "to inspire and disrupt the status quo in ocean research by encouraging other independent thinkers to apply diverse, practical innovation to understanding and protecting our oceans" (Schmidt Ocean Institute, 2017). The report continues by emphasizing how, in exchange for providing this kind of instrumentation to the community, the funder requires all data collected on the vessels to be shared openly with other researchers. "By mandating open sharing of data for all supported projects and by providing end-to-end data acquisition, management, processing, and sharing services to all collaborating researchers, Schmidt Ocean Institute has broken academic glass walls and removed barriers to cooperation among the scientists, research labs, and institutions around the world" (Schmidt Ocean Institute, 2017). Similarly, a recent article reporting on this instrumentation contribution from Schmidt Ocean Institute stressed the importance of having such advanced technological capabilities for conducting ocean science as "creating a space for scientists to both study the ocean as well as test and experiment with new technologies aimed at advancing the pace of ocean science" (Herries & Wiener, 2018, p. 25). There are even other efforts within the Schmidt funding universe that look to further advance the development and commercialization of ocean-related technologies. For instance, an arm of the Schmidt Family Foundation, Schmidt Marine Technology Partners, provides funds to scale businesses working to develop new technologies in this area. As they state on their website, "we created this 'venture philanthropy' model to fill an often-fatal gap in support available for the development of ocean technologies, which typically require something beyond traditional grants in order to achieve full potential and availability" (Schmidt Marine Technology Partners, n.d.).

Beyond Schmidt Ocean Institute, this approach of science philanthropies providing research instrumentation and infrastructure as in-house capabilities, especially in the domain of ocean science, has blossomed in recent years. Individual, high-net-worth donors have started to outfit a growing number of research vessels, in part to compensate for the decline in the number of government-funded ships, which has led to longer researcher wait times and an inability to explore many pressing research questions in ocean science. One news story in *Science* documented the rise in the number of these philanthropically supported expedition research crafts. The article observes that science philanthropies have started to enter this space in part to address the challenges brought on by the aforementioned decrease in government funding for these technologically advanced research vehicles. "Philanthropists have launched several vessels to help shorten the queue," states the article, which profiles the building of a new privately funded craft for science called *Research Expedition Vessel* (Stokstad, 2018, p. 874). Moreover, many of the research liners profiled in this piece are designed to do more than just conduct research. For instance, Dalio Philanthropies, a newer philanthropic entity, has supported a large-scale oceangoing research enterprise, called OceanX. OceanX not only features a suite of state-of-the-art, customized research equipment, but it also includes sophisticated multi-media recording equipment capable of producing a wide range of film and video content that can better share research findings and scientific results with the broader public. As noted on the Dalio Philanthropies website, these expedition vessels are constructed to "provide a platform to support the research of scientists worldwide and serve as a cutting-edge media platform that is used to share exciting discoveries with the public" (Dalio Philanthropies, 2019).

There are other such examples of foundations focusing on supporting the development of instrumentation outside the domain of ocean science as well. For instance, one of the more well-known instances is philanthropic support for the Foldscope paper microscope, an "ultra-low-cost origami-based approach for large-scale manufacturing of microscopes" (Cybulski, Clements, & Prakash, 2014, p. 1). More recently, science philanthropies have been involved in more systematic efforts to advance these kinds of affordable approaches to tool building. The most prominent of these is Tool Foundry, a competitive instrument development process undertaken by the innovation consultancy company Luminary Labs and funded with support from the Moore Foundation and Schmidt Futures. Tool Foundry helps scientists and engineers based at university research centers, companies, and other organizations to build "low-cost, high-quality, and easy-to-use" tools for the purpose of making the conduct of scientific research more accessible to non-experts, thereby helping to "inspire a deeper interest in science and empower people to indulge their curiosity, explore their environments, and solve problems relevant to their own communities" (Tool Foundry, n.d.). Inventor teams connected to Tool Foundry have worked on developing tools such as low-cost microscopes, radiation detectors, pollution monitoring devices, or medical imaging equipment. Building these instruments is being facilitated by the utilization of off-the-shelf parts and standardized hardware components whose design specifications are open source, available for purchase at low cost, or easily manufactured by way of distributed, on-demand printing technologies. These and other kinds of instrumentation development efforts not only help to facilitate citizen science, but they serve as a growing and important link between research conducted in a lab and ensuring positive benefits for society. Furthermore, as this field of open science hardware begins to thrive, there is the potential for philanthropic and government funders to have an impact by helping to create and deploy these novel, accessible instruments as a way of enhancing the responsibility of research and making the conduct of science more societally oriented (Pearce, 2016; Gathering for Open Science Hardware, 2017).

A more inclusive and expansive community of giving: engaging new donors through crowdfunding and more equitable award allocation mechanisms

A second alternative approach to science philanthropy that has been taking place in recent years has been the emergence of crowdfunding platforms that facilitate giving from larger numbers of individuals—often at smaller amounts of money per donation—directly to scientific research projects. One of the effects of this trend is the creation of a more inclusive, expansive pool of donors for research by engaging citizens as supporters of science, not just consumers or users of research results. While still taking place on a relatively small scale, the emergence of these digital platforms to facilitate linkages between members of the public eager to give to science and scientists themselves opens a number of possibilities for science philanthropy going forward. At the moment, this kind of science philanthropy mainly serves to augment and supplement much larger amounts of money that are given through traditional institutional modes of philanthropy to individuals, institutions, and networks. However, one can imagine a situation farther out in the future in which this kind of platform-based giving might challenge the role played by institutional philanthropies, bypassing their priority-setting and strategy development processes. This may accelerate as scientists start to look to source support from larger coalitions of individual donors that they can connect with directly through online giving platforms.

One of the reasons that this kind of crowdfunding for science is taking off is partly due to changes in the ways that science is being conducted. As was discussed earlier in the context of Galaxy Zoo, the Sloan Digital Sky Survey (SDSS), and other larger-scale citizen science collaborations, science is increasingly taking place in a networked manner that encourages diverse groups of experts and citizen scientists alike to engage with one another to collectively solve problems (Nielsen, 2012; Cooper, 2016; Bowser & Shanley, 2013; Guerrini, Majumder, Lewellyn, & McGuire, 2018; Sauermann & Franzoni, 2015; Lintott, 2020). Of course, many citizen science research projects are still funded by existing philanthropic institutions or government funders, not primarily by crowdfunding campaigns. For instance, the website SciStarter is a central hub for information and engagement for over 3,000 citizen science projects, allowing interested individuals to stay up to date on these efforts, join as volunteers, or learn more about results. The platform has been funded by the NSF, universities, local governments, and a number of science philanthropy institutions, including the Burroughs Wellcome Fund, Schmidt Futures, the Sloan Foundation, and the Simons Foundation (SciStarter, 2019). One book examining the rise of citizen science notes that these kinds of citizen science research projects have the potential to be appealing to funders because they strengthen the link between science and society. "Experience shows that citizen science projects open up new sources of potential funding to universities," in part "because many funders and charitable foundations are interested in contributing to projects that benefit society or promote public engagement with science" (Wyler & Haklay, 2018, p. 171). In particular, there is the view from government funders in both United States and Europe that citizen science efforts can serve as a way to better connect science and public engagement by not only diversifying who conducts science but also by engaging a broader range of stakeholders in the research process and helping to train the next generation of scholars (Office of Science and Technology Policy, 2019; UK Research and Innovation, 2019).

One news article from 2015 published in *The Washington Post* documented the rise of crowdfunding platforms for science and articulated the various reasons as to why researchers might be interested in pursuing funding through crowdfunding sites, along with the impacts on the conduct of science that might result from increased reliance on these platforms. "Although the money being raised through crowdfunding sites is only a fraction of the roughly $435 billion spent each year on research and development in the United States, thousands of scientists are building their brands and research coffers on sites such as Experiment.com, Petridish.org, RocketHub.com and others, with the blessing of their universities," writes journalist Ariana Eunjung Cha (Cha, 2015). Cha continues by describing how, "the new money is increasing the momentum for some unconventional or underfunded areas of research…by allowing scientists to bypass the bureaucracy of federal agencies that have acted as gatekeepers for science since World War II" (Cha, 2015). She warns, though, that "the growing popularity of crowdfunding also raises questions about oversight and how to ensure sound project designs, rigorous standards for data collection and safety protocols" (Cha, 2015). Part of the appeal of pursuing funding from these platforms is that securing some amount of backing from these sites is easier than from federal sources, and likely philanthropies as well. "Today, the success rate for a scientist seeking funding is much higher on crowdfunding sites than at the NIH or the NSF," comments Cha, while also noting that the factors that contribute to securing funds from crowdfunding sites are different from traditional government or foundation funding sources (Cha, 2015). "Being able to connect with a large audience through outlets such as Facebook, Twitter and YouTube appeared to correlate with increased levels of funding," she cites (Cha, 2015). She writes that contributors to projects presented on these sites mainly have an interest in connecting personally with the scientists who they choose to support.

Articles in academic publications outline similar reasons for the increase in interest and attention given to crowdfunding for science, taking note of how these approaches do more to engage members of the public in the scientific enterprise. "Crowdfunding is giving researchers the opportunity to take their research in new directions, funding graduate students or undergraduates who can do a lot with a little bit of money, or even paying for a season of field research," assesses Jessica Marshall in a news feature for *PNAS* (Marshall, 2013, p. 4857). Writing in *The Lancet*, Nayanah Siva makes the point that crowd-funding has the potential to fill gaps in funding left by government or philan-thropies, noting that when funding is scarce, it is almost inevitable that "other ways to fund research are likely to gain popularity" (Siva, 2014, p. 1085). Researchers writing in *PLOS Biology* make a similar point, highlighting crowdfunding's dual ability to secure additional resources for science while also bolstering societal engagement with science, arguing that "crowdfunding enables people outside academia to engage with science on a global scale. It can also be an alternative or additional source of funding, given the difficulties of raising funds in the traditional science funding system" (Vachelard, Gambarra-Soares, Augustini, Riul, & Maracaja-Coutinho, 2016, p. 1).

However, given the number of many disparate online platforms, it is difficult to get a full accounting of how much money has been given to science via crowd-funding. The largest crowdfunding website dedicated to science appears to be Experiment; there are other less well-known crowdfunding sites dedicated to sci-ence, including Thinkable and SciFund Challenge, which are dedicated to helping researchers better present their projects on crowdfunding platforms. Other more general crowdfunding sites, such as Kickstarter or Indiegogo, also host science projects for funding. Getting exact numbers on the extent of financial support provided remains challenging. Experiment provides some high-level statistics on its website, indicating that as of October 2019, just over one million "backers" of research projects have collectively given about $8.8 million to 918 projects, with the average project receiving about $4,000 from these donors (Experiment, 2019a). Thinkable notes that over $1 million has been awarded to over 1,400 research institutes (Thinkable, 2018). SciFund Challenge serves more as a guide to help researchers improve their chance of securing support via crowdfunding sites, noting that it has "coached over 200 scientists to collectively raise over $200,000" (SciFund Challenge, 2019). Most of these crowdfunding sites, including the largest in Experiment, work as "an all-or-nothing fundraising platform," in that projects failing to reach their requested threshold of funding in the indicated time do not receive any of the partial funding that has been given (Experiment, 2019b). There are few barriers to a research project being posted on these sites. The Experiment website, for example, describes how its staff reviews the content of proposed research projects along with conducting a "video interview" with the proposers before posting them publicly (Experiment, 2019b). Each of these sites are structured somewhat differently in terms of their corporate form. Both Thinkable and SciFund Challenge appear to be non-profit organizations. On the other hand, and of particular interest regarding this topic of alternative institutional approaches to philanthropy, Experiment describes itself as a "mission-driven for-profit company" that is a "melting pot of science, social entrepreneurship, and technology startup" (Experiment, 2019b).

These crowdfunding sites feature and discuss various kinds of interactions and engagements that take place between scientists and individual donors, often highlighting the societal impact that one person can have by providing funds on these platforms. For instance, the ways in which the Experiment website articulates the value of providing support for scientific research and how it describes the main modes that academic researchers typically use money that is given is noteworthy, given how much it echoes many dimensions of the RRI framework. Experiment frames the "reward" or value proposition of supporting science by emphasizing the direct connection between the financial "backer" of science and academic scientists (Experiment, 2019b). Its website states that, "Experiment researchers share the outcomes of their experiments directly with their backers. Usually this comes in the form of peer-reviewed journal publications, conference proceedings, academic posters, graduate theses, open data sets, and more" (Experiment, 2019b). Their website also summarizes the ways in which academic researchers deploy the money raised on this platform, revealing that it is often used either to explore new areas of work or to complement existing funds. "Experiment is often used to replace small grants for early-stage exploratory research. Other times, it's used to supplement larger projects" (Experiment, 2019b). Yet, quite tellingly, it highlights that there are no grant proposals to write or major bureaucratic hurdles to overcomes to secure this support. "Just don't treat it like a grant, with the expectation of writing a proposal and expecting money to come" (Experiment, 2019b).

It is also difficult to get a comprehensive sense of the scientific results emerging from crowdfunded research activities, as most of the assessments of crowdfunding efforts tend to focus on underscoring the impact of a few high-profile, individual examples. A perusal of the Experiment website indicates that many fields of science are represented in projects open for funding, including mathematics, many disciplines in the natural sciences (including physics, chemistry, biology, and early science), engineering and other applied disciplines (such as materials science and data science), medicine, economics, and the social sciences more broadly. Researchers can share progress on their projects by posting updates on the "Lab Notes" section of the website (Experiment, 2019c), and there are indications of scientific papers or other outputs posted on the "Results" section, which only had 190 postings as of October 2019 (Experiment, 2019d). Marshall (2013) points to two microbiology projects that were successful in securing hundreds of thousands of dollars of crowdfunding support on Indiegogo in 2013, yet they have since diverged in terms of their failures and successes. One of these projects that was designed to develop new tests for measuring human microbiology, called uBiome, was closed down in 2019 due to investigations from law enforcement due to potential misuse of funds and has since filed for bankruptcy (Mathews & Marcus, 2019; Lash, 2019). On the other hand, the American Gut Project, which combines citizen science participation and crowdfunding approaches to measure the gut microbiome of individual participants, has made substantial progress since its early stage. This project, along with a companion effort in the United Kingdom, has succeeded in raising over $2.5 million from over 10,000 participants from crowdfunding sites that include Indiegogo and FundRazr, with individual participants making a financial contribution of $99 each in exchange for receiving a kit that will allow them to collect and submit their own individual microbiology samples for inclusion in the project (Buschman, 2018). A major paper reporting some of the initial results from the American Gut Project study was published in 2018 (McDonald, et al., 2018).

In addition to the production of scientific knowledge, there are other avenues of success for crowdfunding campaigns. For projects that are more technology oriented, the most critical element is likely the ability to secure additional follow-on investment from the private sector. One such example is a crowdfunded project on Kickstarter by the French company Unistellar Optics with the purpose of creating a new, highly sensitive digital telescope called the eVscope that is "100 times more powerful than a classical telescope" (Kickstarter, 2019). This new digital telescope is mainly designed for amateur astronomers to allow for improved viewing of faint objects in the night sky. Beyond mere enjoyment, though, Unistellar has entered into a partnership with the SETI Institute that will facilitate the ability of eVscope owners to participate in citizen science research by taking observations of celestial phenomena that may be of interest to the research community (SETI Institute, 2018). Owners of the eVscope involved in the citizen science program will be able to get alerts regarding important objects to observe and can allow their digital telescopes to be remotely positioned to observe the appropriate location in the sky. Unistellar raised over $3 million in crowdfunding on Kickstarter, with donors at different giving levels having the opportunity to pre-order the telescope when it becomes available. In 2019, Unistellar announced that it raised additional funding provided by venture capital investors to help accelerate the product's commercialization (Unistellar Optics, 2019).

This combination of crowdfunding support with government, philanthropy, or private investment is viewed as being increasingly promising. The ability of a research project to secure crowdfunding support can serve as a positive signal to foundations, governments, or private sector investors that a project warrants additional resources. For instance, research is beginning to show that crowdfunding helps to boost the provision of follow-on private investment in particular regions (Yu, Johnson, Lai, Cricelli, & Fleming, 2017). Studies have also indicated that because crowdfunded projects come from many regions and locales, they are helping to spread follow-on entrepreneurial investment to a wider range of geographies (Sorenson, Assenova, Li, Boada, & Fleming, 2016). One group of researchers has advanced this perspective and argued that crowdfunding mechanisms are particularly well-suited to triangulate among philanthropic modes of giving with early stage private investors and researchers working on societally relevant problems. There is the potential "to create the next generation of crowdfunding to bring together philanthropists and local citizens" and that "doing so will generate a nuanced understanding of the local social context in which research is conducted," they claim (Ozdemir, Faris, & Srivastava, 2015, p. 268).

Though still in its early stages, the academic literature has identified both benefits and drawbacks due to the emergence of crowdfunding as an increasingly viable option of supporting science. One of the most comprehensive analyses of science crowdfunding was published in early 2019, examining data from over 700 science-related research projects on the Experiment platform. This study looked to understand various trends in crowdfunding for research, broken down by the investigator's professional possession, type of institutional affiliation, gender, regional location, research field, budget size, and other characteristics. There were many positives. Of particular interest is that study found that the diversity of those individuals who receive crowdfunding resources is much better than those who typically receive funding from more traditional funding sources. "Crowdfunding seems to differ in important ways from traditional funding mechanisms such as grants from government agencies: Success rates are comparatively high, junior scientists tend to be more successful than senior scientists, and female investigators are more likely to be funded than male investigators" (Sauermann, Franzoni, & Shafi, 2019, p. 19). Sauermann, Fanzoni, and Shafi (2019) also find that projects deemed riskier tend to do just as well in crowdfunding as less risky projects and that funds can be raised faster via crowdfunding mechanisms, although the amounts tend to be substantially smaller and tend not to cover core expenses, such as tuition reimbursement or salaries. Their summary assessment is that crowdfunding succeeds in diversifying who gets resources, but it is not at a level sufficient to replace or supplement more traditional modes of support for science. Their assessment is as follows:

> Our results support the view that crowdfunding of scientific research broadens access to resources for groups that have been excluded or disadvantaged in traditional funding systems, similar to what has been shown in crowdfunding of business initiatives. However, the amount of resources raised—at the level of individual projects but also the platform as a whole—is presently too small for crowdfunding to serve as a substitute for traditional funding mechanisms. As such, crowdfunding for research may best be seen as a complement to such traditional sources.
>
> (Sauermann, Franzoni, & Shafi, 2019, p. 20)

However, they also conclude that there can be an effective interplay between crowdfunded research and more traditional modes of grantmaking for science, such as from philanthropy or governments. Crowdfunding can, in effect, set up a researcher to be better prepared to secure larger grants from these traditional sources later on. "Even a relatively small grant can enable a project to proceed and may also make a long-term difference by allowing researchers to increase their chances of subsequent funding in the traditional system," they determine (Sauermann, Franzoni, & Shafi, 2019, p. 20).

Along with these benefits, a host of challenges exist as well. One difficulty is that crowdfunding involves a skillset and disposition to securing funding that is rather different than preparing grant proposals for foundations or government funders. As noted above, the Experiment website says as much. Researchers need to be able to communicate what they are doing in easy-to-understand language and use engaging visuals to describe their work. Doing so can be time consuming, especially for the relatively small amounts of money that are typically being sought on these platforms. The authors of the *PLOS Biology* paper point to these various challenges by warning that a crowdfunding "campaign is not a miraculous solution, and it requires a significant investment of time and effort in science outreach. The likelihood of successfully fundraising through community participation is directly dependent on the effort you invest in communicating about your research with the public" (Vachelard, Gambarra-Soares, Augustini, Riul, & Maracaja-Coutinho, 2016, p. 3). Perhaps Marshall (2013) puts it best and most straightforwardly by writing, "crowdfunding is not easy money" (p. 4858). She expounds on this statement by conveying that "crafting a message that will appeal to the public, making a video, and putting up a Web page takes a lot of work" (p. 4858). Deploying an effective science crowdfunding campaign requires effort both while the donation period is open and continues once it is closed. "While a campaign is live, success hinges on staying engaged, responding to questions and glitches, and continuing to spread the word on social media and among potentially interested networks, including relevant businesses and the press," she writes (p.4858). "After the campaign, teams need to update backers on the project and distribute the perks, which can include t-shirts, tokens related to the research, or lab tours for larger donors" (p. 4858).

To succeed at raising money via crowdfunding, scientists need to learn to "build an audience for their work," as the creators of the SciFund Challenge site have noted (Byrnes, Ranganathan, Walker, & Faulkes, 2014, p. 1). This team studied the factors that contributed to crowdfunding successes of nearly 160 research projects and found that those with high degrees of online engagement with stakeholders outside of the research enterprise fared best. They note that "researchers should begin by cultivating an audience for their work over time" by adopting a number of strategies: "become active in local public science efforts, foster connections with relevant non-governmental organizations with their own audiences, launch a public science blog (potentially with collaborators), build a Twitter following, and search out as many ways to easily communicate your science to as broad an audience as possible" (Byrnes, Ranganathan, Walker, & Faulkes, 2014, p. 24). They even conclude their article by highlighting the many auxiliary benefits that arise from these kinds of activities, remarking that, "outreach and engagement create public science literacy, new arenas of public support for science, and new connections between scientists and the world that they are trying to understand" (Byrnes, Ranganathan, Walker, & Faulkes, 2014, p. 24).

Beyond these practical challenges of finding effective ways to communicate to the public and staying actively engaged on social media, there are other potentially more serious difficulties that accompany the rise of crowdfunding. Most critical, perhaps, are questions related to ensuring the integrity of research and appropriately addressing research ethics, let alone preventing and addressing potential fraudulent behavior. These questions arise in the context of various types of crowdfunding campaigns (Snyder, Mathers, & Crooks, 2016) and related to the conduct of citizen science projects (Guerrini, Majumder, Lewellyn, & McGuire, 2018). For instance, while Experiment requires that any proposed research project dealing with human subjects has to have received clearance from the university's Institutional Review Board (IRB), those kinds of requirements may not be present or consistent across every science crowdfunding site (Experiment, 2019e). Sauermann, Franzoni, and Shafi (2019) address these ethical considerations as well, observing that, "the crowd may fund projects that are in legal (or political) grey zones, and there may be different views regarding the desirability and value of such research" (p. 20). Moreover, they recognize that projects on Experiment have received IRB approval, it may still be the case that, "it is not clear whether all creators—especially those outside academia—understand and follow guidelines for ethical and responsible research" (Sauermann, Franzoni, & Shafi, 2019, p. 20). In the end, more attention needs to be paid to these and other open questions, especially given that the scale of crowdfunding for science is only likely to continue growing.

It is important to consider that there are other creative ways to think about how to allocate funds via different kinds of crowdfunding-like mechanisms. These new ideas have emerged as a response to the growing recognition that it is challenging—some might even say impossible—for science philanthropies or government funders to determine which scientists or research projects will be successful and able to produce important research results. Moreover, if a researcher does eventually generate valuable and high-impact findings, there is increasing evidence showing that the timing of when such influential work is produced during a scientist's career is hard to predict and tends to arise rather randomly (Sinatra, Wang, Deville, Song, & Barabasi, 2016). Other studies have shown that researchers receiving larger grants do not necessarily publish more impactful publications than researchers who receive smaller grants, leading the study authors to "suggest that funding strategies that target diversity, rather than 'excellence', are likely to prove to be more productive" (Fortin & Currie, 2013, p. 1). Fortin and Currie (2013) go further to contend that science funders should adopt a "many-small model" of grantmaking, in which funders should consider their small-scale support for lots of grantees as representing "an experiment in scientific impact" (p. 7). Furthermore, they note that spreading around modest amounts of support to lots of different researchers is an effective solution to managing the inevitable uncertainty that comes with not knowing which projects might succeed and which may not. "Funding more scientists increases the diversity of fields of research, and the range of opportunities available to students. Greater scientific diversity, like greater genetic diversity, increases the probability that some researcher (like some genetic mutant) will possess characteristics that will flourish in an unpredictable future" (p. 7).

Moreover, researchers in a variety of domains have noted that grantmakers should be cautious when relying solely on peer-review in selecting potential projects for funding. Scholars from the field of science of science, described in Chapter 4, have noted that peer-review can be "subject to biases and inconsistencies," leading social scientists to propose a variety of alternative decision-making processes that funders have begun exploring. One of these approaches is "the random distribution of funding," encompassing a variety of options such as "person-directed funding that does not involve proposal preparation and review, opening the proposal review process to the entire online population, removing human reviewers altogether by allocating funds through a performance measure, and scientist crowdfunding" (Fortunato, et al., 2018, p. 6). Interest in funders experimenting with randomizing at least some of their grant award decisions has grown. In addition to the increased recognition about the vagaries of peer-review (Roumbanis, 2019; Avin, 2019), there has been increased acknowledgment about the inevitable difficulty in making meaningful, fine-grained distinctions when selecting among a large number of proposal submissions, warranting more serious consideration of randomly assigning award decisions to submitted proposals (Osterloh & Frey, 2020; Gross & Bergstrom, 2019; Fang & Casadevall, 2016). As one commentary in *Nature* points out, such randomization processes allow funders to retain quality control while simultaneously achieving more societally equitable outcomes, since "incorporating randomness" into grant decision-making processes can help in "reducing the bias that research routinely shows plagues grant-giving, and improving diversity among grantees" (Adam, 2019, p. 575). Some government and philanthropic funders are already experimenting with these kinds of modified lottery systems to awarding a segment of their grants (Liu, Choy, Clarke, Barnett, & Pomeroy, 2020). Perhaps most notable is the Volkswagen Foundation's decision to adopt a randomized approach to award some of the grants within its "Experiment!" funding program (Walsweer, 2018).

Another idea is scientists allocating research dollars to one another, called scientist crowdfunding, which involves doing away with the whole process of proposal preparation and grantee selection. Instead, this approach proposes that funders give every scientist the same base level of "guaranteed funding" followed by a subsequent funding distribution process conducted by the scientists themselves, in which "everyone must anonymously allocate a fraction of their funds to other researchers of their own choosing" (Bollen, 2018, p. 143). The proponents of this "highly distributed, self-organizing process" contend that funders may still want to utilize separate resource allocation processes to ensure that certain strategic goals are met, such as advancing diversity, and that funders would need to put in place "stringent conflict-of-interest rules" and establish appropriate safeguards so to protect against potential abuse of the system (Bollen, Crandall, Junk, Ding, & Borner, 2014, pp. 132–133). With these caveats, they advance the view that this kind of rather radical approach to distributing science funding could have a number of benefits. These would include reducing the time and financial costs incurred by researchers in preparing proposals that may or may not get funded, facilitating more open data and results sharing among researchers as they seek support for their work, and at the broadest level, leading scientists to focus more attention on "clearly and compellingly communicating the outcomes, scientific merit, broader impact, vision, and agenda" of their proposed research (Bollen, Crandall, Junk, Ding, & Borner, 2014, p. 133). While there are pilot efforts to put some of these ideas into practice, it will be a while before the long-term impact of such adjustments, or any other alternative means of allocating financial resources for scientific research, will be realized.

Reflexively changing decision–making processes: adopting new selection criteria and indicators of success

The third emerging, alternative approach to science philanthropy relates to the utilization of new selection criteria and indicators of research quality that foundations are using to select different kinds of research projects for funding. Many of these changes are coming from new philanthropic institutions interested in directing more philanthropic support toward what they view as high-risk, high-reward research, indicating that these institutions are reflexively looking to change how funding decisions are made within their organizations. Two such philanthropic endeavors that have been particularly involved in implementing these kinds of changes are the Open Philanthropy Project and The Audacious Project, which is based at the TED organization. These changes are also evidenced by the emergence of prize-based science philanthropy, in which funding is provided not at the outset of a research effort but only at its successful conclusion, when it has achieved its desired outcome areas.

The Open Philanthropy Project has made a particular point of looking for high-risk, high-reward research efforts to fund, particularly in the biomedical sciences. As they note on their website, the Open Philanthropy Project primarily looks "to identify scientific research that has the potential for high impact and is under-supported by other funders. We are excited to support high-risk and unconventional science when the potential impact is sufficiently large" (Open Philanthropy Project, n.d.a). Moreover, their decision-making criteria for providing funding explicitly states that the organization looks to support causes that are important, neglected, and tractable, with the second criterion explained with the commentary that, "all else equal, we prefer causes that receive less attention from others, particularly other major philanthropists" (Open Philanthropy Project, n.d.b). As one article in *Science* noted, these selection criteria lead the Open Philanthropy Project to fund research projects that have "high odds of failure" (Callaway, 2018, p. 10). For example, the Open Philanthropy Project has directed over $10 million toward research projects that had previously been rejected by the National Institutes of Health for being too risky but that may still hold the promise for highly impactful discoveries (Callaway, 2018). The Open Philanthropy Project has also been particularly active in supporting research that examines the societal implications of rather futuristic technologies, with a particular interest in studying what they call potentially "global catastrophic risks" from "advanced artificial intelligence" (Open Philanthropy Project, n.d.c). This emphasis has led to multiple grants to establish new research centers examining these kinds of risks to society from developments in artificial intelligence. The organization has provided support to launch the Center for Human-Compatible Artificial Intelligence at the University of California, Berkeley with an over $5 million grant in 2016 (Scutari, 2018) and the Center for Security and Emerging Technology at Georgetown University with an over $55 million grant in 2019 (Williams, T., 2019). The formation of both of these research centers by the Open Philanthropy Project is particularly intriguing given that they go beyond undertaking research that might enable developments in artificial intelligence. Instead, the purpose of these awards is to provide substantial resources to question, probe, and assess the ethical, policy, legal, security, and other societal dimensions that might arise due to significant advancements in artificial intelligence.

The Open Philanthropy Project is not the only philanthropic institution that has become concentrated on deliberately selecting high-risk research projects for support. The Chan Zuckerberg Initiative (CZI) has also come to emphasize this kind of activity, partnering with three California based universities to create the Chan Zuckerberg Biohub program. The Chan Zuckerberg Biohub program awards a series of fellowships to top researchers in multiple fields of science and technology explicitly for the purpose of pursuing projects that are based on "bold ideas that lack preliminary evidence" (Maxmen, 2017, p. 280). Selected winners have come from multiple academic disciplines and have included an array of biologists, engineers, and computer scientists. One of the key requirements accompanying this support provided for high-risk projects is that the award winners are required to meet and share results with one another rather often. The purpose in doing so is to encourage the cross-pollination of ideas and establish a community of scientists interested in pursuing knowledge at the frontiers and intersections of different disciplines.

Another rather new philanthropic effort aimed at advancing high-risk research is The Audacious Project, an offshoot of the well-known and popular TED speaker series. The Audacious Project states that it looks to "select ideas that are truly bold and truly actionable, with the potential to affect millions of lives" (The Audacious Project, 2019a). To do so, The Audacious Project looks bring together funding from multiple high-net-worth individuals and help direct those funds into a few large awards to a select number of potentially high impact projects, amounting to tens or hundreds of millions of dollars per project (Price, 2019). The Audacious Project has adopted a variety of alternative selection approaches aimed at identifying potentially high-risk research projects. First, it uses an open and widely publicized call for submissions to broadly source ideas, with these calls garnering well over a thousand submissions. Second, it has also adopted a rather unusual proposal review process. As an article in *Science* details, "reviewers for these proposals are not typically experts in the relevant fields," and "instead, they look at a team's record of success, the idea's potential for large-scale global impact, its sustainability, and its ability to attract philanthropy" (Price, 2019, p. 317). Proposers whose projects are short-listed for consideration work with a consultant to prepare a brief video to pitch ideas that could attract the interest of the assembled donors. Another article in *Science* describes The Audacious Project as helping to facilitate the connections between individual funders with researchers pursuing high-risk, high-reward science, explaining that, "Audacious raises money from multiple private donors and vets proposals on their behalf, which cuts paperwork for grantees" (Kintisch, 2018, p. 738).

While not all of the awards from The Audacious Project are made in the area of science and technology, in 2019 it funded research projects that looked to study how extensively plants could be used to better sequester carbon dioxide, whether proteins could be engineered to help develop new drugs and vaccines, how to better develop and distribute drugs for neglected diseases, and how to restructure financial debt of island nations to better protect oceans (The Audacious Project, 2019b). Similarly, one scientific project funded by The Audacious Project in 2018 is the Ocean Twilight Zone initiative, a six-year effort to study the region of the ocean that exists in the layer of water between the more easily observable surface and the darker depths. This research will be facilitated by the development of new sensors, cameras, and submersible vehicles to better map and observe the ocean's "mysterious midwater layer," a realm that has been somewhat ignored by other oceanographic research projects, in part because "traditional tools have proved inadequate for exploring midwater ecosystems" (Kintisch, 2018, p. 738). While the projects supported by The Audacious Project are likely to take a long time to produce results or come to fruition, if at all, that is the expectation of the funders going into the process and an inevitable trade-off that comes with looking to support breakthrough projects that boast a high degree of uncertainty.

Finally, another example of philanthropic funders looking to spur high-risk research in science and technology is the emergence of various challenge prizes targeted at spurring breakthrough discoveries. These inducement or innovation incentivization prizes, as they are known, have become more common in the philanthropic and government sectors, as funders look for new ways to encourage researchers to tackle exceedingly difficult scientific or technological questions (Williams, H., 2012; Ubois, 2019; National Research Council, 2007; Patel, 2013). Unlike grants that are awarded at the outset of a project, prizes and challenge awards are only paid out at the conclusion of a project and only if a research team accomplishes the pre-determined terms and requirements of the contest. These awards are generally rather large in size, in the order of many millions of dollars per prize, and thereby receive substantial attention both when the challenge is announced and when the eventual award is made. While the use of incentive prizes has been critiqued for potentially providing perverse incentives for scientists to re-direct their research in directions that may not end up being fruitful or productive (Starr, 2013), they have also been credited with stimulating high-risk research that likely would not have otherwise taken place without the promise of substantial amounts of money being conferred upon completion (Goldhammer, Mitchell, Parker, Anderson, & Joshi, 2014). Perhaps the most well-known donor organization providing prizes is the XPRIZE Foundation, which often partners with corporations or other entities to announce and award large-scale prizes to researchers. Prizes have focused on achieving a wide range of goals within science and technology, such as contests to develop autonomous vehicles in order to more comprehensively map the ocean floor (Rosen, 2018) or challenges to find economically productive ways of using carbon dioxide (Lim, 2015). Given the high-risk attributes of these challenges, it is not uncommon for prizes to be discontinued, canceled, or not awarded for a variety of reasons. These include a low number of participating teams, as was the case with a genomics sequencing prize challenge (Kaiser, 2013), or the inability of teams to accomplish the stated goals of the contest, as was the case with an attempt to develop a new generation of Moon landers (Gibney, 2019).

Challenging the RRI framework: remaking and dissolving the philanthropic form

The fourth alternative approach to science philanthropy is, in many ways, perhaps the most extreme of all and the one that may push the boundaries of the RRI framework. Developments that fall into this category are those that are looking to break apart and perhaps dissolve the philanthropic form altogether, especially in terms of new donor institutions getting established in ways that are radically different from what has come before. In particular, some of the more recently established science and technology funding organizations in the United States are eschewing the traditional non-profit form of institutional philanthropy and, instead, are being set-up in a corporate form known as the limited liability company. The utilization of this approach gained widespread attention when CZI was being established as an LLC, yet the use of this corporate form goes beyond CZI. Along with CZI, both the Omidyar Network and the Emerson Collective, founded by Laurene Powell Jobs, are structured as LLCs (Singer & Isaac, 2015; Montgomery, 2018). There is much debate about the benefits and drawbacks surrounding the establishment of donor institutions as LLCs. Since funding entities established as LLCs act "partly like a corporation and partly like a business partnership," they provide the founding donor with more control over the distribution of funds, ability to invest in "for-profit social enterprises and also supporting political causes," do not require adherence to the annual foundation payout rules, and provide more privacy in that they do not "necessitate the same kinds of disclosures of public tax documents" (Singer & Isaac, 2015, p. B1).

As one analysis of the rise of LLCs in the philanthropic ecosystem by Dana Brakman Reiser (2018) states, these organizations can operate in almost any way they choose, as they "can make charitable grants, manage a diverse portfolio of investments, and engage in political advocacy—all free of the limitations and disclosure obligations to which private foundations are subject" (p. 26). On the other hand, there are critiques that moving away from the traditional construct of the non-profit foundation reduces accountability, challenges transparency, and weakens the independence that these institutions have from their founding donors (Daniels & Wallace, 2015; Lenkowsky, 2015). Reiser (2018) puts this concern most directly by noting that the rise of these philanthropic LLCs not only "gives its founders and leaders carte blanche to make any investment decisions they wish" (p. 29), but there is "very real concern that growth in LLC structures will magnify philanthropy's already problematic elitist nature" (p. 33). She concludes that while "private foundations are hardly democratic paragons…the for-profit LLC structure guarantees the public even less ability to examine, understand, and influence a philanthropy's activities," potentially raising "the risk of amplifying the antidemocratic elements of elite philanthropy and their consequences for society" (p. 33).

As has been discussed so far throughout this book, a number of recently formed philanthropic LLCs have been substantially involved in providing support for scientific research or resources for efforts investigating the connection between science and society. For instance, in addition to the Chan Zuckerberg Biohub program discussed above, CZI supports a range of programs in the biomedical fields, including building connections between patient communities and rare disease experts, developing an atlas of human cells, and funding data science efforts to improve the sharing of research results within the scientific community (Chan Zuckerberg Initiative, 2019). Omidyar Network has coalesced some of its resources around addressing the topic of "beneficial technology" and supports education, research, and networking activities that look to strengthen the connections between technology and society and, as they state, redefine "how tech is created and used in order to articulate a human-centered vision of technology" (Omidyar Network, 2016). One of the main technology-oriented domains of the Emerson Collective relates to addressing the link between environmental and human challenges, in part by investing in companies are developing, testing, and deploying new technological solutions to address climate change (Emerson Collective, 2019).

Beyond the rise of LLCs as a vehicle for new forms of deploying philanthropic-like capital, there are other kinds of interventions that existing philanthropic institutions can utilize to bring to bear investment-like modalities to science philanthropy while simultaneously achieving societal impact. One report points out that in addition to traditional programmatic grantmaking given to non-profit entities conducting basic scientific research, such as universities, foundations are also able to deploy other funding mechanisms, including marshalling the corpus of their endowment, to provide various kinds of investment capital for science and technology start-ups and companies. "Other, under-utilized tools are available, from traditional grants into for-profit start-ups on the one end, to program- or mission-related investments, through to traditional (fiduciary) investment vehicles on the other," write Nicole Systrom, Sarah Kearney, and Fiona Murray (Systrom, Kearney, & Murray, 2017, p. 6). As they note, there are instances where foundations might be able to make grants to for-profit science and technology enterprises, which involves additional oversight responsibilities for the philanthropy, or even taking equity stakes of various kinds in science or technology companies. Philanthropic organizations can also make program related investments (PRIs), which are charitable investments with the potential to be paid back over time, and mission related investments (MSIs), which are investments made from a foundation's endowment that are aligned with its broader societal interests. Additionally, philanthropies can provide funding to non-profit intermediaries or sponsoring organizations, which then can re-grant to for-profit entities. These intermediary entities, often called donor advised funds (DAFs), account for about 10% of total charitable giving and can be appealing because these organizations are able to hold funding on behalf of donors and then subsequently make grants over time (Macpherson, Kearney, & Murray, 2017). DAFs can pool funds from multiple donors, facilitating the ability to give larger amounts of money to particular institutions or causes. Moreover, donor advised funds typically conduct research to analyze the state of various fields and identify potential grantees in order to help funders understand how to direct their resources. These kinds are services are particularly valuable for funders interested in science and technology, for as was discussed in Chapter 6, new donors often face difficulties and barriers to entry when it comes to navigating the landscape of various science and technology fields in which they may have little experience.

Some authors have argued that philanthropies should do more to adopt these and other novel modes of deploying capital, which has become known as the field of impact investing (Bugg-Levine & Emerson, 2011), in the service of funding scientific research. In one article, Kearney, Murray, and Nordan (2014) write "philanthropists…are overlooking the middle ground that lies between their grantmaking to universities and their investment in venture funds," arguing that "philanthropy and impact investment communities can join to create new vehicles that support the creation, translation, and deployment of socially beneficial innovations" (p. 50). Their article highlights a number of examples of foundations that have made these kinds of alternative investments to help new technologies cross the "valley of death" (or, as they write, the "idea-to-impact gap") that often plague new scientific discoveries from translating and scaling into new technological innovations (Kearney, Murray, & Nordan, 2014, p. 50). As they conclude, there is the potential to build "a philanthropic bridge between the ivory tower and traditional capital markets" and a need for "philanthropists of all stripes to pioneer new forms of philanthropic investment—new approaches that support the kind of innovation that the world desperately needs" (Kearney, Murray, & Nordan, 2014, p. 55).

Perhaps nowhere is this need greater than deploying innovative philanthropic capital vehicles to address the challenge of climate change. In an article co-written by some of the authors quoted in the previous paragraph, they argue that these under-utilized forms of early stage capital from the philanthropic sector have unique potential to support "unexplored or nascent climate solutions" (Burger, Murray, Kearney, & Ma, 2018, p. 34). The reason for this is that developing solutions to climate change requires the kinds of financial resources that are hard to secure from other sources. "They require relatively long technical development timelines, demand capital-intensive demonstration tests that may yield negative results, tend not to receive financial valuations commensurate with technology companies of similar sizes or stages, or exist in subsectors that have delivered low financial returns over the past decade" (Burger, Murray, Kearney, & Ma, 2018, p. 34). In particular, the authors of a recent blog post on this topic argue that foundations have a unique role to play in advancing research and analysis in the area of negative emissions and carbon dioxide removal interventions, which aim to reduce the amount of carbon dioxide in the atmosphere through various means (Plechaty, Amador, & Mazurek, 2019). Options for investigation include direct capture of carbon dioxide from the ambient air, storage of carbon dioxide in rocks through accelerated mineralization processes, enhanced sequestration of carbon in soils and crops, and solutions that involve using the ocean as carbon sinks. There are many opportunities for deploying multiple kinds of philanthropic interventions—from grants to PRIs to MSIs and beyond—to advance such lines of inquiry, with foundations being "in a unique position to accelerate progress" and able to "take on risks that governments or the private sector can't or won't" (Plechaty, Amador, & Mazurek, 2019). While only a tiny fraction of philanthropic funding for climate change has been directed into these novel areas of research (Nisbet, 2018; Center for Carbon Removal, 2016), there are a number of opportunities for increased grantmaking on these novel solutions that philanthropic and government funders can pursue (Energy Futures Initiative, 2019).

Beyond addressing climate change, these alternative approaches to giving can have an impact in other areas as well, especially when coupled with the innovations that are taking place surrounding the utilization of DAFs. "The valley of death faced by many of today's most promising ideas in biotechnology, energy, infrastructure, and education requires a patient form of capital only found in philanthropy," states one report on the potential of using DAFs to support science and technology, and that "transitioning more breakthrough ideas from lab bench to market, however, requires DAF participation at scale" (Macpherson, Kearney, & Murray, 2017, pp. 14–15). For instance, a relatively new donor advised fund established in 2015 in the United Kingdom, called Founders Pledge, has emphasized conducting overview analyses on a variety of topic areas in the natural and social sciences, conducted by a number of in-house research experts (Founders Pledge, 2019a). Areas covered in these research reports include the challenges posed by extreme existential risks (Halstead, 2019), policy analysis (Capriati, 2018), and climate change (Halstead, 2018), just to name a few. Founders Pledge has received funding from the Open Philanthropy Project and uses some similar selection and analysis criteria as was discussed above—such as "scale" of the problem, potential for "tractability," and degree of "neglectedness"—to identify promising intervention opportunities (Goldberg, 2018). As a sign of interest in these kinds of DAFs, Founders Pledge has already grown quickly in a short period of time, with nearly $2 billion in total amount pledged, over $400 million in fulfilled grantmaking commitments, and over 1200 giving members from over 30 countries (Founders Pledge, 2019b).

RRI and new modes of science philanthropy

As this chapter has shown, science philanthropy is not a static undertaking. Just as the primary practices of today—providing grants to individuals, institutions, and networks—have made advancements from what was originated in the 20th Century, so too are the seeds for future developments in science philanthropy being germinated now. Both new and existing philanthropies are experimenting with different modes of funding science that will inevitably evolve in unexpected directions. New institutional configurations are emerging, with foundations establishing in-house research centers or serving as hubs for instrumentation management. New kinds of donors are being engaged, including members of the public being able to act as direct funders of research through crowdfunding platforms. New decision-making and grantee selection criteria are being adopted, with more foundations deliberately preferring to fund high-risk, high-reward projects. There are even moves to break away from and dissolve the philanthropic form altogether, as funders have begun embracing for-profit organizational models and investment practices to supplant traditional philanthropic approaches.

What, then, does all this mean in terms of responsible research and innovation (RRI)? There are various plausible views on this front. For one, at the genuine root of many of these developments is a desire to improve upon science philanthropy as it has been, and is currently being, practiced. Funders are looking to address weaknesses they see in the system, and these adjustments to the practice of science philanthropy are part of the result. Second, there is a degree of intentionally underpinning these developments that aligns them well with the dimensions of RRI. The promotion of alternative approaches reflects each RRI dimension. They indicate an anticipatory disposition with the field, with interest in exploring new directions that might prove to be more impactful than current practices. In terms of inclusiveness and diversity, the emergence of new citizen donors to science could help influence the direction that existing science philanthropies take and better prepare these institutions to draw on a more diverse array of perspectives in their work. With some organizations adopting new decision-making criteria, science philanthropies are adjusting how people, projects, and institutions are selected for funding and are showing a capacity to continually and reflexively work on improving what they do and how they do it.

Third, there are additional positive effects that could potentially accompany these developments in terms of strengthening connections between science and society. By creating and fully funding research centers within philanthropies, foundations are freeing up researchers to do what they do best and should be doing all along: conducting research. Facilitating the ability of members of the public to give directly to scientists as they wish is a boon on many fronts: it expands the resource base for science, increases the resiliency of the funding system by providing different funding avenues for scientists to pursue, encourages scientists to find effective ways of communicating their research to wider audiences, and builds relationships and trust between researchers and those outside the laboratory. Explicitly seeking out risky projects brings to the fore philanthropy's privileged ability to allocate patient capital to speculative research ideas that may or may not work out. Increased utilization of traditionally for-profit investment vehicles can allow philanthropies to deploy funding in the manner that is most appropriate for individual research projects.

On the other hand, there are evidently a number of potential pitfalls and drawbacks that must be guarded against with the adoption of these new approaches. One of the biggest difficulties might be that science philanthropies have cultivated and fostered a set of traditions, practices, and approaches over decades that have contributed to a flourishing, if not always perfect, research enterprise. This tried-and-true institutional knowledge, expertise, and heritage that many of these science philanthropies bring—which, in some cases, has been honed for nearly a century—has a lot to offer, learn from, and should be retained. For example, there are reasons of quality control, independence, and efficiency, just to name a few, as to why research institutions were established to be, and still largely remain, separate from their funders. Risk-taking is key, yet science philanthropies also need to allocate resources sensibly and in ways that are best suited to achieving results and generating knowledge, outcomes which are crucial contributions to addressing societal problems. The total amount of funds raised through crowdsourcing remains relatively small and is likely to stay that way for a considerable period of time.

Finally, for all the innovation that may come from new attempts to fund science through for-profit, foundation-like entities, the institutional form of the foundation was established for the very purpose of eschewing profits in favor of creating institutions that have a dedicated societal purpose. The examples in this book have shown that while more can always be done to realize these goals, science philanthropy in particular has a variety of mechanisms at its disposal to make progress on this front. Moving away from the mode of non-profit philanthropy altogether will involve trade-offs and consideration of potentially unforeseen impacts that need to be more fully anticipated before a strong move in that direction is taken. As Karl Zinsmeister (2020) describes in an article about the respective comparative advantages that exist between philanthropy, government, and industry to address societal problems, even with all of their acknowledged weaknesses and potential shortcomings, philanthropic interventions continue to have many positive factors in their favor and are well-situated to realizing responsibility. That essential purpose should not be forgotten nor easily lost.

In the end, I assert that a synergistic relationship between various forms of supporting science is not only possible, but desirable. The future of science philanthropy is likely going to be an amalgam of existing and novel practices, fortified by a commitment to adopt and share best practices across institutions. That is why entities like the Science Philanthropy Alliance are so pivotal, as it provides a dedicated forum for philanthropic funders of science of all kinds to come together, identify opportunities for collaboration, share learning and advice with one another, and marshal their collective resources to encourage new donors to support science. Moreover, all of these science philanthropy activities taken together—traditional or novel, conventional or risky, small-scale or large-scale—help to grow and strengthen the field. It is through a creative combination of approaches that science philanthropies can figure out how best to integrate considerations of societal responsibility into each of their unique organizations and, in doing so, find the most effective ways of blending learning from the past with insights from the present to have an impact in the future.

Bibliography

Adam, D. (2019, November 28). Science Funders Gamble on Grant Lotteries. *Nature*, 575(7784), 574–575.

Avin, S. (2019, September). Centralized Funding and Epistemic Exploration. *The British Journal for the Philosophy of Science*, 70(3), 629–656.

Bollen, J. (2018, August 9). Who Would You Share Your Funding With? *Nature*, 560 (7717), 143.

Bollen, J., Crandall, D., Junk, D., Ding, Y., & Borner, K. (2014, February). From Funding Agencies to Scientific Agency. *EMBO Reports*, 15(2), 131–133.

Bowser, A., & Shanley, L. (2013). New Visions in Citizen Science. Washington, DC: Woodrow Wilson International Center for Scholars.

Bugg-Levine, A., & Emerson, J. (2011). *Impact Investing: Transforming How We Make Money While Making a Difference*. San Francisco, CA: Jossey-Bass.

Burger, S. P., Murray, F., Kearney, S., & Ma, L. (2018, Winter). The Investment Gap that Threatens the Planet. *Stanford Social Innovation Review*, 16(1), 28–35.

Buschman, H. (2018, May 15). Big Data from World's Largest Citizen Science Microbiome Project Serves Food for Thought. Retrieved October 2019, from University of California San Diego School of Medicine: https://health.ucsd.edu/news/releases/Pages/2018-05-15-big-data-from-worlds-largest-citizen-science-microbiome-project-serves-food-for-thought.aspx.

Byrnes, J. E., Ranganathan, J., Walker, B. L., & Faulkes, Z. (2014). To Crowdfund Research, Scientists Must Build an Audience for Their Work. *PLOS ONE*, 9(12), e110329, 1–29.

Callaway, E. (2018, January 4). Facebook Billionaire Pours Funds into High-Risk Research. *Nature*, 553(7686), 10–11.

Capriati, M. (2018, November). Evidence-Based Policy Cause Area Report. Retrieved October 2019, from Founders Pledge: https://founderspledge.com/research/fp-evidence-based-policy.

Center for Carbon Removal. (2016). *Philanthropy Beyond Carbon Neutrality: How Near-Term Grants to Carbon Removal Can Make Long-Term Climate Goals a Reality*. Oakland, CA: Center for Carbon Removal.

Cha, A. E. (2015, January 18). Crowdfunding Propels Scientific Research. Retrieved October 2019, from *The Washington Post*: www.washingtonpost.com/national/health-science/crowdfunding-propels-scientific-research/2015/01/18/c1937690-9758-11e4-8005-1924ede3e54a_story.html.

Chan Zuckerberg Initiative. (2019). Science Programs & Resources. Retrieved October 2019, from Chan Zuckerberg Initiative: https://chanzuckerberg.com/science/programs-resources/.

Cooper, C. (2016). *Citizen Science: How Ordinary People Are Changing the Face of Discovery*. New York, NY: The Overlook Press.

Cybulski, J. S., Clements, J., & Prakash, M. (2014, June). Foldscope: Origami-Based Paper Microscope. *PLOS ONE*, 9(6), e98781, 1–11.

Dalio Philanthropies. (2019). Ocean Exploration and Awareness. Retrieved August 2019, from Dalio Philanthropies: www.daliophilanthropies.org/initiatives/ocean-exploration-and-awareness/.

Daniels, A., & Wallace, N. (2015, December 2). Using For-Profits to Funnel Big Sums to Charities Raises Transparency Concerns. Retrieved October 2019, from *The Chronicle of Philanthropy*: www.philanthropy.com/article/Using-For-Profits-to-Funnel/234429.

Emerson Collective. (2019). Elemental. Retrieved October 2019, from Emerson Collective: www.emersoncollective.com/emerson-elemental/.

Energy Futures Initiative. (2019). *Clearing the Air: A Federal RD&D Initiative and Management Plan for Carbon Dioxide Removal Technologies.* Washington, DC: Energy Futures Initiative.

Experiment. (2019a). Case Studies. Retrieved October 2019, from Experiment: https://experiment.com/start#case-studies.

Experiment. (2019b). Frequently Asked Questions. Retrieved October 2019, from Experiment: https://experiment.com/faq.

Experiment. (2019c). Lab Notes. Retrieved October 2019, from Experiment: https://experiment.com/labnotes?sort=top.

Experiment. (2019d). Results. Retrieved October 2019, from Experiment: https://experiment.com/results.

Experiment. (2019e). Ethics Requirements. Retrieved October 2019, from Experiment: https://experiment.com/guide/extra#ethics.

Fang, F. C., & Casadevall, A. (2016). Research Funding: The Case for a Modified Lottery. *mBio*, 7(2), e00422-16, 1–7.

Fortin, J.-M., & Currie, D. J. (2013, June). Big Science vs. Little Science: How Scientific Impact Scales with Funding. *PLOS ONE*, 8(6), e65263, 1–7.

Fortunato, S., Bergstrom, C. T., Borner, K., Evans, J. A., Helbing, D., Milojevic, S., et al. (2018). Science of Science. *Science*, 359(1007), eaao0185, 1–7.

Founders Pledge. (2019a). Research. Retrieved October 2019, from Founders Pledge: https://founderspledge.com/research.

Founders Pledge. (2019b). Home Page. Retrieved October 2019, from Founders Pledge: https://founderspledge.com/.

Gathering for Open Science Hardware. (2017). Global Open Science Hardware Roadmap: Making Open Science Hardware Ubiquitous by 2025. Retrieved October 2019, from Gathering for Open Science Hardware: http://openhardware.science/wp-content/uploads/2017/12/GOSH-roadmap-smll.pdf.

Gibney, E. (2019, April 18). Israeli Spacecraft Crash-Lands on Moon. *Nature*, 568(7751), 286.

Goldberg, D. (2018, July 1). Our Approach to Charity. Retrieved October 2019, from Founders Pledge: https://founderspledge.com/stories/our-approach-to-charity.

Goldhammer, J., Mitchell, K., Parker, A., Anderson, B., & Joshi, S. (2014). *The Craft of Incentive Prize Design: Lessons from the Public Sector.* San Francisco, CA: Deloitte University Press.

Gross, K., & Bergstrom, C. T. (2019). Content Models Highlight Inherent Inefficiencies of Scientific Funding Competitions. *PLOS Biology*, 17(1) e3000065, 1–15.

Guerrini, C. J., Majumder, M. A., Lewellyn, M. J., & McGuire, A. L. (2018, July 13). Citizen Science, Public Policy. *Citizen Science, Public Policy*, 361(6398), 134–136.

Halstead, J. (2018, May). Climate Change Cause Area Report. Retrieved October 2019, from Founders Pledge: https://founderspledge.com/research/fp-climate-change.

Halstead, J. (2019, January). Existential Risk Cause Area Report. Retrieved October 2019, from Founders Pledge: https://founderspledge.com/research/fp-existential-risk.

Herries, K., & Wiener, C. (2018, November/December). Underwater Paradigm Shift. Retrieved November 2019, from *Eco Environment Coastal & Offshore*, (pp. 24–29): https://www.mydigitalpublication.com/publication/?i=543413&ver=html5&p=24.

Kaiser, J. (2013, August 26). XPrize Pulls Plug on $10 Million Genomics Competition. Retrieved September 2019, from *Science*: www.sciencemag.org/news/2013/08/xprize-pulls-plug-10-million-genomics-competition.

Kearney, S., Murray, F., & Nordan, M. (2014, Fall). A New Vision for Funding Science. *Stanford Social Innovation Review*, 12(4), 50–55.

Kickstarter. (2019, October 17). *eVscope*. Retrieved October 2019, from Kickstarter: www. kickstarter.com/projects/unistellar/evscope-100-times-more-powerful-than-a-classical-t.

Kintisch, E. (2018, August 24). Project Lifts the Veil on Life in the Ocean's Twilight Zone. *Science*, 361(6404), 738.

Lash, A. (2019, September 4). Bankrupt uBiome Says Founders May Have Misled Investors. Retrieved October 2019, from Xconomy: https://xconomy.com/san-francisco/2019/09/04/bankrupt-ubiome-says-founders-may-have-misled-investors/.

Lenkowsky, L. (2015, December 2). Ending Philanthropy as We Know It. Retrieved October 2019, from *The Wall Street Journal*: www.wsj.com/articles/ending-phila nthropy-as-we-know-it-1449100975.

Lim, X. (2015, October 29). How to Make the Most of Carbon Dioxide. *Nature*, 526 (7575), 628–630.

Lintott, C. (2020). *The Crowd and the Cosmos: Adventures in the Zooniverse*. Oxford, UK: Oxford University Press.

Liu, M., Choy, V., Clarke, P., Barnett, A., & Pomeroy, L. (2020). The Acceptability of Using a Lottery to Allocate Research Funding: A Survey of Applicants. *Research Integrity and Peer Review*, 5(3), 1–7.

Macpherson, R., Kearney, S., & Murray, F. (2017). *Donor-Advised Funds: An Underutilized Philanthropic Vehicle to Support Innovation in Science and Engineering*. Cambridge, MA: PRIME Coalition.

Marshall, J. (2013, March 26). Kickstart Your Research. *PNAS*, 110(3), 4857–4859.

Mathews, A. W., & Marcus, A. D. (2019, June 24). FBI Probes Whether Lab Startup uBiome Used Improper Billing Codes, Sought Unnecessary Tests. Retrieved October 2019, from *The Wall Street Journal*: www.wsj.com/articles/fbi-probes-whether-lab-sta rtup-ubiome-used-improper-billing-codes-sought-unnecessary-tests-11561373930.

Maxmen, A. (2017, February 16). 'Riskiest Ideas' on Tap. *Nature*, 542(7641), 280–281.

McDonald, D., Hyde, E., Debelius, J. W., Morton, J. T., Gonzalez, A., Ackermann, G. et al. (2018, May/June). American Gut: An Open Platform for Citizen Science Microbiome Research. *mSystems*, 3(3), 1–28.

Montgomery, D. (2018, June 11). The Quest of Laurene Powell Jobs. Retrieved October 2019, from *The Washington Post*: www.washingtonpost.com/news/style/wp/2018/06/11/feature/the-quest-of-laurene-powell-jobs/.

National Research Council. (2007). *Innovation Inducement Prizes at the National Science Foundation*. Washington, DC: The National Academies Press.

Nielsen, M. (2012). *Reinventing Discovery: The New Era of Networked Science*. Princeton, NJ: Princeton University Press.

Nisbet, M. (2018, July/August). Strategic Philanthropy in the Post-Cap-and-Trade Years: Reviewing U.S. Climate and Energy Foundation Funding. *WIREs Climate Change*, 9(4), e 524, 1–17.

Office of Science and Technology Policy. (2019). *Implementation of Federal Prize and Citizen Science Authority: Fiscal Year 2017–18*. Washington, DC: Office of Science and Technology Policy.

Omidyar Network. (2016). Beneficial Technology. Retrieved October 2019, from Omidyar Network: www.omidyar.com/beneficial-tech.

Open Philanthropy Project. (n.d.a). Scientific Research. Retrieved from Open Philanthropy Project: www.openphilanthropy.org/focus/scientific-research.

Open Philanthropy Project. (n.d.b). Cause Selection. Retrieved from Open Philanthropy Project: www.openphilanthropy.org/research/cause-selection#Exploring_p otential_focus_areas.

Open Philanthropy Project. (n.d.c). Potential Risks from Advanced Artificial Intelligence. Retrieved September 2019, from Open Philanthropy Project: www.openphilanthropy.org/focus/global-catastrophic-risks/potential-risks-advanced-artificial-intelligence.

Osterloh, M., & Frey, B. S. (2020, February). How to Avoid Borrowed Plumes in Academia. *Research Policy*, 49(1), 1–9.

Ozdemir, V., Faris, J., & Srivastava, S. (2015). Crowdfunding 2.0: The Next-Generation Philanthropy. *EMBO Reports*, 16(3), 267–271.

Patel, M. (2013, July). Why Contests Improve Philanthropy. Miami, FL: Knight Foundation. Retrieved October 2019, from Knight Foundation: https://knightfoundation.org/features/open-contests.

Pearce, J. (2016). Return on Investment for Open Source Scientific Hardware Development. *Science and Public Policy*, 43(2), 192–195.

Plechaty, D., Amador, G., & Mazurek, J. (2019, March 6). 2050 Priorities for Climate Action: How Philanthropy Can Help to Scale Carbon Removal. Retrieved October 2019, from ClimateWorks Foundation: www.climateworks.org/blog/how-philanthropy-can-help-to-scale-carbon-removal.

Price, M. (2019, April 26). TED Offers Funding Path, No Just Stage, for "Audacious" Ideas. *Science*, 364(6438), 317.

Reiser, D. B. (2018). The Rise of Philanthropy LLCs. *Stanford Social Innovation Review*, 16(3), 26–33.

Rosen, J. (2018, November 2). Seafloor Mappers to Compete for XPRIZE. *Science*, 362 (6414), 507–508.

Roumbanis, L. (2019). Peer Review or Lottery? A Critical Analysis of Two Different Forms of Decision-making Mechanisms for Allocation of Research Grants. *Science, Technology, & Human Values*, 44(6), 994–1019.

Sauermann, H., & Franzoni, C. (2015, January 20). Crowd Science User Contribution Patterns and their Implications. *PNAS*, 112(3), 679–684.

Sauermann, H., Franzoni, C., & Shafi, K. (2019). Crowdfunding Scientific Research: Descriptive Insights and Correlates of Funding Success. *PLOS ONE*, 14(1), 0, 1–26.

Schmidt Marine Technology Partners. (n.d.). About Us. Retrieved October 2019, from Schmidt Marine Technology Partners: www.schmidtmarine.org/about-1.

Schmidt Ocean Institute. (2017). 5 Years of Science Aboard Falkor. Retrieved August 2019, from Schmidt Ocean Institute, 2017 Annual Report: http://2017annualreport.schmidtocean.org/2018/05/03/2017introduction/.

SciFund Challenge. (2019). Home. Retrieved October 2019, from SciFund Challenge: https://scifundchallenge.org.

SciStarter. (2019). About SciStarter. Retrieved October 2019, from SciStarter: https://scistarter.org/about.

Scutari, M. (2018, January 8). Dept. of Disruption: Can Philanthropy-Backed Oversight Keep Up With the AI Boom? Retrieved September 2019, from *Inside Philanthropy*: www.insidephilanthropy.com/home/2018/1/8/dept-of-disruption-can-philanthropy-backed-oversight-keep-up-with-the-ai-boom.

SETI Institute. (2018, April 19). SETI Institute-Unistellar Partnership Promises to Revolutionize Amateur Astronomy. Retrieved October 2019, from SETI Institute: www.seti.org/press-release/seti-institute-unistellar-partnership-promises-revolutionize-amateur-astronomy.

Simons Foundation. (2017). Flatiron Institute Inaugural Celebration. Retrieved July 2019, from *Annual Report 2017 Edition*: www.simonsfoundation.org/report2017/stor ies/flatiron-institute-inaugural-celebration/.

Sinatra, R., Wang, D., Deville, P., Song, C., & Barabasi, A.-L. (2016, November 4). Quantifying the Evolution of Individual Scientific Impact. *Science*, 354(6312), aaf5239, 1–8.

Singer, N., & Isaac, M. (2015, December 3). Zuckerberg's Philanthropy Uses L.L.C. for More Control. *The New York Times*, p. B1.

Siva, N. (2014, September 20). Crowdfunding for Medical Research Picks Up Pace. *The Lancet*, 384(9948), 1085–1086.

Snyder, J., Mathers, A., & Crooks, V. A. (2016, November). Fund My Treatment!: A Call for Ethics-Focused Social Science Research into the Use of Crowdfunding for Medical Care. *Social Science & Medicine*, 169, 27–30.

Sorenson, O., Assenova, V., Li, G.-C., Boada, J., & Fleming, L. (2016, December 23). Expand Innovation Finance via Crowdfunding. *Science*, 354(6319), 1526–1528.

Starr, K. (2013, August 22). Dump the Prizes. Retrieved October 2019, from *Stanford Social Innovation Review*: https://ssir.org/articles/entry/dump_the_prizes.

Stokstad, E. (2018, November 23). Luxe Research Ship to Explore the Deep Ocean. *Science*, 362(6417), 874–875.

Systrom, N., Kearney, S., & Murray, F. (2017). Foundations: Exploring the Emerging Practice of Philanthropic Investing to Support Innovation in Science and Engineer- ing. Cambridge, MA: PRIME Coalition.

The Audacious Project. (2019a). Homepage. Retrieved September 2019, from The Audacious Project: https://audaciousproject.org.

The Audacious Project. (2019b). 2019 Ideas. Retrieved September 2019, from The Audacious Project: www.audaciousproject.org/ideas#2019.

Thinkable. (2018). Home. Retrieved October 2019, from Thinkable: www.thinkable.org.

Tool Foundry. (n.d.). About Tool Foundry. Retrieved October 2019, from Tool Foundry: www.toolfoundry.org/about/.

Ubois, J. (2019, Winter). The Promise of Incentive Prizes. *Stanford Social Innovation Review*, 17(1) S4–S6.

UK Research and Innovation. (2019). UKRI Vision for Public Engagement. London, UK: UK Research and Innovation.

Unistellar Optics. (2019, March 28). Unistellar Raises €2.1 Million for Its Revolutionary Digital Telescope. Retrieved October 2019, from Unistellar: https://unistellaroptics. com/unistellar-raises-e2-1-million-for-its-revolutionary-digital-telescope/.

Vachelard, J., Gambarra-Soares, T., Augustini, G., Riul, P., & Maracaja-Coutinho, V. (2016, February 17). A Guide to Scientific Crowdfunding. *PLOS Biology*, 14(2), e1002373, 1–7.

Walsweer, Tina. (2018, May 22). Give Chance a Chance. Retrieved December 2019, from Volkswagner Stiftung: www.volkswagenstiftung.de/en/news-press/funding-s tories/give-chance-a-chance-%E2%80%93-a-lottery-decides-which-daring-research-i deas-receive-funding.

Williams, H. (2012). Innovation Inducement Prizes: Connecting Research to Policy. *Journal of Policy Analysis and Management*, 31(3), 752–776.

Williams, T. (2019, March 22). Important But Neglected: Why an Effective Altruist Funder Is Giving Millions to AI Security. Retrieved September 2019, from *Inside Philanthropy*: www. insidephilanthropy.com/home/2019/3/22/why-this-effective-altruist-funder-is-giving- millions-to-ai-security.

Wyler, D., & Haklay, M. (2018). Integrating Citizen Science into University. In S. Hecker, M. Haklay, A. Bowswer, Z. Makuch, J. Vogel, & A. Bonn, eds., *Citizen Science: Innovation in Open Science, Society and Policy* (pp. 168–181). London, UK: UCL Press.

Yu, S., Johnson, S., Lai, C., Cricelli, A., & Fleming, L. (2017, December). Crowd-funding and Regional Entrepreneurial Investment: An Application of the Crowd-Berkeley Database. *Research Policy*, 46(10), 1723–1737.

Zinsmeister, K. (2020, Winter). Natural Advantages. Retrieved January 2020, from *Philanthropy*: www.philanthropyroundtable.org/philanthropy-magazine/article/natu ral-advantages.

8 Opportunities and challenges ahead

Lessons learned and scenarios for the future of science philanthropy

Putting it all together

The preceding chapters have investigated the origins of contemporary science philanthropy, analyzed many of the predominant approaches that these foundations are taking today, and pinpointed newer developments that may characterize a more substantial portion of the field in the years ahead. The responsible research and innovation (RRI) conceptual framework has guided these discussions and, for the first time, has been applied in a systematic way to understanding how philanthropies influence and operate within the research system. The argument has been that science philanthropies have an important, yet often overlooked, role in bringing societal responsibility of research to the forefront. There are already a number of examples and case studies showing how science philanthropies are infusing the mentality of RRI into their grantmaking, even if not alluding to it specifically by name. Science philanthropies are funding individuals, institutions, and networks with more sustained attention to being anticipatory, deliberative, inclusive, and reflexive. Moreover, it is heartening that interviews with foundation staff, leaders, and other practitioners show they are thinking deeply about how to impart a greater degree of societal responsibility into what they do.

A key element here is rethinking what it means to fund and undertake high quality research. Daniel Sarewitz (2016), in his article "Saving Science," nicely summarizes what this kind of shift will entail. He asserts that, "science will be made more reliable and more valuable for society today not by being protected from societal influences but instead by being brought, carefully and appropriately, into a direct, open, and intimate relationship with those influences" (p. 8). Later in the article, Sarewitz captures what such RRI-inspired science might look like. "In the future," he writes, "the most valuable science institutions will be closely linked to the people and places whose urgent problems need to be solved; they will cultivate strong lines of accountability to those for whom solutions are important; they will incentivize scientists to care about the problems more than the production of knowledge" (p. 39). If such a vision is to be realized, science philanthropies will have to play a central role. They will be called on to marry funding of basic science that is methodologically top notch while also being societally relevant in some capacity. As I noted in previous chapters, that is not to say that all science philanthropies need to radically shift their efforts in order to combine these two elements. Funding basic scientific research for its own sake will continue to have an important place in this ecosystem. Yet even there, there are almost always ways to take societal responsibility seriously, as it were, and infuse RRI principles into various steps of decision-making and resource allocation processes. What the examples discussed throughout this book have shown is that there is a broad spectrum of approaches that science philanthropies can adopt, and the hope is that these institutions are motivated to choose deliberately where they fit along this spectrum when deciding how to address questions related to societal responsibility.

Going forward, it is likely that science philanthropies will be called upon by other stakeholders to devote more attention and resources in support of research activities that also include more robust components related to societal engagement. Science philanthropies should prepare now and think through more comprehensively and proactively about how they will answer such a call, if and when it arises. Examples discussed throughout this book have pointed to approaches that foundations have already adopted that move in this direction. In many instances, these approaches combine a deep, abiding commitment to merit review of research with more deliberate attempts to fund people, organizations, and networks that are forward-looking, inclusive, and willing to reflect and improve upon their own practices and procedures. As has been shown, there are numerous ways to do so. Part of the solution may be that science philanthropies looking to fund interdisciplinary research, which generally involves creative applications of different techniques from different fields, requires different communities to come together and interact with one another in new styles, and adopt different success criteria. Part of the solution may be science philanthropies looking to fund researchers who have different backgrounds and experiences than they usually support. Part of the solution may be in embracing more open data sharing practices to disseminate information more broadly. Part of the solution may be having community members impacted by or participating in research involved in funding allocation decisions. Part of the solution may be in increased public engagement and integrating science into a wider array of cultural contexts.

In short, science philanthropies will increasingly be called on to serve in boundary spanning roles, efforts by individuals or organizations to more intentionally link together communities of research and practice. There is an extensive literature identifying and examining the conceptual and practical element of boundary spanning between science and society (Gieryn, 1999; Guston, 1999; Guston, 2001; Crona & Parker, 2011; Parker & Crona, 2012; White, et al., 2010). More recently, a group of researchers and practitioners described the importance of "mainstreaming boundary-spanning" by the research and funding communities in order to "sustain productive interactions between science, policy, and society, lead to increasingly useful science, and ultimately build capacity for science to inform decision-making" (Bednarek, et al., 2018, pp. 1176–1177). They point out that funders are already taking steps in this direction, as "some funding agencies, through their grant-making, actively match the production of science with specific decision-making needs and context using boundary spanners" (Bednarek, et al., 2018, p. 1177). With funders, both philanthropic and government, doing more on this front, they can take steps toward helping boundary-spanning individuals, institutions, and networks "to increase the efficiency by which scientific evidence informs policy, foster the capacity to absorb new evidence and perspectives, enhance research relevance for societal challenges, and open new policy windows" (Bednarek, et al., 2018, p. 1181).

Conversely, if these opportunities are missed or ignored, a number of potential challenges may arise. First, high quality science capable of addressing pressing global problems will be missed and left to the side if the contributions of boundary spanning activities are not sufficiently valued. Second, without the diversity of thought and inspiration that boundary spanning provides, key stakeholders that could be more closely involved in the scientific enterprise—such as researchers at the margins, interested members of the public, or even those skeptical or distrusting of science—will not be brought into the fold as much as they could be. Third, there is the risk that the entire science philanthropy enterprise could be challenged or called into question. This could happen, especially if there is a growing sense that the billions of dollars that science funders give out—even if they lead to a deeper understanding of nature and how the world works—are not translating into useful contributions to society. Finally, some may even argue more strongly that, in exchange for their privileged financial status granted by society at large, science philanthropies have a moral obligation to bridge whatever gaps exists between science and society. In this view, science philanthropies are obliged to play this role in a democratic society. This chapter will expound on these points further. First, it will look back and highlight some of the lessons learned from the discussion presented throughout this book. Then, it will look forward and consider some plausible, alternative future scenarios about the ways in which science philanthropy may evolve in different directions.

Lessons learned for science philanthropy

There are a number of lessons that can be drawn from the discussion and analysis contained in the previous chapters, both in terms of high-level findings and more targeted conclusions. It is evident that for a number of reasons, *foundations are likely to play an increased and outsized role in supporting science and in shaping the research enterprise*, even more so than was the case in recent decades. This is due to a number of factors, including uncertainties surrounding federal funding for science, increased competition for these federal dollars within the research community, indicators of growing interest in funding science by newer philanthropies, and a broader recognition of the need for scientific research to address complex, pressing societal problems. A second finding that emerges from this analysis is that *philanthropic support for science will continue to be focused on providing research fellowships for individual scientists, supplying critical support for research centers and institutions, and establishing and sustaining research networks.* As Chapter 4 demonstrated, these forms of science philanthropy serve as the primary kinds of interventions that foundations undertake. Moreover, each of these types of efforts can be intentionally steered toward taking better account of societal responsibility when attention is paid to these matters. Science philanthropies have traditionally had preferences in terms of how funding in each of these modes was directed. Fellowships for early career scientists are popular, as they allow funders to support the next generation of researchers. High profile research centers and universities tend to receive large amounts of funding, as there is the expectation that this is where scientific breakthroughs are likely to originate. Convening networks that bring researchers together has been the primary mode of disseminating findings. Yet, as the discussion has shown, science philanthropies are already taking steps to improve the societal relevance of these grantmaking approaches. Diversity, equity, and inclusion criteria are being added as key selection metrics, as philanthropies reassess their priorities and practices. Funders are increasingly looking to diversify the institutions that they support, seeking to support discovery wherever it may be housed. Networks are no longer confined to the research community and, instead, are moving toward inclusion of other stakeholders and members of the public.

Third, *multi-sectoral funding partnerships are becoming more of the norm*, as researchers and institutions look to develop more sustainable funding models and are under pressure to pool resources from multiple sources in order to maintain sufficient funding levels. Science philanthropies are increasingly working to develop these partnerships at the outset of a funding program to ensure that necessary resources are available. Scientists themselves are becoming more entrepreneurial, working to create funding coalitions on their own, which may involve combining support from philanthropy, government, industry, and even crowdfunding.

As noted in Chapter 7, while such alternative modes of giving to science are on the rise, it is likely these new approaches will mainly augment, not replace, traditional forms of science philanthropy. In this model, given the combination of the traditional and the novel, stakeholders throughout the research enterprise will need to become more facile in working with an even wider spectrum of donors than was previously the case. Funding from foundations set up as limited liability companies (LLCs) might coincide with government grants and foundation money. Crowdfunded resources might be used to fill in the gaps. Researchers based at universities might look to find new ways of collaborating with the in-house research centers that science philanthropies have started to create.

Likewise, these multi-sectoral partnerships can potentially help mitigate the impacts when philanthropic funding runs its course and winds down. Science philanthropies and other funders need to pay close attention at these moments and think about how to help grantees prepare for ongoing success when a project or research effort comes to a conclusion. This could involve a host of considerations. Science philanthropies need to think through how branding and communication elements, such the use of the foundation's name in a project's title, could help or hinder the ability of researchers to secure funds in the future. Foundations may choose to sequence their grants in a certain way in response to funding from other sources to help give researchers a longer runway to secure additional support. Science funders may also want to dedicate resources to grantees to develop sustainability plans or conduct other longer-term strategic planning assessments. In these ways, science philanthropies can strengthen the development of an anticipatory mindset from the outset of a project all the way through to its end.

Fourth, one of the critical lessons arising from this analysis is that even though it may be time consuming and challenging, *science philanthropies should regularly conduct evaluation as a core feedback mechanism*, which not only helps identify whether the goals of a program have been met but can also give a sense as to whether societal responsibility is being adequately addressed. Soliciting feedback and using evidence-based practices to adjust a science philanthropy's own practices is a sign of a sound organizational culture and an indicator of effective organizational governance (Jones, et al., 2018). Part of the challenge of conducting evaluations to assess the impact of funding for basic scientific research is that it is hard to identify counterfactual conditions that would give an indication as to what would happen in the absence of such funding. One workshop report on this question of how to evaluate the impact of philanthropy for basic science asserts that "assessing the impact of basic science funding is more complex than measuring the impact of applied science research or direct service interventions common in the health and human service arenas" (Cosentino, Foster, & Klebanov, 2017, p. 1). This is due to a range of factors, including that the importance of results only "becomes evident many years after a typical grant period," because "basic science does not follow a linear path," and since many "scientists, projects and institutions rely on many sources of financial support" (Cosentino, Foster, & Klebanov, 2017, p. 1). Not only is there increasing interest in the science philanthropy community in evaluating the impact of their programs, but steps can be taken to design funding programs at the outset to better prepare for evaluation at the conclusion. There are methodological adjustments that can be adopted, such as comparing grant winners with those applicants who just missed receiving funding, identifying and following other comparison groups to those in a foundation's funded portfolio, expanding the view beyond assessing publications and looking at broader impacts on a field, or in getting a more holistic view of foundation funding on the direction of a researcher's career (Li & Conti, 2018). Understanding the wider impact of various types of societal impact that could arise from science philanthropy funding is key, as there is growing evidence that researchers themselves want to produce research products that are better designed to have a stronger impact on society (Parks, Rodriguez-Rincon, Parkinson, & Manville, 2019).

There are various tactics that science philanthropies can adopt to approach evaluation in different contexts (Basco, 2018). Some funders conduct external evaluations on a grant by grant basis; others may conduct summative evaluations at the conclusion of the program or undertake evaluations at different points in a program's lifecycle, including formative evaluations at the outset or mid-term assessments. As has been discussed, grant-level evaluations are generally conducted through peer review by subject matter experts. For program-level reviews, however, foundations can outsource these evaluations to external consultants, trained academic evaluators, or even from visiting committees of subject matter experts to conduct one-off reviews. In some cases, program personnel responsible for oversight and management are tasked with conducting evaluations alongside their other duties. In other instances, where resources are available, science philanthropies are able to hire an evaluation expert on staff or create an entire evaluation team to conduct and oversee program evaluations as an in-house capability. Funders differ as to whether program evaluations are mainly designed for internal use or to be more widely shared with the research community, yet the more these materials are made publicly available, the more a foundation demonstrates the extent to which it values openness and engagement with external constituents.

The Moore Foundation, for instance, is a good example of a science philanthropy that regularly adopts this practice and shares its program review learning with the wider community. The Moore Foundation not only has a section on its website dedicated to sharing findings from external program evaluations that have been conducted, but these detailed reports and evaluation documents are often accompanied by blog post summaries prepared by foundation staff. In the second half of 2018 alone, the Moore Foundation shared the results of three evaluations associated with their science programs. These included evaluations of the Moore Foundation's Emergent Phenomena in Quantum Systems Initiative (RTI International, 2018), Data-Driven Discovery Initiative (Abt Associates, 2017), and Marine Microbiology Initiative (Science-Metrix Inc., 2018). Collectively, these external evaluations employed a range of research methodologies—including qualitative interviews, document analysis, online surveys, bibliometric analyses, site visits, and assessment by a panel of experts—to assess the impact of these programs and inform conclusions about what was accomplished. Other foundations have adopted similar approaches as well. For instance, in 2018, The Rockefeller Foundation also shared the results of a multi-method evaluation of its Digital Jobs Africa Initiative (Genesis Analytics, 2018). Similarly, the Sloan Foundation has supported program evaluations that have utilized these various techniques to assess impact, including those focused on reviewing the Moore-Sloan Data Science Environments effort (Abt Associates, 2019) and bibliometric and network analysis of the Sloan Foundation's Microbiology of the Built Environment program (Hicks, Coil, Stahmer, & Eisen, 2019). Making evaluation results public contributes to science philanthropies being more accountable and transparent, and it helps to engage various stakeholders within and beyond the research community.

Expanding this practice can be a key element in contributing to how these institutions address concerns about societal responsibility.

Lastly, this analysis indicates that *science philanthropies should ensure that the notion of responsibility is made more explicit within various dimensions of their work.* Examples, case studies, and interviewee perspectives shared in the preceding chapters have indicated how this can be done, from informally keeping issues of societal responsibility top-of-mind, to updating proposal evaluation criteria, to seeking out individuals and institutions who are looking to make strides in this area. This gets to the heart of what it means for science philanthropies to take these matters seriously. As discussed in Chapter 7, recent economics, public policy, and social science research is beginning to show that funders are likely to get more bang for their buck if they look to diversify their efforts on a number of fronts. For instance, new studies have shown that the provision of larger grants does not necessarily correlate with increases in the novelty or significance of research that is conducted, findings that should encourage funders to diversify their research budgets (Lerchenmueller, 2018; Mairesse, Pezzoni, Stephan, & Lane, 2018). Scientists that have previously been declined funding may end up being just as productive, if not more so, than those that may have won funding awards, so early career researchers that do not boast as strong a track record may warrant renewed attention by funders given their likelihood to succeed at subsequent stages of their careers (Ayoubi, Pezzoni, & Visentin, 2019; Wang, Jones, & Wang, 2019). Implicit bias can arise during the peer review and proposal assessment process at various stages, so steps need to be taken to make these dynamics visible and find effective ways of addressing them at the outset of review processes. (Kolev, Fuentes-Medel, & Murray, 2019; Teplitskiy, et al., 2019). Most of these studies that, collectively, point to the need for funders to be more reflexive in the practices they adopt and how they implement their programs have looked predominantly at these factors in the context of government funding. More empirical research that looks at how these dynamics play out in the context of philanthropies that support science is needed.

Chapter 4 described the many ways in which science philanthropies have already taken steps to think through these issues more comprehensively and apply them in a reflexive manner to their own institutions. Some foundations have adopted a requirement that proposers address how they will take account of diversity issues as part of their standard grant proposal application package. Others have brought in social science experts to conduct reviews of foundation practices and to help make improvements along these lines. Still others have established dedicated programs to focus on diversity, equity, and inclusion in science. In short, science philanthropies need to intertwine what they do with how they do it. As Christopherson, Scheufele, and Smith (2018) write in their article about civic science, previously mentioned in Chapter 4, "philanthropists can contribute to these conversations by communicating the core values that drive their own support of science, civic life, and their intersection" (p. 51). In their view, doing so allows science philanthropies to enhance their potential for effectiveness and impact, as they conclude that, "philanthropy can contribute to the formation of new ties among scientists, scientific institutions, and diverse stakeholders directly, as well as to bodies of knowledge to make them more effective" (p. 52).

While this book has illustrated the many ways in which science philanthropies are already making progress on this front, science philanthropies can also continue to learn from other funders in terms of how to be even more forward-looking when it comes to improving their own procedures and evaluation practices in order to better account for considerations of societal responsibility more directly. One good example that science philanthropies could pay more attention to, drawn from another funding domain, is how Canada's International Development Research Centre (IDRC) has developed a new conceptual framework that places stakeholder and user engagement at the core of assessing research impact. Known as Research Quality Plus (RQ+), this framework recognizes that judging the quality of funded research has to go beyond simply accounting for traditional indicators of "scientific merit" (Ofir, Schwandt, Duggan, & McLean, 2016, p. 4). Instead, the team at IDRC has conceived of a more integrative, well-rounded point of view on understanding research impact that accounts for "how an abiding interest in scientific values as the basis of assessing research quality might be effectively combined with considerations of user involvement in, and user-oriented criteria for, judging quality" (p. 4). In particular, the RQ+ framework makes evident that "the determination of research effectiveness is not solely in the hands of the researchers, or of the research funders or research project managers," meaning that multiple stakeholders and actors can and should have a say as to whether a research effort should be judged as being successful (p. 4).

While this perspective may be easier to implement in research settings that are more applied, as in the international development context rather than in a laboratory, there are still lessons that can be learned here for funders of basic science. This is especially true in that the often desired end-goal of basic science research is to eventually have some kind of broader societal impact, whether that means gaining a deeper appreciation of the workings of nature or developing a new product or process. As the originators of the RQ+ framework describe in a commentary article in *Nature*, assessing "scientific merit is necessary, but not sufficient" to fully account for societal impact, and to do so systematically requires "attention on how well scientists position their research for use, given the mounting understanding that uptake and influence begins during the research process, not only afterwards" (Lebel & McLean, 2018, p. 24). An application of the RQ+ framework in assessing the societal impact of hundreds of research projects across multiple countries found that scientific quality and societal utility often go hand-in-hand. As this analysis states, "contrary to conventional wisdom, there is no clear trade-off between the rigor and the utility of research and that research capacity-strengthening effort is positively correlated with the scientific merit of a project" (McLean & Sen, 2019, p. 123).

Of course, as discussed in Chapter 1 and Chapter 3, this notion that rigor and responsiveness can be intentionally and effectively combined serves as the bedrock principle of the RRI framework and the various related concepts that have preceded it, such as participatory technology assessment, real-time technology assessment, and anticipatory governance. To return to the introductory essay to the *International Handbook on Responsible Innovation* that was referenced in Chapter 1, von Schomberg and Hankins (2019) nicely encapsulate this view, and it is one which science philanthropies would be well-served to adopt. They write that, "the innovation process is neither steerless nor inherently good. Instead of being steerless, innovation can be managed and a growing body of research constitutes a testimony on how we can manage innovation and shape technologies in accordance with societal values and expectations as well as (re-)direct them towards normative targets such as sustainability goals" (von Schomberg & Hankins, 2019, p. 1). In the concluding section to this chapter and this book as a whole, let us turn to look ahead and consider some of the different directions that the societal responsibility of science philanthropy might take under different scenarios.

Scenarios for the future of science philanthropy

In recent years, there have been many valuable attempts that look ahead and try to discern the future of philanthropy. Some of these analyses examine the changing factors that underpin philanthropic practices as a whole (Fulton, Kasper, & Kibbe, 2010). Others look at the ongoing potential of philanthropy to make large contributions to address intractable societal challenges (The Bridgespan Group, 2019). Some studies look more specifically at how changes in the tax code might impact future philanthropic giving (Indiana University Lilly Family School of Philanthropy, 2019). Yet still other assessments take a global perspective to assess how philanthropy might change in different cultural and political contexts (Future Agenda, 2018).

Prominent practitioner and academic thought leaders in the field have also generated their own outlooks on the future of philanthropy, such as those from heads of foundations in Ford Foundation President Darren Walker (Walker, 2019) and former Hewlett Foundation President Paul Brest (Brest & Harvey, 2018). Researchers who study philanthropy have also provided their takes on the direction that the field is headed, with scholars such as Rob Reich (Reich, 2018) and Lucy Bernholz (Bernholz, Skloot, & Varela, 2010) sharing their views on these issues. Bernholz has produced a series of annual forecasts for the field over the past decade, which focus on the points of intersection between philanthropy, technology, and social entrepreneurship (Bernholz, 2018). Relatedly, university presidents, center directors, and faculty have laid out their visions about how to move institutions of higher education to become more societally responsible, whether in terms of addressing the issue of diversity more directly (Hrabowski III, Rous, & Henderson, 2019; Posselt, 2016), restructuring how universities function and are structured (Crow &

Dabars, 2015; Staley, 2019), or suggesting how to better link the social, research, and teaching missions of academic institutions (Owen-Smith, 2018; Gavazzi & Gee, 2018). Lastly, even consulting organizations and think tanks have developed a variety of tools to help philanthropies anticipate future trends, prepare for unexpected changes, and envision new trajectories for their institutions. These analyses have included the development of dedicated guides that outline how to conduct scenario analysis in non-profit settings (Scearce & Fulton, 2004) and maps to help visualize alternative futures for philanthropy (Institute for the Future, 2019).

However, to my knowledge, there does not yet exist a scenario framework that specifically looks at the future of science philanthropy. As discussed in Chapter 3, Murray presented a helpful typology that applied the Pasteur's Quadrant model to understand different kinds of historical and contemporary giving to science, yet it was not much focused on looking ahead (Murray, 2013). To be clear, the intention of scenario thinking exercises is not to make specific forecasts about how an issue will unfold in the future or devise pinpoint predictions about the years ahead. Matters such as science philanthropy are too complex and intertwined with other factors in society to allow for that kind of prescient foresight. Instead, the goal is to develop a mindset willing to consider the different ways in which key trends might interact with one another, become comfortable with uncertainty, and devise strategies that may be robust and applicable across alternative states of the world.

Typically in scenario planning, two underlying forces are identified, with each driver capable of evolving in at least two different directions. When considered in tandem, this creates four different, hypothetical future states of the world that can serve as conceptual guides for thinking in more nuanced ways about what may lay ahead. These speculative worlds can be explored in depth through stories and vignettes, identification of signals indicating how these forces are changing, or using other creative modalities to better imagine potentially surprising developments. Figure 8.1 provides a scenario analysis matrix that points to four different kinds of futures for science philanthropy in the years and decades ahead. The driver on the vertical axis is the extent to which science philanthropy *slows or accelerates* in the future. The driver on the horizontal axis is the extent to which the realization of societal responsibility is *low or high* in the future. When intersected, consideration of these drivers points to at least four different futures regarding the ways in which the style, impact, and scope of societally responsible science philanthropy might play out under these differing conditions.

The future world represented in the bottom left section of the figure arises when societal responsibility is low and science philanthropy slows. This scenario, titled *Failure to Launch*, is the most pessimistic and represents a world in which the excitement and promise of science philanthropy fails to live up to its potential over the long run. Hard as it may be to envision, one can imagine this world being characterized by a decline in philanthropic giving toward science. There could be a slowing, if not reversal, in the number of prominent philanthropies interested in funding science, with fewer new donors entering the space.

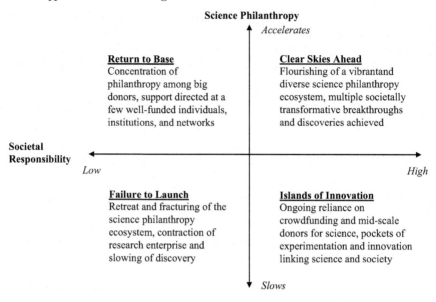

Figure 8.1 Scenarios for the future of science philanthropy

Presumably such a world could arise due to a backlash against science philanthropy caused by scandals, fraud, or other forms of negative attention that lead the pool of philanthropic resources for science to shrink. In this scenario, while science philanthropy may not disappear, it could be challenged and would contract in size and scale. Research institutions would have to scramble for a diminishing supply of resources. Competition for dollars would become even more fierce, and discovery would slow as the availability of funding dries up. If government spending on research further declines or becomes harder to secure due to further political polarization, this could create negative feedback loops and further reduce the resources available for research. Without government funding partners, foundations or high-net-worth individuals—who might have once focused on giving to science—might become disincentivized to provide funds for research. In this world, success stories of new researchers receiving funding awards would be few and far between, and funders may be less inclined to address diversity, equity, and inclusion as a central element of their grantmaking. What research is conducted would be restricted to achieving scientific output only, as concerns about research becoming more societally responsive fall by the wayside in this hard-pressed funding environment. Researchers once pursuing a more societally oriented research agenda might retrench. Remaining science philanthropies would also likely face a dilemma in how to respond. Some might choose to narrow their focus further to concentrate resources on a few longstanding priorities and pay more attention to already existing grantees in their funding portfolio. Other institutions may decide that it is necessary to band together more closely as a field and potentially develop a more regularized, collective set of research funding priorities if resources across multiple domains of science become unexpectedly scarce or hard to come by. This would likely make it difficult to establish new fields, adopt alternative methods, or conduct interdisciplinary research. Instead of supporting what is new, science philanthropies would likely have to focus on simply maintaining the status quo.

The world represented in the bottom right quadrant, called *Islands of Innovation*, would arise with a combination of factors in which science philanthropy slows, yet attention to societal responsibility becomes high. This is a more complicated future state of the world, where perhaps the larger-scale resources provided by institutional philanthropies fails to grow as hoped for—or are redirected to address other societal challenges—and other forms of smaller-scale science philanthropy become more prevalent. This world could feature, for example, a more sustained rise of crowdfunding, both in the United States and abroad. While perhaps not able to serve in the same role as larger philanthropic institutions, one could envision crowdfunding becoming more the norm than the exception, with a broader and growing base of researchers able to secure small or even modest amounts of funding from a larger pool of individual donors from the public. Furthermore, this world could see more of the newer science philanthropy institutions that are established choosing different organizational structures, such as incorporating themselves as LLCs, in order to be able to support other kinds of non-charitable undertakings along with whatever support for science is provided. Yet in this kind of environment, even as traditional science philanthropy fails to grow significantly and may even falter, whatever philanthropic funding does exist and is eventually provided actually starts to pay more attention to matters of societal responsibility. If crowdfunding has a more central presence in funding science and in shaping the direction of research, these developments could be accompanied by researchers being more interested in making the societal implications of the work they undertake more evident and engaging in public engagement activities that more closely link science and society. Existing science philanthropies might even move toward adopting more of the qualities of online crowdfunding platforms, for instance by encouraging grantees to regularly share research updates publicly via social media. Support for a more diverse cohort of researchers begins to arise more seamlessly, given the diversification of funding across a larger number of small donors. Following these trends, science philanthropies could become more interested in funding citizen science research projects to accompany, or perhaps supplant, their support for more traditional laboratory-based studies. This world might still feature a problematic fracturing of the science philanthropy community, however, as different funders pursue different goals and agendas without much coordination or sense of common purpose. As a result, societal responsibility might be better accounted for, but ultimately it is hindered by a lack of sufficient resources.

The area in the top left, termed *Return to Base*, symbolizes a future embodied by low attention paid to societal responsibility yet an acceleration and growth in science philanthropy. Here, funding provided for science philanthropy grows due to many factors. New donors at the individual and institutional level become interested in supporting specific topic areas based upon their personal preferences. Established foundations that were previously less focused on supporting science look to diversify their grantmaking portfolios in response to difficulties faced in successfully solving persistent challenges in other domains. This growth in science philanthropy would occur not only in the United State, but in Europe and elsewhere as well, as donors increasingly view science as a global enterprise. Drops in government funding are smoothed, if not wholly accounted for, by this rise in philanthropic giving for research. Yet in this world, such a rise in funding papers over worrying trends. Much of this new money would remain siloed and concentrated, largely dedicated to a small number of high-profile individuals and institutions working within the confined disciplinary boundaries that funders have prioritized. Individual, high-net-worth donors would come to have even more of an outsized impact on the direction of fields they decide to support. While a few disciplines and research institutions would be able to publicize and showcase large awards, many others would continue to scramble for resources, perhaps even more than previously. In this rich-get-richer scenario, efforts that are already well-resourced would continue to dominate. Expected outcomes from science philanthropy grantmaking would focus primarily on achieving academic research results and leading to new discoveries, with funders showing little interest in supporting or enhancing any potential societal components of research projects. Considerations of diversity would inevitably suffer as a result. Researchers from different disciplines working on similar problems would become further isolated, with little to no incentives to share findings across disciplinary boundaries or in more societally engaging ways. In many of its features, the *Return to Base* scenario mirrors in opposite the characteristics of the *Islands of Innovation* world. Both feature some positive trends, yet here the constraint on the scientific enterprise comes less from the availability of resources and more about restrictions due to funder interests and preferences. *Return to Base* sees science philanthropies following in one another's footsteps more so than setting out on their own or being willing to chart a new path to merge scientific impact with societal responsiveness, leading to an inclination for funding more inward-focused activities.

The final scenario represented on the top right quadrant, named *Clear Skies Ahead*, epitomizes a world in which both science philanthropy and societal responsibility advance considerably, with philanthropic giving for science accelerating and concern for societal responsibility hitting a high level. A well-rounded, flourishing funding ecosystem arises in this world, with effective science philanthropy existing at all levels, as philanthropies increasingly recognize the importance of giving to science. Small-scale donors are able to spread funding by leveraging crowdfunding platforms. Mid-scale institutions provide resources on a wide array of research topics to a diverse set of scholars and institutions. A growing number of philanthropic institutions and high-net-worth individuals capable of making larger contributions to science choose this area as a way to help lay the groundwork for improving society over the longer term. Even existing foundations that may have historically only supported scientific research on the margins devote more of their resources to this purpose. Science philanthropies increasingly work together in concert and through coordinating mechanisms, providing funds that complement one another's approach wherever possible and intentionally structuring their grantmaking to help balance each funder's strengths and interests. Additionally, multiple forums arise for funders to share knowledge and evaluate results. Although the scope of the challenges that funders are interested in addressing may continue to exceed available resources, science philanthropies help foster multi-sectoral partnerships, which become more of the norm than the exception. Furthermore, in this world science philanthropies strive to integrate mechanisms for addressing societal responsibility wherever possible. For instance, an abiding interest in achieving both scientific and societal impact leads philanthropies to support individuals, institutions, and networks that are not only committed to spanning disciplinary, methodological, and geographic boundaries, but that also integrate public engagement activities as critical constituent elements of the research effort. Researchers demonstrate a genuine interest in marshalling their scientific findings to address societal challenges, and science philanthropies help them achieve these goals by supporting an array of activities that include extensive public deliberation about their potential implications. Science philanthropies also look to serve as exemplars for the broader scientific community, reflexively applying best practices to improve the way they operate and intentionally working to account for diversity, equity, and inclusion dimensions throughout their grantmaking. Foundations would look to embrace new ways of identifying and supporting under-represented minority researchers. This world might see some science philanthropies trying to experiment with democratizing how they award a portion of their grant funding, potentially engaging users or local communities that may eventually be impacted by a research project to have more of a direct say in how and where funding is allocated. In short, *Clear Skies Ahead* results in a future in which the myriad financial resources of the philanthropic community are coupled with an unequivocal commitment to improving societal well-being.

Of course, not only is the actual future unknowable, but it is likely to be characterized by a subtle combination of factors, trends, and elements from each of these fictitious worlds. What is important is the ability to spot signals that point to these different directions, which may help inform an understanding of which future scenario state might be becoming more predominant or which scenario may need to be explored further. The Institute for the Future defines a signal as "a small or local innovation or disruption that has the potential to grow in scale and geographic distribution" and that it "catches our attention at one scale and in one locale and points to larger implications for other locales or even globally" (Institute for the Future, 2019). In fact, there are already real-world signals that can serve as early indicators for each of the possible futures discussed above. Regarding *Failure to Launch*, there have been a number of examples pointing to how the unceasing push for funding for scientific research can create problematic dynamics between philanthropies, individual donors, universities, and scientists (Thorp, 2019; Williams, 2019; Rogers, 2019). These instances not only can have the effect of eroding public trust, but they also can raise fundamental questions about the commitment of various stakeholders to act in the best interests of society at large. There are signs pointing in the direction of *Islands of Innovation*, including funders banding together to support the adoption of guidelines and practices that promote transparency and openness in sharing research results (Open Research Funders Group, n.d.; Center for Open Science, n.d.). There is also ongoing interest in funders utilizing the methods of "participatory futures" to engage the public in the research enterprise (Ramos, Sweeney, Peach, & Smith, 2019) and, as discussed in Chapter 7, there are indications that crowdfunding has disproportionately been beneficial for junior scholars and women in successfully raising money for research (Sauermann, Franzoni, & Shafi, 2019). There are also many signposts pointing in the direction of the *Return to Base* scenario. These signals tend to be high-profile announcements of individual donors making large awards—on the scale of hundreds of millions of dollars—to establish or expand schools or institutes at universities in order to conduct cutting-edge scientific research (Caltech, 2019; MIT, 2018; University of Chicago, 2019; Princeton University, 2019).

Most optimistically, there are signs that a *Clear Skies Ahead* future is possible, indicated by many new endeavors over the past few years aimed at enhancing the collective impact of science philanthropy. For instance, the Science Philanthropy Alliance has achieved a five-fold increase in membership growth since its formation, from its six initial members to its roster of 30, with four organizations joining in late 2019 alone (Science Philanthropy Alliance, 2019a; Science Philanthropy Alliance, 2019b). The Science Philanthropy Alliance has also succeeded in accomplishing many of the goals it set out to achieve over its first five years in existence (Science Philanthropy Alliance, 2019c). The examples presented throughout this book make clear that science philanthropies are increasingly interested in expanding diversity, equity, and inclusion programs and are taking steps to apply best practices of reflexivity and responsiveness to their own organizations. As noted in Chapter 4, there are a host of recently formed, philanthropically supported efforts designed to better understand the impacts of foundation giving for science and strengthen interactions between science philanthropies, academia, industry, and government, including the Science of Science Funding Initiative at the National Bureau of Economic Research (NBER) (National Bureau of Economic Research, 2018) and the Research on Research Institute (RoRI) (Research on Research Institute, 2019) at the Wellcome Trust. Similarly, philanthropic support has been devoted to help better connect scientists and researchers to decision-making processes, as exemplified by the creation of a new Center for Scientific Evidence in Public

Issues at the American Association for the Advancement of Science (AAAS) (Ham, 2018). Furthermore, Chapter 7 showcased that new developments are arising that are pushing the boundaries of science philanthropy, and while the outcomes there remain highly uncertain, just the very volume of activity across many fronts reveals the energy that is apparent across the field. As one assessment put it about the potential for science philanthropy in the years ahead, "a given for the foreseeable future is that there will be myriad small, medium-sized, and moonshot-scale problems for which philanthropic money could make a difference" (Amato, 2019) In sum, there is no shortage of societally oriented, collaborative opportunities for science philanthropies to pursue, and these institutions are already making progress on building a bedrock of experience advancing these approaches that can create a pathway for additional interventions going forward.

Moving the conversation forward

There is much still to be learned about science philanthropies. Each one has its own backstory, its own way of working, its own set of desired outcome areas. This book has shown, however, that there are ways to make sense of the field as a whole and that much can be learned when examining how this collective set of institutions is looking to have an impact on society. Nevertheless, a number of open questions still remain that offer promising avenues for future research. How does the unique history of individual science philanthropies influence their ability to implement the principles of RRI? What practices aimed at realizing the societal responsibility of research work best in different contexts? How does the introduction of societal responsibility as a guiding framework change the ways that science funders operate? How might data be better collected and shared across institutions to help science philanthropies determine whether they are making collective progress on this front? What changes would grantees—individual scientists, academic institutions, and research networks—want science philanthropies to make regarding these matters? How might traditional and novel forms of grantmaking more seamlessly interact with one another?

The more that science philanthropies work to integrate societal responsibility into everything they do, the more they will be able to shape the future of science and technology in a mindful and productive way. The more these institutions reflect on their own practices and set high expectations for themselves, the more they can help guide their grantees to be attentive to considerations of societal responsibility. Achieving responsible research and innovation is a continual process of adjustment and improvement. Yet it is a project that these organizations—with their long legacies behind them and the ability to take a long-term view toward the future—are perhaps best situated to pursue. By making the pursuit of societal responsibility one of their distinguishing characteristics, science philanthropies can truly exemplify the spirit of giving for research: to generate knowledge that improves people's lives and create a better world.

Bibliography

Abt Associates. (2017). *Mid-Term Evaluation of the Gordon and Betty Moore Foundation's Data-Driven Discovery (DDD) Initiative*. Cambridge, MA: Abt Associates.

Abt Associates. (2019). *Evaluation of the Moore-Sloan Data Science Environments*. Cambridge, MA: Abt Associates.

Amato, I. (2019, December 9). A Calling for Moonshot Philanthropy. Retrieved December 2020, from Medium: https://medium.com/the-moonshot-catalog/a-calling-for-moonshot-philanthropy-d372f0c837ac.

Ayoubi, C., Pezzoni, M., & Visentin, F. (2019, February). The Important Thing is Not to Win, It is to Take Part: What if Scientists Benefit from Participating in Research Grant Competitions? *Research Policy*, 48(1), 84–97.

Basco, D. (2018). *Strengthening Federal Capacity to Conduct Evaluations to Inform Future R&D Program Planning*. Santa Monica, CA: RAND Corporation.

Bednarek, A., Wyborn, C., Cvitanovic, C., Meyer, R., Colvin, R., Addison, P., et al. (2018, July). Boundary Spanning at the Science–Policy Interface: The Practitioners' Perspectives. *Sustainability Science*, 13(4), 1175–1183.

Bernholz, L. (2018). *Philanthropy and Digital Civil Society: Blueprint 2019*. Stanford, CA: Center on Philanthropy and Civil Society, Stanford University.

Bernholz, L., Skloot, E., & Varela, B. (2010). *Disrupting Philanthropy: Technology and the Future of the Social Sector*. Durham, NC: Center for Strategic Philanthropy and Civil Society, Duke University.

Brest, P., & Harvey, H. (2018). *Money Well Spent: A Strategic Plan for Smart Philanthropy, Second Edition*. Stanford, CA: Stanford University Press.

Caltech. (2019, September 26). Stewart and Lynda Resnick Pledge $750 Million to Caltech to Support Environmental Sustainability Research. Retrieved November 2019, from Caltech: www.caltech.edu/about/news/stewart-and-lynda-resnick-pledge-750-million-caltech-support-environmental-sustainability-research.

Center for Open Science. (n.d.). Transparency and Openness Promotion, Current Signatories. Retrieved November 2019, from Center for Open Science: https://cos.io/top/.

Christopherson, E. G., Scheufele, D. A., & Smith, B. (2018, Spring). The Civic Science Imperative. *Stanford Social Innovation Review*, 16(2), 46–52.

Cosentino, C., Foster, L., & Klebanov, J. (2017). *Evaluating Basic Science Investments: Toward a More Robust Practice*. Palo Alto, CA: Gordon and Betty Moore Foundation.

Crona, B. I., & Parker, J. N. (2011). Network Determinants of Knowledge Utilization: Preliminary Lessons From a Boundary Organization. *Science Communication*, 33(4), 448–471.

Crow, M. M., & Dabars, W. B. (2015). *Designing the New American University*. Baltimore, MD: Johns Hopkins University Press.

Fulton, K., Kasper, G., & Kibbe, B. (2010). *What's Next for Philanthropy: Acting Bigger and Adapting Better in a Networked World*. San Francisco, CA: Monitor Institute.

Future Agenda. (2018). *Future of Philanthropy: Insights from Multiple Expert Discussions Around the World*. London, UK: Future Agenda.

Gavazzi, S. M., & Gee, E. G. (2018). *Land-Grant Universities for the Future: Higher Education for the Public Good*. Baltimore, MD: Johns Hopkins University Press.

Genesis Analytics. (2018). *Evaluation of Impact: The Rockefeller Foundation's Digital Jobs Africa Initiative*. New York, NY: The Rockefeller Foundation.

Gieryn, T. F. (1999). *Culture Boundaries of Science: Credibility on the Line*. Chicago, IL: The University of Chicago Press.

Guston, D. H. (1999). Stabilizing the Boundary Between US Politics and Science: The Role of the Office of Technology Transfer as a Boundary Organization. *Social Studies of Science*, 29(1), 87–111.

Guston, D. H. (2001). Boundary Organizations in Environmental Policy and Science: An Introduction. *Science, Technology & Human Values*, 26(4), 399–408.

Ham, B. (2018, September 28). AAAS EPI Center Launch Brings Evidence to Policy-Makers. *Science*, 361(6409), 1327–1328.

Hicks, D. J., Coil, D. A., Stahmer, C. G., & Eisen, J. A. (2019). Network Analysis to Evaluate the Impact of Research Funding on Research Community Consolidation. *PLOS ONE*, 14(6), e0218273, 1–14.

Hrabowski III, F. A., Rous, P. J., & Henderson, P. H. (2019). *The Empowered University: Shared Leadership, Culture Change, and Academic Success*. Baltimore, MD: Johns Hopkins University Press.

Indiana University Lilly Family School of Philanthropy. (2019). *The Philanthropy Outlook 2019 & 2020*. Indianapolis, IN: Indiana University Lilly Family School of Philanthropy.

Institute for the Future. (2019). Signals. Retrieved November 2019, from Institute for the Future: www.iftf.org/what-we-do/foresight-tools/signals/.

Institute for the Future. (2019). *The Future of Philanthropy: Networked Action for Social Impact*. Palo Alto, CA: Institute for the Future.

Jones, M., Lepetit, L., Krapels, J., Lichten, C., Spisak, A., & Manville, C. (2018). *Organising for Excellence: An International Review of Good Practice in Organisational Design and Governance of Research Funding Bodies*. Santa Monica, CA: RAND Corporation.

Kolev, J., Fuentes-Medel, Y., & Murray, F. (2019). *Is Blinded Review Enough? How Gendered Outcomes Arise Even Under Anonymous Evaluation*. Cambridge, MA: National Bureau of Economic Research.

Lebel, J., & McLean, R. (2018, July 5). A Better Measure of Research from the Global South. *Nature*, 559(7712), 23–26.

Lerchenmueller, M. (2018, July). Does More Money Lead to More Innovation? Evidence from the Life Sciences. Retrieved November 2019, from National Bureau of Economic Research: http://conference.nber.org/conf_papers/f113989.pdf.

Li, D., & Conti, A. (2018). *An Advancing the Science of "Science Funding Impact" White Paper on Impact Evaluation for Science Funding*. Cambridge, MA: National Bureau of Economic Research.

Mairesse, J., Pezzoni, M., Stephan, P., & Lane, J. (2018, June). Publication Outcome of Public Funding in Science: A Panel Data Analysis of Grant Attribution, Scaling and Bundling Issues. Retrieved November 2019, from National Bureau of Economic Research: https://conference.nber.org/conf_papers/f114408.pdf.

McLean, R. K., & Sen, K. (2019). Making a Difference in the Real World? A Meta-Analysis of the Quality of Use-Oriented Research Using the Research Quality Plus Approach. *Research Evaluation*, 28(2), 123–135.

MIT. (2018, October 15). MIT Reshapes Itself to Shape the Future. Retrieved November 2019, from MIT: http://news.mit.edu/2018/mit-reshapes-itself-step hen-schwarzman-college-of-computing-1015.

Murray, F. (2013). Evaluating the Role of Science Philanthropy in American Research Universities. In J. Lerner & S. Stern, eds., *Innovation Policy and the Economy, Volume 13* (pp. 23–60). Chicago, IL: University of Chicago Press.

National Bureau of Economic Research. (2018). The Science of Science Funding Initiative. Retrieved November 2019, from National Bureau of Economic Research: https://projects.nber.org/drupal/SOSF/home.

Ofir, Z., Schwandt, T., Duggan, C., & McLean, R. (2016). *Research Quality Plus (RQ+): A Holistic Approach to Evaluating Research*. Ottawa, Canada: International Development Research Centre.

Open Research Funders Group. (n.d.). About. Retrieved November 2019, from Open Research Funders Group: www.orfg.org/about.

Owen-Smith, J. (2018). *Research Universities and the Public Good: Discovery for an Uncertain Future*. Stanford, CA: Stanford University Press.

Parker, J., & Crona, B. (2012). On Being All Things to All People: Boundary Organizations and the Contemporary Research University. *Social Studies of Science*, 42(2), 262–289.

Parks, S., Rodriguez-Rincon, D., Parkinson, S., & Manville, C. (2019). *The Changing Research Landscape and Reflections on National Research Assessment in the Future*. Santa Monica, CA: RAND Corporation.

Posselt, J. R. (2016). *Inside Graduate Admissions: Merit, Diversity, and Faculty Gatekeeping*. Cambridge, MA: Harvard University Press.

Princeton University. (2019, May 29). Gift from Eric and Wendy Schmidt to Create a New Home for Computer Science at Princeton University. Retrieved November 2019, from Princeton University: www.princeton.edu/news/2019/05/29/gift-eric-and-wendy-sch midt-create-new-home-computer-science-princeton-university.

Ramos, J., Sweeney, J. A., Peach, K., & Smith, L. (2019*). Our Futures: By the People, For the People*. London, UK: NESTA.

Reich, R. (2018). *Just Giving: Why Philanthropy Is Failing Democracy and How It Can Do Better*. Princeton, NJ: Princeton University Press.

Research on Research Institute. (2019, September). Research on Research Institute. Retrieved October 2019, from Research on Research Institute: http://researchonre search.org/.

Rogers, A. (2019, September 15). How Rich Donors Like Epstein (and Others) Undermine Science. Retrieved November 2019, from WIRED: www.wired.com/story/the-problem-with-rich-people-funding-science/.

RTI International. (2018). *External Evaluation of the Emergent Phenomena in Quantum Systems Initiative: Final Evaluation Report*. Research Triangle Park, NC: RTI International.

Sarewitz, D. (2016, Spring/Summer). Saving Science. *The New Atlantis*, pp. 5–40.

Sauermann, H., Franzoni, C., & Shafi, K. (2019). Crowdfunding Scientific Research: Descriptive Insights and Correlates of Funding Success. *PLOS ONE*, 14(1), e0208384, 1–26.

Scearce, D., & Fulton, K. (2004). *What If? The Art of Scenario Thinking for Nonprofits*. San Francisco, CA: Global Business Network.

Science Philanthropy Alliance. (2019a, September 9). The Brinson Foundation, Ross M. Brown Family Foundation, and Sergey Brin Family Foundation Join the Science Philanthropy Alliance. Retrieved November 2019, from Science Philanthropy Alliance: www. sciencephilanthropyalliance.org/the-brinson-foundation-ross-m-brown-foundation-and-sergey-brin-family-foundation-join-the-science-philanthropy-alliance-alliance-news/.

Science Philanthropy Alliance. (2019b, October 28). John Templeton Foundation Joins Science Philanthropy Alliance. Retrieved November 2019, from Science Philanthropy Alliance: www.sciencephilanthropyalliance.org/john-templeton-foundation-joins-science-philanthropy-alliance/.

Science Philanthropy Alliance. (2019c). Science Philanthropy Alliance: Advancing Basic Science. Retrieved December 2019, from Science Philanthropy Alliance: www.scien cephilanthropyalliance.org/advancing-basic-science/.

Science-Metrix Inc. (2018). *Evaluation of the Marine Microbiology Initiative*. Montreal, Canada: Science-Metrix Inc.

Staley, D. J. (2019). *Alternative Universities: Speculative Design for Innovation in Higher Education*. Baltimore, MD: Johns Hopkins University Press.

Teplitskiy, M., Ranu, H., Gray, G., Menietti, M., Guinan, E., & Lakhani, K. R. (2019). *Do Experts Listen to Other Experts? Field Experimental Evidence from Scientific Peer Review*. Cambridge, MA: Harvard Business School.

The Bridgespan Group. (2019). *Unleasing Philanthropy's Big Bets for Social Change*. Stanford, CA: Stanford Social Innovation Review.

Thorp, H. H. (2019, November 8). Beyond Vetting Donors. *Science*, 366(6466), 667.

University of Chicago. (2019, May 28). $100 Million Commitment Launches Pritzker School of Molecular Engineering. Retrieved November 2019, from University of Chicago: https://news.uchicago.edu/story/100-million-commitment-launches-prit zker-school-molecular-engineering.

von Schomberg, R., & Hankins, J. (2019). Introduction to the International Handbook on Responsible Innovation. In R. von Schomberg & J. Hankins, eds., *International Handbook on Responsible Innovation: A Global Resource* (pp. 1–11). Cheltenham, UK: Edward Elgar.

Walker, D. (2019). *From Generosity to Justice: A New Gospel of Wealth*. New York, NY: The Ford Foundation.

Wang, Y., Jones, B. F., & Wang, D. (2019). Early-Career Setback and Future Career Impact. *Nature Communications*, 10(4331), 1–10.

White, D. D., Wutich, A., Larson, K. L., Gober, P., Lant, T., & Senneville, C. (2010, April). Credibility, Salience, and Legitimacy of Boundary Objects: Water Managers' Assessment of a Simulation Model in an Immersive Decision Theater. *Science and Public Policy*, 37(3), 219–232.

Williams, T. (2019, September 3). Epstein, Science, and the Power of Saying No to Money. Retrieved November 2019, from Inside Philanthropy: www.insidephilanthrop y.com/home/2019/9/3/epstein-science-and-the-power-of-saying-no-to-money.

Index

Note: Page locators in **bold** refer to tables and in *italic* refer to figures.

Printed in the United States
by Baker & Taylor Publisher Services